A Practical Guide to Exemplary Professional Development Schools

A Volume in
Research in Professional Development Schools
and School-University Partnerships

Series Editors:
JoAnne Ferrara, *Manhattanville College*
Ronald Beebe, *University of Houston-Downtown*
Drew Polly, *UNC Charlotte*
Jennifer McCorvey, *University of South Florida*

Research in Professional Development Schools
JoAnne Ferrara, Ronald Beebe,
Drew Polly, and Jennifer McCorvey, Editors

*A Practical Guide
to Exemplary Professional Development Schools* (2024)
Michael N. Cosenza, JoAnne Ferrara, Diane W. Gomez, Editors

The Impact of PDS Partnerships in Challenging Times (2020)
Keli Garas-York, Pixita Del Prado, Editors

*Exploring Cultural Competence
in Professional Development Schools* (2020)
JoAnne Ferrara, Janice L. Nath, Ronald Beebe, Editors

Clinically Based Teacher Education in Action (2020)
Eva Garin, Rebecca West Burns, Editors

A Pathway to PDS Partnership: Using the PDSEA Protocol (2019)
Emily Shoemaker, Michael Cosenza,
Thierry Kolpin, Jacquleine May Allen, Editors

*Doing PDS: Stories and Strategies
From Successful Clinically Rich Practice* (2018)
Keli Garas-York, Pixita Del Prado, Leslie Day, Editors

*Visions From Professional Development School Partners:
Connecting Professional Development and Clinical Practice* (2018)
Meryln Buchanan, Michael Cosenza, Editors

Expanding Opportunities to Link Research and Clinical Practice (2017)
JoAnne Ferrara, Janice Nath, Irma Guadarrama, Ronald Beebe, Editors

Creating Visions for University-School Partnerships (2014)
JoAnne Ferrara, Janice Nath, Irma Guadarrama, Editors

Investigating University-School Partnerships (2011)
Janice L. Nath, Irma N. Guadarrama, John Ramsey, Editors

*University and School Connections: Research Studies in Professional
Development Schools* (2008)
Irma N. Guadarrama, John Ramsey, Janice L. Nath, Editors

Advances in Community Thought and Research (2005)
Irma N. Guadarrama, John Ramsey, Janice L. Nath, Editors

Forging Alliances in Community and Thought (2002)
Irma N. Guadarrama, Editor

A Practical Guide to Exemplary Professional Development Schools

Edited by

Michael N. Cosenza
California Lutheran University

JoAnne Ferrara
Manhattanville College

and

Diane W. Gómez
Manhattanville College

Information Age Publishing, Inc.
Charlotte, North Carolina • www.infoagepub.com

This book is endorsed by the National Association for School-University Partnerships.

This book is endorsed by the California Association of School-University Partnerships.

Library of Congress Cataloging-in-Publication Data

CIP data for this book can be found on the Library of Congress website:
http://www.loc.gov/index.html

Paperback: 979-8-88730-568-4
Hardcover: 979-8-88730-569-1
E-Book: 979-8-88730-570-7

Copyright © 2024 IAP–Information Age Publishing, Inc.

All rights reserved. No part of this publication may be reproduced, stored in a retrieval system, or transmitted in any form or by any electronic or mechanical means, or by photocopying, microfilming, recording or otherwise without written permission from the publisher.

Printed in the United States of America.

CONTENTS

Foreword vii

Acknowledgments ix

Introduction
   Michael N. Cosenza xi

1. Thirty Years of Partnership: Sustaining Our PDS Work
   Douglas W. Rogers, Rachelle Myer Rogers, Krystal Goree, Madelon McCall, Barbara Purdum-Cassidy, and Suzanne Nesmith 1

2. Bowie State University PDS Network: A Trailblazing Historically Black University
   Eva Gavin 21

3. The Buffalo State Professional Development School Consortium: A Shared Goal While Responding to Varying Needs
   Pixita Del Prado Hill and Keli Garas-York 41

4. California Lutheran University PDS Network: Sustaining Successful Partnerships
   Michael N. Cosenza 53

5. Mason's Elementary PDS Program: Leveraging a History of Collaboration to Grow and Sustain School/University Partnerships
   Audra Parker 73

6. Rooted in a Commitment to Change: How a PDS Network Renews and Rebuilds Its Implementation of Best Practices
   Stacey Leftwich, Cathy Brant, Michelle Damiani, and Robert Eisberg 89

7. Engaging and Impactful Practices in an Award-Winning PDS Network
   Sara Elburn, Diallo Sessoms, and Ron Siers Jr. 105

8. School-University Partnerships: Lessons Learned From the UNC Charlotte-Kannapolis City Schools Initiative
   S. Michael Putman and Drew Polly 123

9. Common Characteristics and Challenges of Successful School-University Partnerships
   Michael N. Cosenza 141

10. Resources 149

    Resource I: Memoranda of Understanding 151

    Resource II: Roles and Responsibilities 179

    Resource III: Recommended Readings for Professional Development 189

    Resource IV: Organizational Charts 193

    Resource V: Problem Solving Protocol 197

    Resource VI: Job Descriptions 199

    Resource VII: Application Solicitation 207

    Resource VIII: Grant Narrative 209

About the Contributors 213

FOREWORD

JoAnne Ferrara, Ronald Beebe, Drew Polly, and Jennifer McCorvey

In this volume of the book series the editors decided to showcase the National Association for Professional Development Schools (NAPDS) award winners for Exemplary Professional Development School Achievement. These PDSs are recognized for distinctive PDS partnerships and their ongoing contributions to the mission and vision of NAPDS. The association acknowledges that exemplary achievement takes place in large, multi-institutional partnerships as well as in single-site arrangements between P–12 and higher education; in well-funded and in budget-challenged partnerships; in long-standing collaborations as well as in recently established PDS's (NAPDS, 2023). With this in mind, *A Practical Guide to Exemplary Professional Development Schools* provides readers with a wealth of resources and insights from successful practitioners in the field. Each case presents the local context and rationale for becoming a PDS along with structures and ways to support school, universities, and stakeholders. Regardless of where schools and universities are on their partnership journey, the contributing authors provide a clear roadmap for what works, what are the benefits/challenges, and what is needed for growth and sustainability.

We are honored to share these thoughtfully designed PDS models that create rich learning communities and set the stage for school transformation and renewal.

—JoAnne, Ron, Drew, and Jennifer

REFERENCES

National Association for Professional Development Schools. (2023). Awards Information. https://napds.org/pds-award/

ACKNOWLEDGMENTS

We would like to extend our sincere gratitude to all the contributing authors who shared stories about their award-winning professional development schools (PDSs). Each story centers on policies, procedures and best practices that each reader can replicate or adapt to advance their own partnership work.

A special thank you goes to Elizabeth Sweeny for her copyediting skills. Elizabeth checked each chapter thoroughly to ensure the manuscript was in publishable form. We extend our thanks to the staff of Information Age Publishing, for guidance and good counsel. We also thank the series editors, JoAnne Ferrara, Ronald Beebe, Drew Polly, and Jennifer McCorvey for their support and encouragement.

Lastly, we would like to recognize all the work and effort of the people who dedicate themselves to school-university partnership and PDS work. The work they do provides high quality and inspirational educational experiences for P–12 students, university students and veteran teachers.

INTRODUCTION

Michael N. Cosenza

The professional development school (PDS) movement is often described as a response to the 1983 report that was commissioned by President Ronald Reagan entitled, *A Nation at Risk: The Imperative for Educational Reform*. The release of this report inspired three Deans of Schools of Education to collaborate about how educator preparation could be reformed in response to the concerns outlined in the report. The deans, who were from the Schools of Education at the State University of New York-Albany, Michigan State University, and the University of Wisconsin, formed an organization known as the Holmes Group (Homes Partnership, 2007). Henry Holmes, the namesake of the group, was the dean of the School of Education at Harvard University during the 1920s. Henry Holmes had a vision for preparing teachers in the same manner as physicians, attorneys, and other professionals. He created such a program at Harvard, but it gained little support and was short lived. The founders of the Holmes Group used the name to honor Holmes' ideas and utilize them as they developed a model for teacher education reform in the 1980s (Cosenza & Buchanan, 2018, p. 5).

The Holmes Group revived the ideas of Henry Holmes by developing a concept called the PDS, which centered on the relationship between medical schools and teaching hospitals as the foundational model for teacher preparation. With a series of three books published between 1986 and 1995 (combined into one volume in 2007), the PDS design was put forward as an educational reform that would provide high quality teacher preparation centered in high quality clinical field experiences.

The movement caught on in the years to follow and by the year 2000 the PDS model was widespread (Cosenza & Buchanan, 2018, p. 9). Educational accreditation organizations and state education agencies began to recognize the potential of the PDS. A prominent accreditation organization at the time, the National Council on the Accreditation of Teacher Education (NCATE), created standards to guide the implementation and sustainability of PDSs (Cosenza & Buchanan, 2018; NCATE 2001; Shoemaker, et.al, 2020). In 2005, the National Association for Professional Development Schools (NAPDS) was established as the first professional association devoted to providing resources and support for the PDS movement. Three years after its founding, NAPDS published a policy paper, *What It Means to Be a Professional Development School: The Nine Essentials* (NAPDS, 2008) which provided universities and their partner P–12 schools a set of guidelines to create collaborative partnerships focusing on new teacher preparation, student achievement, collaboration and professional development for veteran teachers. These nine essentials became fundamental to the PDS movement and a basis for PDS research and literature. In the year 2021, NAPDS revised and published an updated version of the nine essentials in a document entitled, *What It Means to Be a Professional Development School: The Nine Essentials* (2nd ed.).

Annually, NAPDS recognizes exemplary PDS work between university and P–12 school partners. The award is intended to recognize outstanding partnerships experiencing long term success. Through a rigorous peer review process anchored in the *Nine Essentials*, universities and P–12 schools are awarded the Exemplary PDS Award with public recognition during an awards luncheon at the association's annual conference. After the award winners are recognized, breakout sessions are led by each recipient allowing conference attendees to hear detailed stories about their PDS work. The chapters of this book contain the stories of eight of these award winners from the years 2017–2021. Each chapter is similarly formatted to tell the narrative of why each partnership began and how they have been successful over many years of collaboration.

As the title of this book suggests, each chapter serves as a guide by documenting a story which provides practical ideas, procedures and policies that can be implemented by the reader to begin new partnerships or help improve and sustain existing partnerships. Each chapter also explores some challenges that have been identified and overcome as well as challenges that are still being deliberated.

In addition to the eight stories from PDSs spanning seven different states, there is a resource chapter and a summary chapter. The resource chapter is a place where the award winning partnerships share specific documents that may be adapted by the readers of this book for their own use. The summary chapter looks at common practices and challenges found across the partnerships. The editors and contributors of this book hope you find it to be a practical guide for your own school-university partnership.

As previously stated, the decision to grant an award is rooted in the NAPDS nine essentials which are reprinted below.

NAPDS NINE ESSENTIALS (NAPDS, 2021)

Essential 1: A Comprehensive Mission

> A PDS is a learning community guided by a comprehensive, articulated mission that is broader than the goals of any single partner, and that aims to advance equity, antiracism and social justice within and among schools, colleges/universities, and their respective community and professional partners.

Essential 2: Clinical Preparation

> A PDS embraces the preparation of educators through clinical practice.

Essential 3: Professional Learning and Leading

> A PDS is a context for continuous professional learning and leading for all participants, guided by need and a spirit and practice of inquiry.

Essential 4: Reflection and Innovation

> A PDS makes a shared commitment to reflective practice, responsive innovation, and generative knowledge.

Essential 5: Research and Results

> A PDS is a community that engages in collaborative research and participates in the public sharing of results in a variety of outlets.

Essential 6: Articulated Agreements

> A PDS requires intentionally evolving written articulated agreement(s) that delineate the commitments, expectations, roles, and responsibilities of all involved.

Essential 7: Shared Governance Structures

> A PDS is built upon shared, sustainable governance structures that promote collaboration, foster reflection, and honor and value all participants' voices.

Essential 8: Boundary-Spanning Roles

A PDS creates space for, advocates for, and supports college/university and P–12 faculty to operate in well-defined, boundary-spanning roles that transcend institutional settings.

Essential 9: Resources and Recognition

A PDS provides dedicated and shared resources and establishes traditions to recognize, enhance, celebrate, and sustain the work of partners and the partnership.

CHAPTER OVERVIEW

Chapter 1: Baylor University, Texas (NAPDS Exemplary PDS Award Winner in 2017 and 2018)

- The PDS work at Baylor University began in 1993 and continues to flourish. Their story includes how PDS work began and how the work has grown to include several elementary, middle and high schools in two school districts. Additionally, Baylor served in a 3-year field study for the development and piloting of the NCATE PDS Standards.

Chapter 2: Bowie State University, Maryland (NAPDS Exemplary PDS Award Winner in 2021)

- Bowie State University began its PDS work in the early 1990s by serving as a pilot program for the Maryland State Department of Education. Bowie's story comes from the perspective of a historically black college/university (HBCU) which makes a meaningful contribution to this book. Bowie also played a role in reviewing the NCATE PDS standards and adopting similar standards for the State of Maryland, which was the first state to mandate PDS in all teacher preparation programs.

Chapter 3: Buffalo State University, New York (NAPDS Exemplary PDS Award Winner in 2018)

- Buffalo State first began its PDS work in 1991 and shares a story about the importance of collaboration and meeting the needs of all stakeholders. The Buffalo PDS program is very large and has expanded to include more than 100 schools and community part-

Introduction xv

ners. Additionally, Buffalo has expanded the concept of PDS work internationally, with partner schools outside the United States in nine different countries.

Chapter 4: California Lutheran University, California (NAPDS Exemplary PDS Award Winner in 2021)

- California Lutheran began PDS work in 2002 with one elementary school in a nearby school district. This chapter focuses on the importance of collaboration when working with various stakeholders and the value of transparent communications. This chapter also explores lessons learned from a failed partnership which contributed to changes in policies and procedures that have permitted the PDS program to grow into a thriving network across three school districts.

Chapter 5: George Mason University, Virginia (NAPDS Exemplary PDS Award Winner in 2020)

- George Mason University began its PDS work in 1991 and focuses on a long history of work with local school districts. The chapter focuses on how the *Nine Essentials* (NAPDS, 2021) and quality clinical fieldwork influences its work. Since its inception, the George Mason program has grown to include 30 schools across six school districts.

Chapter 6: Rowan University, New Jersey (NAPDS Exemplary PDS Award Winner in 2020)

- Rowan University began its PDS work in 1991. The chapter tells a story about how PDS work began, was restructured in 2013, and has continued to grow to include 11 P–12 partner schools. This chapter discusses Rowan's fidelity to the original Holmes Group PDS model (Holmes, 2007) and how those principles are nonnegotiable in their PDS work.

Chapter 7: Salisbury University, Maryland (NAPDS Exemplary PDS Award Winner in 2011, 2015, 2017, and 2021)

- Salisbury University is the most recognized NAPDS award recipient having won the Exemplary PDS Award four times as well as three other recognitions since 2009. This chapter tells the story of a large PDS network that includes 33 PDS partners including elementary, middle, and high schools. Managing a large network requires many stakeholders and this chapter focuses on the roles and responsibilities of the partners and overall oversight of the network.

Chapter 8: University of North Carolina-Charlotte, North Carolina (NAPDS Exemplary PDS Award Winner in 2021)

- UNC Charlotte has a large and demographically diverse program that focuses a great deal on high quality clinical practice. This chapter also discusses the value of collaboration in partnership oversight, clarity in the components of the partnerships, and the importance of communication. Shared governance and decision making is a key factor in this network's success as well as learning from struggles and challenges.

Chapter 9: Common Themes and Challenges

- This chapter attempts to identify commonalities among the eight award winning programs in an effort to uncover key ideas and concepts that may contribute to the success of PDS work. Additionally, common challenges are identified with the hope of finding potential solutions for long-term sustainability.

Chapter 10: Resources

- This is a collection of artifacts provided by the eight award winning programs. These documents are shared with permission to help those who would like to implement the various policies, procedures and structures that are discussed in this book. The various MOUs, organizational charts and other forms can be used as templates for any program intending to replicate the work of these eight programs.

REFERENCES

Cosenza, M., & Buchanan, M. (2018). A short history of professional development school: Looking backward and forward. In M. Buchanan & M. Cosenza (Eds.), *Vision from professional development school partners: Connecting professional development and clinical practice* (pp. 3–10). Information Age.

Holmes Partnership. (2007). *The Holmes partnership trilogy*. Peter Lang.

National Association for Professional Development Schools. (2021). *What it means to be a professional development school: The nine essentials* (2nd ed.). [Policy statement]

National Council for Accreditation of Teacher Education. (2001). *Standards for professional development schools.* [Policy statement].

Shoemaker, E., Cosenza, M., Kolpin, T., & Allen, J. (2020). *A pathway to PDS partnership: Using the PDSEA protocol.* Information Age.

U. S. States. National Commission on Excellence in Education. (1983). *A nation at risk: the imperative for educational reform: A report to the Nation and the Secretary of Education, United States Department of Education.* National Commission on Excellence in Education. [Superintendent of Documents, U.S. Government Printing Office distributor]

CHAPTER 1

THIRTY YEARS OF PARTNERSHIP

Sustaining Our PDS Work

Douglas Rogers, Krystal Goree, Rachelle Myer Rogers, Madelon McCall, Barbara Purdum-Cassidy, and Suzanne Nesmith

Rationale

At Baylor University, the professional development school (PDS) model of teacher preparation is based on the historical success of a pilot program at a single elementary campus. In the fall of 1993, Baylor University's School of Education (SOE) and Waco Independent School District (WISD) entered a new era for both organizations. After several bleak years consolidating attendance zones and shuttering campuses to account for population shifts within the district boundaries, WISD wanted to reconstitute select campuses to relieve overcrowding that had become a problem at some school sites. In addition, WISD wanted to create some unique environments within the district to experiment with several popular reform initiatives of the time (e.g., multiage classes, outdoor education, fine arts, and technology emphases). The WISD Superintendent found a more-than-willing partner in the dean of the Baylor University SOE.

For a year, while the Hillcrest Elementary campus underwent renovation, collaborative groups from the district and the university met, discussed, and decided what would happen in this "new" shared facility. The district brought several ideas to the campus: year-round schooling, multiage and outdoor learning environments, full inclusion, district waivers from benchmark testing, and the concept of a fine arts/technology magnet. A unique aspect of this magnet campus was that student applicants were placed in a lottery and drawn to match the ethnic diversity of the district. The SOE brought ideas among the nation's premier research institutions about teacher preparation to the campus. One such idea, the PDS, came from the Holmes Group and was published in *Tomorrow's Schools* (Holmes Group, 1990). The PDS concept centered around early and extended clinical experiences for preservice teachers, dedicated campus space for university courses to be taught on-site, reciprocal faculty appointments, joint faculty development, and a focus on student learning.

When the newly christened Hillcrest PDS opened its doors in August 1993, it became the first of its kind in the community and to this day, the only elementary school in the state of Texas that uses "Professional Development School" in its official name (Texas Education Agency, n.d.). This venture placed Baylor's SOE and the Waco community at the forefront of a national movement articulated in the third volume of the Holmes Group's trilogy *Tomorrow's Schools of Education* (Holmes Group, 1995, p. 79) that concluded, "Nothing like the PDS has ever before existed in American education." The inaugural enrollment at Hillcrest PDS was approximately 220 students grouped into five multiage learning environments, roughly the equivalent of two traditional classrooms at each of the first through fifth grade levels. To avoid traditional grade-level designations, each of the learning environments was named after a candy (e.g., Skittles, Starburst, Snickers, etc.) produced locally at the M&M Mars factory in Waco, a community partner with the campus. The inaugural group of Baylor preservice teachers (PST), selected from a pool of applicants, was limited to ten individuals pursuing Texas' elementary special education certification or elementary certification with a gifted and talented endorsement. At the time, neither the WISD nor the Baylor SOE anticipated the impact this joint venture would have on their collective future (Goree et al., 2019).

Within 3 years, WISD and the SOE would recommend the creation of a second PDS at G. L. Wiley Middle School. Conceived as a full-service campus, the G. L. Wiley PDS would offer "comprehensive and integrated social services to children and families in the school community" (Messer, 1996, p. 1). Unfortunately, the G. L. Wiley PDS would never fully materialize primarily due to leadership changes at both organizations; however, the Hillcrest PDS model gained local attention and planted the seed for expansion. In early 1998, the WISD/Baylor University partnership at Hillcrest PDS garnered national attention as one of only eighteen PDS sites (the only one in Texas) selected nationally to participate in a 3-year field-test of PDS standards proposed by the National Council for the Accreditation of Teacher Education (NCATE; Fogleman, 2001). The Standards for Professional Development Schools (NCATE, 2001) were released on October 16, 2001 at Washington D.C.'s National Press Club. The person who had joined the Baylor University SOE faculty as Dean in 1998, participated in the press conference and summarized the standards' significance, "we now know how to create effective Professional Development Schools through standards that are based on documented successful practices" (Fogleman, 2001). During the press conference, the Dean announced the SOE's intention to have *all* preservice teachers involved in PDSs. This marked a monumental transition for teacher preparation at Baylor University and area school districts. The successful 5-year history of Hillcrest PDS, the development of the national standards, and the dean's vision for the SOE within the Baylor context served as the rationale for comprehensive adoption of the PDS model across all teacher preparation programs on campus.

DEMOGRAPHICS

As a private faith-based institution, Baylor's SOE enrolls approximately 100 freshmen annually with an average total enrollment of 402 undergraduates. The University's gender distribution is approximately 60% women and 40% men. Teacher preparation programs are closer to 85% women and 15% men. The ethnicity of the SOE's students is primarily White (77%), followed by Hispanic (13%), Asian (4%), Black/African American (3%), and Multiracial (3%).

Baylor's PDS partnerships exist in two primary districts—WISD, a primarily urban school district, and Midway Independent School District (MISD), a primarily suburban district. District demographic data are reported in Table 1.1 because PDS work has shifted to various campuses within these two districts over the course of almost 30 years of partnership work.

Network Description

The current configuration of the nine PDS P-12 partner campuses contains two high schools, two middle schools, and five elementary schools. The campuses are split between the two districts; MISD hosts one addi-

Table 1.1 Ethnic and Gender Distribution of Districts With PDS Campuses

District/Characteristic	n	%
WISD	14,428	
Ethnicity		
African American	4,042	28.0
Hispanic	8,815	6.1
White	1,209	8.4
American Indian	9	0.1
Asian	41	.3
Pacific Islander	6	0.0
Two or more races	306	2.1
Sex		
Female	7,068	49.0
Male	7,360	51.0
Economically disadvantaged	13,167	60.0
MISD	8,253	
Ethnic distribution:		
African American	921	11.2
Hispanic	2,025	24.5
White	4,557	55.2
American Indian	22	0.3
Asian	383	4.6
Pacific Islander	11	0.1
Two or More Races	334	4.0
Sex		
Female	4,086	49.5
Male	4,167	50.5
Economically disadvantaged	2,767	33.5

Source: Texas Education Agency, Texas Academic Performance Report, https://rptsvr1.tea.texas.gov/perfreport/tapr/tapr_srch.html?srch=D)

tional elementary P–12 campus. The program makes every effort to give PSTs experiences in both districts. When neither district has the capacity to host Baylor's PSTs, additional campuses in local districts accept Baylor PSTs. These campuses and districts are referred to as "partner campuses" or "partner districts." They do not receive the same level of support provided to PDSs and districts with PDSs.

The Teacher Preparation Program

The concept of PDSs is built on extensive clinical experiences. The Baylor SOE model could be characterized as "early and often." The initial implementation required six semesters of clinical work across eight semesters of a PST's program. Over time, most programs reduced the number of courses associated with clinical experiences to create flexibility for students who transfer into teacher education from other programs on campus or from other institutions.

PSTs are introduced to field experiences during the first semester of enrollment. Labeled novice candidates, these first-year students are introduced to the essential cycle of pre-assessment, planning, delivery, and evaluation as they provide individual or small group tutoring on a local campus for 2 hours per week for 8 weeks. Additional novice field experiences for first- or second-year PSTs are provided through a course on social issues in education. Though these may not be classroom experiences, they introduce PSTs to the socio-cultural communities served by the partnership districts.

Third-year PSTs are considered teaching associates (TAs) and participate in content and grade specific field experiences for 8 hours per week for 12 weeks of at least one semester. Some certificate programs include a second TA experience.

The culminating field experience was redesigned to replace the traditional single semester of student teaching with a year-long internship. The internship for senior-level PSTs represents a full-time multi-day, multi-week, two-semester experience in a public school classroom.

The SOE made significant curricular changes to support these extensive field experiences. New courses associated with the field experience hours required University Curriculum Committee approval. Three courses were deleted from the program sequence; the content was shifted to other courses. Courses with field components were scheduled for early morning, allowing PSTs to meet at their campuses prior to the beginning of the school day. Content in all courses within the certificate programs were modified to reflect the extended clinical opportunities and to accommodate additional content consolidated from removed courses. Curricular changes also were negotiated with departments across the University campus that provided content courses. These negotiations dealt with course content and the schedule for offering courses taken by PSTs—

both impacted by the shift to extensive field work and the need for PSTs to travel between their clinical sites and the University campus.

In addition to the extensive field experience component of the program, three additional elements are cross-certificate requirements: 1) the development of a personal digital portfolio that includes PST-selected evidence and written narratives that address the program's nine benchmarks (generally fashioned after the Interstate Teacher Assessment and Support Consortium standards) (Council of Chief State School Officers, 2011); 2) the completion of an action research project during the senior internship year; and 3) the implementation of co-teaching models in cooperation with the campus-based clinical instructors (with junior level teaching associates) and mentor teachers (with senior level interns)

STRUCTURE

Policies and Procedures

Currently there is an extension of the model that began at Hillcrest PDS that has continued through the transitions of eight superintendents in WISD, four superintendents in MISD, and five deans (plus five interim deans) in the SOE. It is a resilient work fueled by the shared commitment of the partners. The transition from a small group of PSTs at a single campus to all (300+) PSTs involved at multiple PDSs required significant modifications to policies and procedures.

Partnership Development

Other than the initial implementation at Hillcrest PDS, all other P–12 campuses complete an application process. The application process includes a written component that describes why the campus wants to be a PDS and what aspect of pre-service teacher preparation is a good fit for the campus (e.g., content area focus, pedagogical methods, student clientele, etc.). The P–12 campus is asked to conduct a capacity analysis to determine the number of professionals on campus that are qualified to support PSTs and to document that a campuswide discussion of the PDS model occurred and that the campus faculty voted to complete the application process. Often, university faculty who have established relationships for research or programmatic experiences at individual campuses collaborate in crafting the written application.

A review committee of representatives from the university and from existing PDSs is appointed by the associate dean. The review committee reads the applications, makes site visits, and submits a recommendation to the SOE administration. A draft memorandum of understanding

(MOU) (see resources) detailing the financial obligations is prepared. Currently, the financial obligations are evenly distributed across the SOE and the district of the P–12 campus. The MOU enumerates site coordinator salaries, mentor teacher and clinical instructor stipends, professional development funds, and perishable resource funding based on the number of PSTs placed on a P–12 campus. Many campuses absorb additional costs for items designed to assimilate PSTs into the campus community including faculty shirts, campus ID badges and lanyards, etcetera. In some cases, iPads are provided to interns and TAs placed at PDSs with one-to-one technology initiatives. The SOE also recognizes the need to make explicit the connections between the University campus and the individual P–12 campuses and district offices; the SOE created and installed matching signage in each of the district central offices and in each P–12 campus.

Organizational Oversight and Governance

The authors wish they could share a governance structure that supported flawless communication; however, the partnership's history is recorded as a never-ending series of governance modifications [as this manuscript is being written a new governance proposal is in the works] to eradicate the inevitable miscommunication, even after 29 years of experience. Regardless of the iteration or the arrangement of the boxes in an organizational chart, the purpose remains the same: How do the individuals and groups participating in this collaborative effort share information within their own organizations and across and between the other organizations in the partnership?

One of the strengths of the Baylor University, WISD, and MISD partnerships is that the individuals who implement the vision at the grassroots-level do the bulk of the daily planning, reflecting, and communicating. Campus-level concerns, ideas for professional development or the improvement of clinical experiences, and strategies for addressing P-12 student learning are communicated to a PDS Steering Committee on each campus. In some instances, local campuses merge the PDS Steering Committee with the state-mandated Campus Decision Making Committee, which facilitates the incorporation of PDS goals in the Campus Improvement Plan submitted to the Texas Education Agency. Issues and ideas that transcend a single campus are shared with a district-appointed liaison (usually an assistant superintendent associated with the district's human resources or professional development). This liaison function is paralleled in the SOE as a task assigned to the Director of the Office of Professional Practice (OPP). These individuals are responsible at the district-level and SOE-level, which differs from the university liaison (UL) assigned at the program level to a single campus. The district liaison and the Director of OPP present issues and ideas that impact more than one entity to the Coordinating Council. As indicated by the name, the council works to coordinate partnership activities across multiple campuses and to facilitate communication from individual campuses to the Oversight Council. The Oversight Council, composed of senior leadership from the school district and from the SOE, provides overall direction for the partnership and addresses policy issues, resource allocations, legal constraints, organizational cultures, and any major changes to the partnership (McCall et al., 2017). Three core elements of the current program originated at the campus level, made their way through the structures described above, and were adopted across the partnerships: 1) the use of action research as a capstone experience for interns; 2) the implementation of coteaching strategies rather than the traditional strategy of solo teaching by the intern; and 3) the requirement for PDSs to reapply for PDS status at select intervals.

Just as PDSs are represented by a multitiered governance structure, the University faculty share a multitiered structure as well. All members of the University faculty both within the SOE and in academic units external to the SOE who provide instruction to PSTs are designated members of the Professional Education Faculty (PEF), which serves as the University's advisory committee for teacher education as required by Texas Administrative Code (State Board for Educator Certification, 2020). Within the SOE's departmental structure (Curriculum & Instruction, Educational Psychology, and Educational Leadership), individual faculty responsible for course instruction and clinical experiences are assigned to certificate level groups: Elementary, Middle Grades, and Secondary. While Baylor's SOE also provides certificate teams for Special Education and the Gifted and Talented endorsement, none of the PDSs are exclusively associated with those programs. Certificate teams select members to serve on the PEF Executive Committee (PEFX) with two members selected at-large from the departments and one member selected from the academic units external to the SOE. The PEF and PEFX are chaired by the Associate Dean for Undergraduate Education, who also sits on the Oversight Council (see Figure 1.1).

Organizational Leadership

Creating a network of PDSs to support extensive field work required the enhancement of existing or the creation of new organizational structures. The major change was the concentration of PSTs on a limited number of P–12 campuses within two primary school districts, rather than widely dispersed across as many as ten area school districts historically. The initial implementation called for 10 P–12 campuses; however, that number was insufficient for all field experiences for all PSTs in all certifi-

Figure 1

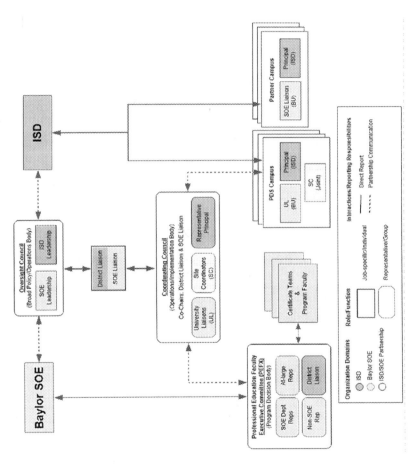

cate programs. Additional campuses were needed; these campuses were identified as partner campuses to distinguish them from PDSs. The two designations were critical because PDSs receive considerably more support for hosting significantly more preservice teachers.

The shift from a single P–12 campus to multiple P–12 campuses also required new designations for personnel at both the P–12 campuses and the University. Public school teachers who worked with 4th-year (senior-level) interns were designated as mentor teachers; those working with 3rd-year (junior-level) teaching associates as clinical instructors. Both mentor teachers and clinical instructors receive stipends each semester for their work with PSTs ($500/intern and $250/TA respectively). To help manage the increased number of PSTs working with public school teachers, the position of site coordinator was created. Site coordinators, one at each P–12 campus, serve as half-time employees of the districts in which the P–12 campuses are located. The responsibilities of the mentor teachers, clinical instructors, and site coordinators are listed in a document entitled, Roles and Responsibilities (see resources).

Baylor's SOE retains the designation of university supervisor for those individuals working directly with senior-level interns and mentor teachers. The SOE assigns a faculty member to each P–12 campus to serve as the UL. The primary responsibility of the UL is to be a regular and consistent program presence at the PDS. The UL functions as the essential conduit for communicating the needs and expectations of the P–12 campus to the teacher preparation program and for communicating the needs and expectations of the teacher preparation program to the P–12 campus. In recognition of the unique workload of primarily nontenure track faculty members working in this field-experience intensive program, the SOE Dean spearheaded a campuswide effort to approve a new nontenured classification of Clinical Faculty. Recognized by the University in 2011, the classification provided a promotion process for individuals in this category to move through the ranks of Clinical Assistant Professor, Clinical Associate Professor, and Clinical Professor, with appropriate compensation increases.

In the fall of 2003, as the first cohort of all senior interns started their full-year internships, no one could have anticipated the role the Office of Professional Practice (OPP) would play over the next almost 30 years. Originally responsible for one-semester student teaching placements, state licensure exam preparation, and university documentation for state certification, the OPP emerged as the nexus for the PDS initiative at Baylor University. Preservice teacher placements that increased from one semester to four semesters with every intention of not duplicating a placement. Additionally, PST admissions to certification programs, the documenting of PST performance over time, mentor teacher and clinical instructor vetting and training, state certification exam preparation, and student remediation were all moved under the OPP umbrella in addition to the preexisting responsibilities. Designated the SOE Liaison to PDS and partner districts, the Director of OPP became the programmatic ambassador of the SOE and the pragmatic first responder to PSTs or campus issues.

SUPPORT

All the curricular, organizational, fiscal, and physical modifications are essentially logistics—*how* the partnership originally operated and how it continues to operate. But the heart of the partnership, the energy that drives the participants, is a shared vision around four overarching goals: 1) the continuous improvement of K–12 student learning; 2) the development of effective PSTs; 3) the joint professional development of all individuals (public school and university) engaged in educator preparation; and 4) the improvement of educational practice through educator inquiry (Holmes Group, 1990). While the first two goals represent the primary goal of public schools (P–12 student learning) and the primary goal of schools of education, neither are exclusive domains. Neither the public schools nor the teacher preparation institution can ignore the need to strengthen and enhance their individual expertise based on a structured and systematic investigation of practices that work. This was the essence of the first PDS and remains the essence of the joint PDS work between Baylor University, WISD and MISD. But vision and logistics are not enough. There must be support from both organizations—the SOE and the P–12campus/district.

Because the PDS network between Baylor University, Waco ISD and Midway ISD traced its proverbial roots back to Hillcrest PDS, one element of that history was the "Baylor Room" on the Hillcrest campus. Dedicated space at each PDS, required unless prohibited by extreme circumstances, provides a location for PST seminars, collaborative planning, PST support conferences, shared professional development activities, and a wide array of events that would have been problematic if PDS participants (PSTs, faculty, administrators) had to travel between the P–12 campus and the University.

The Characteristics of Partnership Resilience

As the authors considered almost three decades of partnership history, their reflections focused on the traits that seemed to stabilize and sustain the partnerships across time and across leadership changes at the university, the districts, and the individual P–12 campuses. The characteristics of resilience enumerated by the three Certificate Coordinators, the Director of the Office of Professional Practice, a former Associate dean, and the current Associate dean include but are not limited to: 1) the PDS principal as campus champion; 2) the freedom to differentiate programs at the certificate level; 3) the relationships-informed decision making; 4) the focus on addressing a campus/certificate need; and 5) the support to make critical decisions at the certificate and campus levels.

The PDS Principal as Campus Champion

The three certificate coordinators contributing to this manuscript unanimously identified the critical role played by PDS P–12 campus principals. The involvement of the campus principal is a key factor in the success of the partnership. Principals set the tone for a campus; many established open-door policies for PDS personnel and met monthly to plan PDS activities. Among the unique contributions made by PDS principals were conducting simulated hiring interviews, providing campus shirts, and allocating technology on 1-to-1 campuses. One middle school PDS principal hosted monthly "coffee and conversation" meetings with all interns and available administrators to discuss topics suggested by the interns. Another PDS principal cotaught an intern seminar on classroom management. As campus champion, the principal embodies both the vision and logistics for PDS work on the campus. Examples of the remaining characteristics of resilience at each of the three certificate levels are described below. The examples that follow have been the subject of partnership presentations at the NAPDS annual conference and the Association for Teacher Educators (ATE) annual conference or written about in appropriate professional journals.

The Elementary Certificate

Certificate Level Variations. Perhaps the single most significant variance at the elementary level is the need to prepare PSTs in multiple subject areas. This distinction is most notable in the focus of the P–12 campuses. Prior to 2014, the junior-level TA field experience in the elementary certificate program included only two content areas (a literacy block and a mathematics block) delivered on a P–12 campus to which a PST was assigned for a full year. Piloted on two campuses in AY2015, the elementary certificate faculty reconfigured the TA experience to include four core subject areas, and in AY2016 formally integrated the change in four PDSs with one of two subject-area designations: a Social Studies/English Language Arts (SELA) campus or a Science Technology Engineering Mathematics (TAs on a SELA campus one semester and on a

STEM campus in another semester). The alternating placements on content-specific campuses allowed for specialized, content-specific support, mentoring, and pedagogical experiences for PSTs as well as all individuals involved in the content-specific clinical experiences.

Relationship-Informed Decisions. Collaborative work on the PDS partner campuses is characterized by decisions that reflect the magnitude of the relationships. A prime example at the elementary certification level is the modification of master schedules to accommodate specialized campus content area teaching and PST travel time between the clinical site and the university campus. Likewise, based on the depth of the PDS relationship, P–12 campuses engaged in one-to-one technology initiatives in which they assigned interns and TAs the same devices assigned to fulltime campus personnel.

Addressing a Campus/Certificate Need. The best example of addressing a need at the elementary level arose during a periodic reapplication process for elementary PDSs. The process revealed the need to improve the consistency and quality of the initial novice experience for first-year PSTs. Historically, elementary PSTs were scattered across several different campuses for their initial field experiences, which impacted the levels of collaboration as well as the quality of the overall experience. Meeting the need required the identification of a single site to host all elementary PSTs for their inaugural clinical experiences. The newly identified PDS also serves as the site for the special education certificate's third-year TA experience.

Support for Making Critical Decisions. Many of the examples cited above could appear in this category as well, as could others mentioned earlier in the narrative (e.g., c-teaching, action research, content-specific campuses, etc.). But it is not the number of decisions that matter; it is the partnership support to make and implement such critical decisions that matters. Another example is when the elementary certificate coordinator identified more major decisions that illustrated the support of the partnerships: deciding to reduce time PSTs in all programs spent at a PDS from five days a week to four and one day a week on the Baylor University campus and deciding to provide all elementary PSTs with both urban and suburban teaching experiences.

The Middle Level Certificate

Certificate Level Variations. An exclusive variation within the middle level certificate is a data analysis and instruction course, designed to give middle level PSTs experience interpreting national, state, campus, and class data and preparing instruction based on the analyses. The course also provides additional TA field experiences and the unique experience of conducting a simulated parent-teacher conference to discuss the results of standardized state assessments.

Relationship-Informed Decisions. The best example of a decision based on the PDS relationships at the middle level is the adoption of the unique data analysis and instruction course previously described. The decision was the result of conversations initiated by the members of the PDS steering committee.

Master schedules at the PDSs are critical to facilitating PSTs' timely arrivals at the PDSs and returns to the Baylor University campus. The coordinator of the middle level certificate program reported that at one of the two middle school PDSs, the administration initiated a master schedule change that had all middle school students participating in a character education class during the first period of the day, which effectively eliminated the opportunity for junior-level TAs to conduct content-specific field work at that PDS. Based on relationship-oriented conversations within the PDS, the character education class was moved to the third hour of the day, which not only restored the first and second hours for content-specific work by TAs, but also allowed TAs to remain on campus for the character-education class if their schedules on the Baylor University campus allowed. A similar issue occurred at the second middle level PDS that uses professional learning communities (PLCs) in which content area teachers meet each day for a class period to collaborate on lesson plans and students' performance and to engage in professional learning. The administration scheduled the English/Language Arts (ELAR) department to have their PLC during the first hour and the mathematics department to have their PLC during the second hour. This impacted the ability to place PSTs in mathematics and ELAR classrooms for a two-period teaching experience. ELAR and mathematics are the two largest content areas for the middle level program at Baylor University. Once again, when the school-university partners discussed the impact scheduling PLCs for core content areas had on the PDS program, the PDS administrators immediately changed the schedule so that all core content areas engaged in PLCs after second period each day. These changes might not have been necessary if communication among partners had occurred earlier in the process. The outcome in which decisions already at work in the campuses' master schedules were altered to support the work of the PDS partnership illustrates the depth of the PDS relationships.

Addressing a Campus/Certificate Need. One of the middle-level PDSs identified a need for specific individual tutoring for PDS students performing below grade level. The partnership agreed to focus the tutoring provided by first-year novice PSTs on this identified need. Using technology-based communication systems, the novice PSTs were able to record tutoring sessions that could be used with more than one student and could be curated for future use.

Support for Making Critical Decisions. As with the elementary certificate, implementing the activities described above illustrates support for many critical decisions. Another example of the partnership's support for critical decisions is an action research project as a partnershipwide capstone experience for all interns. At one middle school PDS, the principal hosts a spring faculty meeting to discuss the findings of action research conducted on the campus. In at least two instances, the findings of PST-initiated action research led to campus changes: using flipped classroom techniques in mathematics instruction (Rogers et al., 2017) and various instructional strategies in ELAR classrooms.

The Secondary Level Certificate

Certificate Level Variations. Like the middle school certificate, the secondary certificate is supported by two PDSs, one in each district. Two significant variations are incorporated in the secondary program. A single UL supports both high school PDSs, and the secondary PDSs support PSTs pursuing the traditional certification program, other University students pursuing education minors or concentrations, and PSTs in a 5-year joint degree that leads to a Master of Arts in Teaching (MAT). Minor and MAT PSTs complete a one semester-long internship. Also unique to the secondary certificate program is the opportunity for junior TAs and senior interns to complete their clinical experiences on a middle school campus in grades 7 or 8. Secondary certifications in Texas bridge the upper middle grades and high school; therefore, an experience at a middle or junior high school better prepares secondary preservice teachers for employment opportunities.

Relationship-Informed Decisions. While the decision to use coteaching models spread across the three certificate levels, the idea originated in the secondary certificate. The secondary certificate coordinator credits the principal of one of the secondary PDSs for initiating the shift. The principal wanted to decrease the student-to-teacher ratio in classrooms that hosted clinical instructor/TA pairs and mentor teacher/intern pairs, rather than allowing the solo teaching/observation model that was prevalent. Coteaching strategies were investigated, discussed, and piloted at that secondary PDS (McCall et al., 2018; Rogers et al., 2021). The Saint Cloud University Co-Teach Model (St. Cloud State University, n.d.) was implemented and the initiative became a requirement for all PDSs at all certificate levels.

Addressing a Campus/Certificate Need. Consistent with the national decline in teacher preparation programs, enrollment in the secondary certificate began to decline. The certificate team and its PDS partners made significant changes to the program, primarily reducing the junior-level TA clinical experience from two semesters to one semester. This was done to integrate PSTs seeking education minors and PSTs seeking the MAT degree. To offset the loss of that second semester of clinical experience, clinical rounds were implemented in a different junior-level course that previously had no clinical experience. The structure and processes for the instructional rounds were established by the PDS administrators, university liaisons, and site coordinators. The primary purpose of the instructional rounds is to provide campus experiences on at least four different campuses in different districts. These experiences are designed to better prepare PSTs for the cultural, campus, and instructional diversity they will experience during their TA semester and internship year. Like their colleagues at the elementary and middle school PDSs, the principals at the secondary PDSs conduct simulated interviews. The secondary certificate also addressed an identified need by providing resume writing support for secondary PSTs.

Support for Making Critical Decisions. Changes to the master schedules were also identified as critical decisions to support PDS work at the secondary level. These decisions made potential clinical instructors in core content areas available during first and second period to work with secondary TAs. The decision to move to a 4-day-a-week/Baylor day on Friday schedule for interns at the secondary level was also identified as a critical decision supported by the PDS partners.

CHALLENGES

The Baylor SOE, WISD, and MISD share three decades of partnership work dedicated to the ideals of PDSs: 1) the continuous improvement of P–12 student learning; 2) the development of effective preservice teachers; 3) the joint professional development of all individuals (public school and university) engaged in educator preparation; and 4) the improvement of educational practice through educator inquiry (Holmes Group, 1990). Collaboratively, the University and two districts operate nine PDSs. Each district has one secondary PDS, one middle school PDS, and a combined five elementary PDSs. The authors, whose experience spans the origination of PDS work through the current implementation, offer the following observations about the challenges and opportunities of PDS work.

Communication across the partnership is both a strength and a challenge. While a sophisticated multilayered organizational structure serves as the vehicle for regular and meaningful communication, it is an ongoing effort to maximize timely communication and minimize miscommunication. The current effort to modify the organizational structure illustrates the partnership's commitment to reflect on its efforts and make changes where necessary.

One contributing factor to the communication challenge is the impact of leadership changes at every level. As previously mentioned, the partnership has absorbed the transitions of eight superintendents in WISD, four superintendents in MISD, and five deans (plus five interim deans) in the SOE, and that does not include the countless campus principal changes. The partnership often feels as if it is constantly starting over, reestablishing both the shared vision and the commitment to PDS work with new leaders.

The partnership has also endured the inevitable stress of school reconfiguration. From the inception of PDS work at Hillcrest, when the opportunity to reconstitute a shuttered elementary campus was part of a districtwide plan to rebalance attendance at crowded consolidated campuses, the partnership has weathered the population shifts within both urban and suburban school districts. Whether accommodating district growth with new campuses or adjusting attendance zones to encompass the meandering concentrations of families with school-age children, the partnership districts have been required to shuffle personnel. Personnel changes on public school campuses have the potential to impact the capacity for Baylor University to place PSTs with experienced clinical instructors and mentor teachers.

Building and maintaining the capacity for effective PST placements at PDSs remains a consistent challenge. Whether the result of district initiatives or the natural attrition of professional retirements, advancements, or departures, the need to maintain a cadre of high-quality experienced teachers is a substantial challenge for district human resource departments and campus principals. When layered with the additional expectations for teachers at PDS sites (e.g., accepting PSTs as peers or the increased responsibilities of professional mentoring and partnership work), the challenge is magnified.

OPPORTUNITIES

Each of the challenges identified also represents an opportunity. There are some overarching opportunities for the partnerships. Chief among them is identifying new ways to increase enrollment in the teacher preparation program. Nationally, enrollment in teacher education has dropped by almost a third (Partelow, 2019). This is consistent with enrollment declines at the University. The Baylor SOE's approach to PDS work is to get PSTs into clinical experiences early and often (field work in six of eight semesters) initially attracted potential PSTs to the program. As other universities adopted similar experiences, the unique draw to Baylor diminished. There is currently a task force examining the Baylor programs to identify unique aspects that currently exist or can be added to increase the potential draw to the institution. In addition, the task force may make recommendations about how the SOE can use its scholarship funds to attract additional enrollments.

A second opportunity is related to one of the challenges mentioned earlier—leadership turnover. The School of Education has hired a new dean, has an interim department chair, and is reconstituting the Office of Professional Practice, after the retirement of the only director the OPP has ever known. These do not include the personnel changes anticipated within the two partnership districts, one of which will be opening a new campus configuration that will require arbitrary movement of key personnel. From a positive perspective, these changes provide opportunities to rearticulate the PDS work, to engage new leaders in the partnership, and to reaffirm the value of the partnership to a continually expanding constituency.

Similarly, there are anticipated changes in the capacity of the PDS partner districts to provide sufficient placements and there are anticipated changes to the adjunct faculty who supervise those placements. Feedback from the current adjunct faculty, mentor teachers, and clinical instructors is that the current process of on-boarding is overwhelming—too much information presented in too short a time frame. This has initiated the development of a website that would provide a "just-in-time" resource for new partnership teachers and adjunct faculty.

NEXT STEPS/SUMMARY

As the partnership moves into its fourth decade, there will be new challenges addressing learning declines that have emerged as a result of education's shift to remote instruction. As this manuscript is being prepared, yet another mass shooting at a school has engulfed the education profession with questions about how to prepare future teachers to stand in between their students and whatever potential harm comes through the classroom door.

Herein lies the value of PDS work, none of these challenges will be faced as a singular institution; the strength of the partnerships, the collegial bonds created by a shared vision and shared work are formidable. When K–12 educators perceive themselves as teacher educators and university faculty accept responsibility for K–12 student learning, then both environments are enriched. The PSTs and their future students are the beneficiaries. Our best example of what the future holds is embedded in our partnership work during COVID. Though the challenges can appear daunting, the COVID pandemic had the potential to completely undermine more than 25 years of collaborative work. However, it was the nature of the long-standing relationships between the SOE, WISD, and MISD, that even during the pandemic, Baylor SOE PSTs taught alongside their in-service counterparts, whether collaborating on remote instruction or the various forms of in-person instruction shaped by COVID-mitigation protocols. It is a testament to the partners' commitment to the work that allowed for 86 novice PSTs to participate in field experiences on campuses during the pandemic. At one point during the pandemic, a single campus hosted all middle and secondary PSTs. It is due to this dedication to the goals of the partnership that the work did not stop. The work did go on. The work will go on.

REFERENCES

Council of Chief State School Officers. (2011). Interstate Teacher Assessment and Support Consortium (InTASC) Model Core Teaching Standards: A Resource for State Dialogue. https://ccsso.org/sites/default/files/2017-12/2013_INTASC_Learning_Progressions_for_Teachers.pdf

Fogleman, L. S. (2001, October 16). *Baylor teacher education partnership in national spotlight*. Baylor University. https://www.baylor.edu/mediacommunications/news.php?action=story&story=3716

Goree, K., Williams, Y., Hamilton, S., Mathews-Perez, A., Talbert, S., Strot, R., Barrett, S., Bolfing, D., Miller, S., Almaguer, D., Gilbreath, D., Martinez, D., Rubio, B., Ward, V., Edison, R., Henry, M., Mechell, R., Pritchard, M., & Welsh, K. (2019, Spring). The Baylor University and Waco Independent School District: A twenty-five-year partnership that began with a plan in a van. *School-University Partnerships, 12*(1), 10–15. https://files.eric.ed.gov/fulltext/EJ1220179.pdf

Holmes Group. (1990). *Tomorrow's schools: A report of the Holmes Group*.

Holmes Group. (1995). *Tomorrow's schools of education: A report of the Holmes Group*

McCall, M., Howell, L., Rogers, R., Osborne, L., Goree, K., Merritt, B., Cox, H., Fischer, J., Gardner, P., & Gasaway, J. (2017, Fall). Baylor University and Midway Independent School District: An exemplary partnership. *School-University Partnerships, 10*(2), 8–12. https://files.eric.ed.gov/fulltext/EJ1169297.pdf

McCall, M., Rogers, R., Gasaway, J., & Veselka, M. (2018). Clinical experiences in middle and high schools: Results of a one-year implementation of the co-teach model. *School-University Partnerships, 11*(1), 26–35. https://files.eric.ed.gov/fulltext/EJ1179957.pdf

Messer, M. (Ed.). (1996, Spring). SOE considers additional PDS site. *Baylor Pedagogue: School of Education Newsletter, 14*(2), 1.

National Council for the Accreditation of Teacher Education. (2001). *Standards for professional development schools*.

Partelow, L. (2019, December 3). *What to make of declining enrollment in teacher preparation programs*. Center for American Progress. https://www.americanprogress.org/article/make-declining-enrollment-teacher-preparation-programs/

Rogers, R., McCall, M., & Crowley, B. (2021, Fall). Implementing co-teaching: What mentors believe and what they do. *School-University Partnerships, 14*(2), 105–114.

Rogers, R., Rogers, D., Choins, J., & Cox, H. (2017, Special Issue). Deliberate investigations of a flipped class. *School-University Partnerships, 10*(4), 95–111. https://napds.org/wp-content/uploads/2020/07/SUP-104-Teacher-Inquiry-Rogers.pdf

State Board for Educator Certification, Texas Administrative Code 19 § 228.20 (2020). https://texreg.sos.state.tx.us/public/readtac$ext.TacPage?sl=R&app=9&p_dir=&p_rloc=&p_tloc=&p_ploc=&pg=1&p_tac=&ti=19&pt=7&ch=228&rl=20

St. Cloud State University. (n.d.). *The Academy for Co-Teaching and Collaboration*. https://www.stcloudstate.edu/coeld/coteaching/default.aspx?utm_source=website&utm_medium=redirect

Texas Education Agency. (n.d.). *AskTED*. https://tea4avholly.tea.state.tx.us/TEA.AskTED.Web/Forms/ViewDirectory.aspx

CHAPTER 2

BOWIE STATE UNIVERSITY PDS NETWORK

A Trailblazing HBCU

Eva Garin

Context

Rationale

In the early 1990s Bowie State University (BSU) was one of two original universities identified by the Maryland State Department of Education (MSDE) to pilot the first professional development schools (PDS). BSU began working with a local high school to develop the first high school PDS in the state and another university piloted the elementary site. This introduction to a PDS launched a long, successful PDS history that has continued through the years. We believe that the rationale for including BSU into this pilot was our history in Maryland as being the oldest Historically Black College and University (HBCU) and the fact that BSU began as a teaching institution (BSU, 2022). BSU is an outgrowth of a school opened in 1864 in Baltimore, Maryland by the Baltimore Association for the Moral and Educational Improvement of Colored People, an organization dedicated to offering educational opportunities for its Black citizens. The association opened its first Baltimore school on January 9, 1865, in the African Baptist Church in Crane's Building on the corner of Calvert and Saratoga streets. The school offered courses in the elements of education. Courses to train teachers were added in 1866. By 1910, the state decided to relocate the school to Bowie, MD, purchasing a 187-acre tract formerly known as Jericho Farm dating to 1716. The school opened at its current location in 1911 with about 60 students.

Our history as the first secondary PDS in Maryland and the oldest HBCU in Maryland has influenced our work in teacher education in a variety of ways. We mention our important history as being the first HBCU in Maryland because as a PDS Network, we focus on the tenets of equity and social justice in all aspects of our collaborations.

Piloting a PDS for our state allowed us to be at the table when important decisions regarding PDSs were made. For example, MSDE convened a group of university and school district leaders to examine the National Council for the Accreditation of Teacher Education (NCATE) PDS Standards and develop PDS standards for the state of Maryland. BSU professors and PDS teachers and administrators were an important part of this process that continued until 2001 when the Superintendents and Deans Committee of the Maryland Partnership for Teaching and Learning K–16 was proud to present *Professional Development Schools: An Implementation Manual.* This document (MSDE, 2003) was revised in 2003 and is still used today as a model for PDS partnerships in Maryland along with *What it Means to Be a Professional Development School: The Nine Essentials Second Edition* (NAPDS, 2021).

BSU and PDS Demographics

Our PDS program is housed in the College of Education, the Department of Teaching, Learning and Professional Development, where we offer three undergraduate programs: elementary education, early childhood/special education, and secondary education. We graduate approximately 40 students annually in our undergraduate programs. Our undergraduate students complete a yearlong internship in one of our seven elementary schools or two secondary schools (one middle and one high school) spanning two school districts.

BSU offers 23 undergraduate majors, 19 master's degrees, 14 post-bachelor's certificates and two doctoral programs. Our overall enrollment is around 6,000 students with 5,000 of those students being undergraduate. Our student body is predominantly local from the Baltimore, DC region and is 85% minority with 81% African American and 4% Latinx. BSU ranks among the nation's top comprehensive universities, cultivating next-generation leaders by providing opportunities for students to discover their strengths through focused academic experiences and opportunities to tackle real-world problems.

PDS Network Description

Our PDS sites are located in two school districts in Maryland, Prince George's and Anne Arundel County Public Schools. We have one elementary school in Anne Arundel County Public Schools and the other PDS sites are in Prince George's County Public Schools. Both school districts are located near the university and have a long history of partnering with us. Anne Arundel County (AACPS, 2022) has a dedicated person who works with PDSs across sites and universities and has many universities working with them. We are hoping to expand that partnership to other sites. The remainder of our PDS sites are in Prince George's County (PGCPS, 2022) where our original pilot PDS was located. Prince George's County also has a dedicated person who works with university partners.

We have Memorandums of Understanding (MOU) with each of these districts. The MOUs (see resources) represent the differing approaches to PDSs that the districts used. One is a legal document and the other outlines roles and responsibilities. Our relationships with the districts and with individual PDS sites are not influenced by these MOUs as much so as the NAPDS Nine Essentials (NAPDS, 2021) and the MSDE PDS Standards.

These two school districts offer diversity of setting and opportunity. Anne Arundel County Public Schools (AACPSs) has 6,351 teachers, and 94.4% hold advanced or standard certificates. They rank second in the state with 541 National Board Certified teachers. 38% of the students attending school in AACPS are Hispanic/Latino or African American. Our second district partner, Prince George's County Public Schools (PGCPSs), is one of the nation's 20th largest school districts and the second largest in the state of Maryland. Fifty-five percent of the students are Black or African American and 36% are Hispanic/Latino. The school district has over 20,000 employees.

Description of Teacher Education Programs

BSU offers three programs in our Teacher Education Program. We offer a traditional elementary education program that certifies teachers in Grades 1 to 6. Our early childhood/special education program is a dual certification program meaning that students are certified in both areas ages birth to Grade 3. We also offer a Master's Degree in Teaching (MAT) program for career changers. A fourth program is offered by our College of Arts and Sciences for secondary education students who major in their disciplines of English, Mathematics, Sciences and History and minor in secondary education. We collaborate closely with our Arts and Sciences faculty. All of our Teacher Education programs are fully certified by the Maryland State Department of Education.

Oversight Positions

The College of Education has a PDS Coordinator who receives a two course release to coordinate the BSU PDS Network. This position reports to both the chair of the Department of Teaching, Learning and Professional Development and to the College Dean. The university PDS coordinator works closely with the Director of Field Studies in coordinating intern placements but mostly coordinates professional development for the faculty in both the university and PDS sites. The university PDS coordinator liaisons with the school districts, PDS Principals and site-based PDS coordinators and mentor teachers. Each PDS site has a site-based PDS Coordinator. Most of our methods faculty are PDS teachers who are current in the pedagogy of their disciplines. Our PDS Network meetings bring all of the oversight members together on a monthly basis.

Structure

Partnership Creation

Since beginning our PDS work in the late 1990s we have continued to work with the two original sites. Others were added in a variety of ways. Informally our relationships with administrators and teachers helped us open new schools as BSU PDS sites. For example, when a new elementary school opened near our university with a principal and reading specialist who had worked with us previously, both the university and the principal advocated to become a PDS as part of their opening the school and interviewing prospective teachers. This worked out well for the university and the site. When another new elementary school opened, a group of teachers transferred from one of our PDS sites to this new school, and again the principal and teachers advocated for our partnership, and we were successful in creating another PDS for our BSU PDS Network (PDSN).

Vetting Process

The formal vetting process for selecting new PDS sites begins with the BSU PDS Network as we identify our needs for additional PDS sites. These needs could range from additional placements needed to a current PDS needing a break from hosting interns. Each school district liaison attends our Network meeting. We collaborate on our needs and the school district needs, and we are given a few schools to consider. Often, we begin placing early field experience students at these sites and get to know our new partners before moving to a PDS partnership. We visit the school and attend faculty meetings to talk about PDS in general and our BSU signature programs. The last step is for the entire public school faculty to vote on whether they want to be a PDS site. We use a voting procedure that allows anonymous votes and comments. This is an important step for us as the teachers play a major role in our PDS partnerships.

Shared Resources and Participant Recognition Across P–12 and Higher Education

The BSU PDSN has a history of both human and financial shared resources. Table 2.1 outlines the flow of these resources to the network. Each of the two school districts pays their site based PDS coordinators a yearly stipend for their work. Both BSU and the districts provide a robust professional development (PD) program for these coordinators. BSU offers a three-tiered mentor teacher series that includes three sets of four-session workshops led by PDS teachers and university faculty. Both school districts offer a stipend to teachers who take the first level course, and teachers who complete our three-tiered mentoring program receive a BSU certificate and award for PDS Leadership. The school districts also pay the teacher facilitators for coplanning the workshops with university faculty and serving as workshop leaders. The university pays one teacher a stipend who coordinates the paperwork and payments with the school districts. A university PDS coordinator works with both PDS faculty and university faculty to be sure that these workshops are meeting the needs of all constituents. The PDS coordinator receives a two-course release from the university for PDS coordination.

BSU pays the mentor teachers, and the school district supplements this payment by providing a stipend for the first part of the yearlong internship. In addition, the school districts support PDS summer strategic planning by providing payment for participating teachers, and the university provides meals. For inquiry groups, the university provides books and materials for PDS teachers and yearlong interns, and the school district provides curriculum workshop pay for after school meetings. PDS teachers serving as methods faculty receive adjunct faculty pay through the university and receive support from university faculty program coordinators who meet with them on a regular basis.

For the grants supporting PDS work, stipends are paid to participating PDS teachers and faculty. PD is offered to university (College of Education and College of Arts and Sciences) and school district partners.

Table 2.1. Contributions to PDS Resources

	University	School District
Personnel	• University PDS Coordinator • Adjunct Faculty from PDS Sites	• Yearly stipend for Site-Based PDS Coordinators
Professional development	• PD for Site-Based PDS Coordinators • 3-Tiered Mentor Teacher Series • Meals for Summer Strategic Planning • Books and Materials for Inquiry Groups	• PD for Site-Based PDS Coordinators
Stipends	• PDS Teacher Stipend for Coordination of Paperwork and Payments • Mentor Teacher Stipend	• Stipend for Mentor Teacher Series (Tier 1) • Stipend for Teacher PD Facilitators • Mentor Teacher Stipend Supplement • Stipend for Summer Strategic Planning • Stipend for Inquiry Group Participation
Conferences	• Teacher Candidate Registration and Travel for NAPDS Conference • Registration for State PDS Conference	• PDS Teacher Registration for NAPDS Conference • Travel Expenses for Teacher Candidates

    The university pays for teacher candidate registration for the National Association for Professional Development Schools (NAPDS) Conference, and the Parents Teachers Organization (PTO) and principals fund registration for PDS teachers. Both the PDS sites and the university cover travel expenses for teacher candidates. The university funds PDSN member registrations for the state PDS Conference.

    Both the university and school districts recognize and reward PDS partners in our network. Each year the College of Education sponsors a Star Awards evening. PDSN members are honored by the Dean and the university PDS Coordinator in presentations summarizing their work with the university and presentations of awards of appreciation. We also recognize students for such PDS recognitions as presentations at state and national PDS conferences and the Outstanding Action Research Award. In two cases, BSU PDS teachers were recognized by the school district as the Outstanding Educator of the Year (2015 and 2018), and these teachers who also taught methods courses for BSU were recognized by the college and the university. BSU's Center for Research and Mentoring of Black

Male Students and Teachers regularly recognizes Black Male PDS site-coordinators and new teachers in our PDSN.

We celebrate our site-based PDS coordinators at monthly PDSN meetings and during summer strategic planning by recognizing their roles in our teacher education programs and by offering multiple pathways to leadership roles including adjunct faculty, mentor teacher workshops leaders, inquiry group leaders, university committee and panel members, PDS conference presenters and/or attendees, coauthors of articles and book chapters, and national leadership positions which we believe has had a positive impact on retention of teachers in our PDS sites (Garin, 2017).

Unique Partner Features

BSU PDSN is a small, close-knit learning community whose members support the advancement of the 9 Essentials (2021) and the State of Maryland PDS Standards (2003) that are based on the previous NCATE Standards (NCATE, 2001). We represent university faculty, PDS faculty, and state and school district liaisons and work across two school districts and three undergraduate programs—elementary, early childhood/special education and secondary education.

The mission of the BSU PDS Network (Bowie State University, 2023) is to create and sustain a collaborative partnership that impacts student learning by exploring models of effective teaching and learning; facilitating extensive, clinically rich yearlong internship practices for prospective teachers; conducting needs-based professional development; and sharing best practices among PDS Partners.

BSU's unique PDS Initiatives include:

- PDS Leadership Certificate via a three-tiered program including Teach-Coach-Reflect, Advanced Teach-Coach-Reflect and PDS Leadership Workshop,
- Focused professional development on culturally responsive teaching pedagogies (CRP), literacy, mathematics, science and technology, lesson planning, and student engagement,
- Focused response to the new reality of mentoring and completing a yearlong internship in a virtual classroom,
- Yearlong internship assessment through a performance-based electronic portfolio,
- Multisite monthly planning including extended Summer Strategic Planning,
- On-Site Methods Courses (math, science and reading taught by PDS teachers),

- Methods course assignments that are conducted in mentor teachers' classes while working with children during the courses held at a PDS site (e.g., reading clinic – which is rotated between PDS sties each semester, science club, and math club),
- Attention to issues of equity and social justice,
- State, local and national PDS leadership opportunities,
- Coauthored articles, book chapters and studies,
- Site-Based Inquiry Groups,
- Action research conducted by teacher candidates and mentor teachers, and
- A shared mission across institutions.

Opportunities for Teacher Leadership in Boundary Spanning Roles

As stated in NAPDS Essential 8: Boundary-Spanning Roles (NAPDS, 2021) PDSs work best when there are clearly defined formal and informal roles assumed by individuals from both schools and universities. According to Garin and Burns (2020), "Boundary spanners are the heartbeat of any PDS. These are individuals who work across the institutional settings of schools and universities daily to ensure that the PDS functions and thrives" (p. 191). The BSU PDSN features many boundary-spanning roles, including PDS teachers serving as adjunct faculty, PDS teachers teaching mentoring workshops, University faculty and PDS teachers coauthoring studies and publishing journal articles, PDS teachers and university faculty serving as coeditor and assistant editor of a journal, PDS teachers and university faculty collaborating on conference presentations, and PDS teachers and university faculty creating and testing departmental surveys. What initially propelled our PDSN into having a collaborative spirit was the edict from a former dean that any methods course not being taught by tenure track faculty would be taught by PDS teachers. Over the years, methods courses have been taught on site at rotating PDSs where interns have worked with P–12 students in a PDS reading clinic and math and science clubs. Just this year, our math methods course is being instructed for the first time by a PDS teacher who was an undergraduate in our elementary education program 16 years ago! These boundary spanning roles help link theory to practice and provide leadership opportunities for PDS teachers.

We consider many of these boundary spanning roles as a way to reward members of our PDSN. As a PDS Network we offer many opportunities to take leadership roles in the state and national PDS arena. Our PDS Network has been awarded both state and national grants to support our work with university faculty, PDS teachers, and pre-K–12 students. We were the recipients of a Maryland State Department of Education (MSDE) Race to the Top subgrant that focused on our secondary PDS. As part of this teaching consortium, university faculty and PDS faculty met with state coordinators and other universities to create a Maryland Teaching Consortium Manual that is comprised of modules for teaching culturally and linguistically diverse students. This recently released document, which members of our Network coauthored with others across the state of Maryland, will provide a framework for professional development of PDS partners at Network meetings and Summer Strategic Planning.

Other grant opportunities that expanded the reach of our PDS Network and provided learning opportunities for many of our members in four main areas:

Strengthening Writing through Culturally Responsive Practices

This grant funded project began with an inquiry group of 22 teachers focused on CRP for teachers who work in culturally, linguistically, and socioeconomically diverse schools. Teachers were guided through lesson planning sessions to incorporate their knowledge of CRP with writing and technology. The project culminated in the creation of video cases to demonstrate teacher learning. Participating schools were identified by numbers of limited English Proficiency and students receiving free or reduced lunch. Although the grant was originally written to target our entire PDSN, we learned that only one of our PDSs qualified. One of the benefits of this project was pairing our participating PDS with a neighboring middle school for the inquiry group. As a result of this partnership, the middle school became our new middle school PDS. In addition, our collaborations with Arts and Sciences faculty increased because one of the PIs on this grant was from the English and Modern Languages Department.

This has resulted in increased momentum for our secondary PDSs. This grant paved the way to another research grant that focused on the diversity conversations between and among 10 preservice teachers: 5 from BSU and 5 from a Midwestern predominately white university. Conversations focused on social justice as well as stereotypes and biases. This resulted in a staged reading at BSU and ultimately to the creation of a play, *How Can I Say This So You Will Stay?*, that was performed at the Kennedy Center for the Performing Arts.

Preparing and Retaining Diverse, High-Quality Secondary School STEM Teachers

This ongoing grant, funded by the National Science Foundation and the Noyce Scholarship Program provides internship opportunities, academic scholarships, pedagogical training, and mentoring activities to attract, prepare, support, and retain talented underrepresented minority secondary teachers in Maryland high-need school districts. The PIs on this grant include the BSU PDS Coordinator and the BSU Arts and Sciences Math and Science liaisons to education. Our Secondary PDS sites serve on the advisory board for this project. Scholarship recipients receive training in best practices in tutoring, tutor students in our middle school PDS site, complete their yearlong internship in one of our secondary PDS sites, and participate in inquiry groups and action research. In addition, BSU students and faculty will attend and present at conferences, supported by grant funding.

Computer Science Teacher Educator Program

This project funded by Maryland Center for Computing Education (MCEE) focuses on BSU faculty, PDS teachers, and teacher candidates by creating a learning community whose mission and vision is to become an exemplar first class university in teaching Computer Science Fundamentals in undergraduate and graduate programs of study and to promote a computer science, computational thinking, and teaching culture through collaboration on teaching computer science fundamentals.

To date, participants have written lesson plans and kept reflective journals that were shared in a poster session on campus. Next steps include development of a website, a revised lesson plan format being integrated into science and math methods courses, and development of workshops for mentor teachers and preservice students on computational thinking. Finally, we hope to develop a computer science education major collaboratively planned by Education faculty, Arts and Sciences faculty, and PDS teachers. This collaborative group is in the process of writing an additional grant to fund workshops for PDS partners in computational thinking.

The Collaborative Video Lab:
Enhancing Preservice Teacher Experiences Through CRP

This project included workshops on CRP for preservice teachers and mentor teachers. Preservice students created video journals and presentations on their reflections on aspects of CRP and shared them with mentor teachers and university supervisors. Workshops included topics such as growth mindset, embracing social media as an instructional tool to create positive learning environments for students, CRP classroom management and learning environments to support student learning, and using CRP to empower African American learners. Students filmed their journals to fulfill a student teaching seminar assignment and developed a collaborative rubric with supervisors and mentor teachers.

These elements of our PDS context reflect a strong commitment to Essential 4's "shared commitment to innovative and reflective practices by all participants" (NAPDS, 2021, p. 4) through collaboration between Education and Arts and Sciences faculty, PDS teachers and administrators, PDS site-based coordinators, teacher candidates, and community partners; our innovative and reflective focus on P–12 learning; and support of effective practices through our PDSN, including inquiry groups, action research, and attention to CRP.

National Leadership Opportunities

Nationally, representatives from the BSU PDS Network have served in PDS leadership capacities. One member of the Network has served as one of the past presidents of National Association for Professional Development Schools (NAPDS). Another member of the Network served as the American Educational Research Association (AERA) PDS Research-SIG Chair. Additionally, two members of the Network served as associate editors of the NAPDS Journal, *School-University Partnerships*. One member of the Network has served a coeditor of PDS Partners: Bridging Research to Practice and a teacher in our Network served as Assistant Editor. While the BSU PDS Network is a small, close-knit learning community, the members of the Network support the advancement of PDS on a national scale.

As previously mentioned, our PDS Network is guided by the Maryland State Department of Education *Professional Development Schools: An Implementation Model* (2003), which outlines PDS standards and a redesign in teacher education. This manual guides our commitment to the role of teacher inquiry in impacting student learning, extended internships and the requirement that all students must complete their internships in a PDS site. Additionally, we focus on the NAPDS (2008, 2021) documents, *What it Means to be a Professional Development School*. Each of these documents and organizations has provided impetus as we developed our BSU PDS Network Signature Programs.

Signature Programs of the PDSN

Signature Programs are those programs that epitomize an institution's mission and define its distinctiveness. For the BSU PDS Network, identifying Signature Programs has facilitated PDS partners' identification of the network's programming strengths and nonnegotiables (Kelly, 2008). This list of signature programs has been revisited at each Network meeting with site based PDS coordinators and university faculty. Furthermore, each summer our Signature Programs are discussed and refined with the greater community of site based PDS coordinators, mentor teachers, school administrators, student teachers, and university faculty.

Network Signature Programs (Garin, 2015) evolved from discussion to print to reality through a 5-year process. To advance the vision of our PDS Network, new programs are added and those that are no longer needed are omitted. The process of identifying and refining our Signature Programs is a collaborative effort between all PDS stakeholders, all of whom work together for the greater good of the Network and the pre-K–12 students who we support. While each signature program stands as a unique initiative, they each share several underlying characteristics. Specifically, these programs:

- Build on existing strengths
- Work on interdisciplinary and interagency levels with MSDE, Prince George's County and Anne Arundel County school districts, and Bowie State University
- Support the development and growth of PDS teachers, university faculty, and students
- Offer potential to tap into external and internal funding opportunities
- Distinguish our PDS Network from others
- Possess tremendous potential for development and start-up ventures
- Support the Maryland State Department of Education PDS Standards (MSDE, 2003) and the National Association for Professional Development Schools Nine Essentials (NAPDS, 2008, 2021)

BSU's PDSN focuses on five signature programs: (1) action research, (2) mentoring workshops, (3) PDS meetings, panels and committees, (4) on-site methods courses and the PDS reading clinic, and (5) publications and conference presentations.

Action Research. Within the Bowie State University PDS Network, both PDS teachers and teacher candidates participate in action research. Interns use action research during their student teaching semester to support a school improvement goal or their mentor teacher's Student Learning Outcomes (SLOs) and work with a small group of students to offer additional support. Teacher candidates present their action research to a panel of PDS stakeholders consisting of university and PDS faculty members who use a rubric to score and give feedback to each teacher candidate. This occurs towards the end of the student teaching semester and is one of the graduation requirements and part of our assessment system. In addition, often PDS sites are invited to apply for action research mini grants, which are open to all teachers within the PDS, whether or not they serve as mentor teachers. To apply for an action research minigrant, PDS teachers are invited to an information meeting on campus where the Request for Proposals (RFP) is presented, and questions are answered. Mentor teachers who enroll in our mentoring workshops also have the opportunity to conduct and share their action research. This Signature Program addresses NAPDS Essential 2: Clinical Preparation, Essential 3: Professional Learning and Leading, and Essential 4: Reflection and Innovation (NAPDS, 2021).

While action research is the most recognized form of teacher research, another lesser-known and less formal type of teacher research is the inquiry group (Garin, 2015; Garin, 2005). Inquiry groups are defined by the MSDE as "a group of PDS stakeholders who collaboratively examine and asses their practices and the outcomes achieved" and who "raise specific questions related to teaching and learning, seek to systematically answer their finding to others" (MSDE, 2003, p. 20). In the BSU PDS Network, inquiry groups include teachers and teacher candidates (supported by their university faculty) who choose a topic of interest and meet regularly to discuss research literature and examine instructional practice, both theoretical and actual, as they implement new instructional strategies in their classrooms and collect data and student work samples to analyze collaboratively.

To date, BSU inquiry groups have read over 100 professional books including such titles as *The Café Book: Engaging All students in daily Assessments in Literacy* (Boushey & Moser 2009), *Strategies that Work* (Harvey & Goudvis, 2007), *The Book Whisperer: Awakening the Inner Reader in Every Child* (Miller, 2009), *Boys and Girls Learn Differently* (Gurian, 2011), *The Distance Between Us* (Grande, 2012), *Mathematical Mindsets* (Bouler, 2022), and *The Distance Learning Book* (Fisher et al., 2021). See a list of inquiry group books read by the PDSN in the resources chapter.

Mentoring Workshops

The BSU PDS Network offers a three-tier professional development program developed by PDS teachers and university faculty. Tier 1 is a mentoring workshop, Teach-Coach-Reflect (TCR), which is offered once a year and is rotated to each PDS site. The workshop is delivered by PDS teachers and is open to university faculty and PDS teachers from all our sites. Tier 2 is an Advanced TCR course collaboratively planned and delivered by PDS teachers. This four-session workshop is open to any university faculty or PDS faculty who successfully completed the initial TCR course (Tier 1). Tier 3 is a PDS Leadership Workshop for university and PDS faculty who completed Tiers 1 and 2. This workshop provides opportunities for PDS research, presentations, and exploration of PDS through collective readings and discussions of books and articles. Through the successful completion of this three-tier professional development program, our educators are afforded the opportunity to earn a PDS Leadership Certificate. This signature Program addresses NAPDS Essential 5: Research and Results (NAPDS, 2021).

PDS Network Meetings, Review Panels, and Campus Committees

The BSU PDS Network holds the following meetings: PDS Network monthly meetings, PDS Summer Strategic Planning meetings, and BSU Teacher Education Council meetings. Site PDS Coordinators, BSU faculty, preservice mentor teachers, and BSU supervisors are invited to participate in these meetings. The PDS Network meets monthly to discuss professional development needs, PDS conferences, inquiry groups, action research, and school improvement plans that involve PDS partners. Attendees include Site PDS Coordinators, principals, university faculty, and school district partners. The first meeting of the year is held in October, and this meeting's agenda includes revisiting our Network's Signature Programs, the roles and responsibilities of each PDS Partner, and supports and professional development needed within the partnership. Other topics discussed during the year include site based PDS meetings, planning for our Summer Strategic Planning, and mentoring workshops. We also revisit the NAPDS Nine Essentials and the MSDE PDS Standards.

The PDS Summer Strategic Planning is considered the fourth Network meeting, it involves partners reflecting on the school year and planning for the upcoming year. Summer Strategic Planning provides an opportunity for school system liaisons and site based PDS committees to meet with one another to develop and refine policies, procedures, programs, and larger PDS activities. During these meetings research agendas are discussed, and the NAPDS 9 Essentials and MSDE PDS Standards are used to reflect upon the progress of the PDS sites and the overall Network. As a Network, we reflect on our Signature Programs and formally vote on each program's modifications and continued inclusion on the list.

BSU PDS partners also serve on the Teacher Education interview panel, action research review panels and e-portfolio review panels. Site PDS Coordinators, BSU faculty, preservice mentor teachers, school district liaisons, and BSU supervisors meet as a committee to interview candidates seeking admittance to a Teacher Education program at BSU. At the end of the internship, Site PDS Coordinators, BSU faculty, preservice mentor teachers, and BSU supervisors also serve on e-portfolio and action research panels. This Signature Program addresses NAPDS Essential 5: Research and Results (NAPDS, 2021).

On-Site Methods Courses and the PDS Reading Clinic

Our methods courses in the elementary and early childhood/special education programs are offered at a PDS. This has enabled greater collaboration, more opportunities for classroom visits, and copresentations between PDS teachers and university faculty. Methods courses are instructed by tenure-track faculty or PDS teachers serving as adjunct faculty, a policy created and endorsed by our College Dean.

The Science Methods instructors, who are PDS teachers serving as adjunct faculty, collaborate with the Site PDS Coordinators to determine course content. The course objectives are often aligned with action research and inquiry groups conducted at the PDS site. The BSU teacher candidates are required to teach a science read aloud in their mentor teacher's classroom. In addition, each PDS site has a science club that meets monthly during the science methods course. During this time, teacher candidates facilitate and implement club activities and field trips in order to build intern and student interest in science. This type of course delivery gives PDS partners the opportunity to examine and share best practices specific to achievement in science.

The Reading Methods course is also taught at a PDS site by one of our PDS teachers or principals. The assignments address K–5 best practices in reading curriculum and state objectives and enrich the current literacy program. One such assignment is the implementation of an author study in the mentor teachers' classroom. This assignment promotes opportunities for teacher candidates and mentor teachers to collaborate on best practices in literacy instruction.

Since 2004, BSU has partnered with elementary PDS sites to host a PDS Reading Clinic as part of the Assessment for Reading Instruction course. This innovative format, which serves a different PDS site each year, offers another opportunity for examining best practices. The Assessment for Reading Instruction teachers, who are BSU faculty and PDS teachers serving as adjunct faculty, meet with BSU teacher candidates at a PDS site and collaborate with the site-based reading specialist to provide instruction on assessments and appropriate reading interventions. Then, BSU teacher candidates practice these assessments and interventions with students who have been referred to the Reading Clinic by their classroom teacher. These students are tutored weekly for a total of 10–12 forty-five-minute tutoring sessions with their BSU tutor. At the end of the semester, the Assessment for Reading Instruction teacher holds conferences with the classroom teacher who referred the students, the reading specialist, and the BSU intern/tutor to discuss the student achievement results of the reading clinic intervention.

Publications and Conference Presentations

Conference attendance and presentations provide another opportunity for PDS partners to examine and share best practices and PDS Signature Programs on local, state, and national levels. The BSU PDS Network stakeholders gather in May at the BSU PDS Research Conference to share results of individual and collaborative action research, book study, and inquiry groups. Over 80 teacher candidates, PDS teachers/administrators, and university faculty attend this PDS Network Signature Program. At our last Summer Strategic Planning meeting, PDS partners identified this conference as a vital aspect of our partnership.

Each May, The Maryland PDS Network sponsors a statewide PDS conference where PDS partners share their best practices during breakout sessions. A gallery walk is also hosted where teacher candidates share their action research studies with conference attendees. BSU sponsors registration for teacher candidates and university and PDS faculty to attend this conference.

An important aspect of our PDS Network is that we collaborate on local, state and national conference presentations. At the national level, PDS partners, including university faculty and PDS faculty, present their examination of best practices at the NAPDS Annual Conference, the American Educational Research Association Conference and the American Association of Colleges of Teacher Education Conference. These collaborative conference presentations have been an important aspect of our partnership as far back as 2004.

As an example, the PDS Network Coordinator led a study (Garin, 2017) that used survey research and interviews to learn about PDS teachers' experience participating in action research and inquiry groups and yielded a finding of interest to PDS research regarding teacher career paths. Through this study we learn that PDS teachers are less likely to seek new leadership roles and promotions both within and outside of their schools. Non-PDS respondents were nearly four and a half times more likely to seek new leadership roles. The results of this study indicate that PDS teachers experience teacher leadership roles as part of their PDS partnership including participation in their own action research,

Table 2.2. Proudest Accomplishment

Accomplishment	Aligned NAPDS Essentials
• Staying together as a Network across school districts rather than dividing by school level or initial certification programs. This commitment has led to cross-district sharing and increased the effectiveness of the entire Network.	1, 6, and 7
• Developing a culture of inquiry through inquiry groups and action research	3, 4, 5, and 6
• Developing and implementing Signature Programs that have grown over time and represent who we are as a Network	1-9
• Agreeing that the entire school is the PDS, not just the mentor teachers, and providing opportunities for all teachers, which results in the entire PreK-12 setting embracing teacher candidates	1, 2, 3, 4, and 5
• Providing continual and collaborative needs assessment, reflection, and planning during Network meetings	1, 3, 4, 7, 8, and 9
• Providing leadership at the local, state, and national levels in the PDS arena through PDS conference presentations and publications co-authored and copresented by university faculty and PDS teachers	3, 4, and 5
• Leading the state of Maryland by implementing a PDS Leadership Certificate workshop program for university faculty and PDS teachers consisting of a three-tier professional development series	3, 4, 5, 8, and 9

mentoring interns through their action research as well as participating in inquiry groups with other mentor teachers and teacher candidates. They reported that they remain in the classroom because the PDS opportunities provide the leadership experiences they seek. While the accomplishments of the BSU PDS Network are many, we are proudest of those found in Table 2.2

Challenges

One of our greatest challenges is securing funding for our PDS initiatives. As stated above, both school districts pay a stipend to their site based PDS Coordinators and a stipend to mentor teachers; however, workshop pay, books and refreshments are not as available as they once were. The university also pays a stipend to mentor teachers and purchases books for inquiry groups. What challenges us most is the inconsistent availability of funds. We continue to make the best of limited resources and use grant opportunities to strengthen our PDS Network.

The other challenge we are experiencing is one that is a national trend. Both school districts, MSDE, and state leaders are grappling with the terms *PDS* and *school university partnerships* and defining the similarities and differences. Even MSDE who led the nation in developing PDS structures and guidelines is pondering these terms and moving towards the term *school university partnerships*. At BSU, we have created cohorts for paraprofessionals, Master of Education students and PDS students to help us distinguish between PDS and other types of partnerships. We continue to seek ways to address the needs of all constituents without working in silos.

The University Systems of Maryland is also currently involved in redesigning teacher education under the Blueprint for Maryland's Future (MSDE, 2022), a piece of landmark legislation passed in 2021 that calls for a yearlong internship of over 200 days, a required passing score on a performance assessment such as edTPA and a required passing score on Praxis. This legislation has provided an opportunity for us to reexamine and redesign our teacher education program, PDS program, and involve our greater Network to be part of this journey.

Over the past several years, we have experienced unprecedented challenges including the COVID-19 pandemic and the bomb scares called into HBCUs throughout the nation. We learned a great deal about the strength of our PDS Network as we faced these challenges. Our monthly Network meetings were vital in addressing the challenges of fully online courses, virtual PDS sites, and supervision of interns. For a while we met bimonthly to forge a plan that felt like changing the tire while the car was still moving. As safety measures changed, schools closed, and campus lockdowns were put in place, we worked to develop and revise mentoring plans and workshops, protocols for supervision, and support for members of the Network.

We used our virtual mentor teacher happy hours to learn about the challenges our mentor teachers were experiencing and offered one happy hour that included mentor teachers and their interns. This led to action research conducted by a university faculty member, a graduate student and a fifth-grade teacher on mentoring during the pandemic. This action research study was submitted to the AERA PDS Research Special Interest Group, and Bowie State University was awarded the Claudia A. Balach Teacher as Researcher Award. In addition, this work can be found in two articles in the NAPDS Journal School University Partnerships (Garin, 2021; Marshall-Kraus et al., 2021).

Opportunities

The BSU PDS Network has a long history of collaboration, commitment to continuous improvement of all partners, boundary spanning roles, and dedication to student achievement. Network members actively contribute to the knowledge of the network as a whole and also to the larger PDS community within Maryland and nationwide. We pride ourselves on our professionalism. All members of the Network are professionals with parity, and all seek to advance the profession of teaching through cultivation of excellence within our newest members and ourselves, and through deliberate research into effective practices that result in improved school cultures and student outcomes. We believe that we will be leaders in the Blueprint for Maryland's Future (MSDE, 2022) as we continue to lead in exemplary PDS partnerships, serve as leaders in recruitment of minority teacher candidates and demonstrate through our graduates what it takes to retain teachers.

REFERENCES

Anne Arundel County Public Schools. (2022). http//:aacps.org

Boaler, J. (2022). *Unleashing students' potential through creative mathematics, inspiring messages and innovative teaching.* Jossey-Bass.

Boushey, G., & Moser, J. (2009). *The café book: Engaging all students in daily assessments in literacy.* Stenhouse.

Bowie State University. (2023). About the PDS network. https://bowiestate.edu/academics/colleges/college-of-education/departments/teaching-learning-and-professional-development/pds-network/about/

Bowie State University. (2023) Historic timeline. https://bowiestate.edu/about/history/timeline.php

Fisher, D., Frey, N., & Hattie, J. (2021). *The distance learning playbook, grades k-12: Teaching for engagement in any setting.* Corwin.

Garin, E., & Burns, R. (2020). *Clinically based teacher education in action: Cases from professional development schools.* Information Age.

Garin, E., (2017). Action research in professional development schools: Does it make a difference? *School-University Partnerships, 10*(4), 13–29.

Garin, E. (2015). PDS network signature programs: What we have learned. *PDS Partners, 10*(2), 14-16.

Garin, E. (2005, February). *Using action research and inquiry groups to enhance student learning in a professional development school context* [Paper presentation]. American Association of Colleges of Teacher Education (AACTE) Annual Meeting, Washington, DC.

Grande, R. (2012). *The distance between us: A memoir.* Simon and Schuster.

Gurian, M. (2011). *Boys and girls learn differently.* Jossey-Bass.

Harvey, S., & Goudvis, A. (Eds.). (2007). *Strategies that work: Teaching comprehension for understanding and engagement.* Stenhouse.

Kelly, R. (2008, September). Setting academic priorities, identifying signature programs. *Faculty Focus.* http://www.facultyfocus.com/articles/curriculum-development/setting-academic-priorities-identifying-signature-programs

Maryland State Department of Education. (2003). *Professional development schools: An implementation manual.*

Miller, D., (2009). *The book whisperer: Awakening the inner reader in every child.* Jossey-Bass.

National Association for Professional Development Schools. (2008). *What it means to be a professional development school: The nine essentials.* [Policy statement].

National Association for Professional Development Schools (2021). *What it means to be a professional development school: The nine essentials* (2nd ed.). [Policy statement].

National Council for Accreditation of Teacher Education. (2001). *Standards for professional development schools.* [Policy statement].

Prince George's County Public Schools. (2022). https://pgcps.org

CHAPTER 3

THE BUFFALO STATE PROFESSIONAL DEVELOPMENT SCHOOL CONSORTIUM

A Shared Goal While Responding to Varying Needs

Pixita del Prado Hill, Keli Garas-York, and Selenid Gonzalez-Frey

Context

Teaching is an endeavor that encompasses community and continual progress. It is a community of educators, administrators, family, guardians, peers, and others that interact to help impact the outcome of students in the classroom. It is a community of faculty, educators, staff, organizations, and scholars that helps to advance the field of education and improve the practices of instructors in institutions of higher education (IHE). These forces combine to help build a foundation for future teachers in IHE. At its core, a Professional Development School (PDS) brings together the different forces in the community and the stakeholders within these communities to leverage their strength and resources, build connections, and help to address needs for continual growth.

In 1991, Buffalo State established a PDS consortium to foster a dynamic and reciprocal relationship between the university and school partners. The set goals are to provide teacher candidates authentic experiences in the field to supplement their learning in the classroom, to provide professional development geared towards supporting the growth of all stakeholders within P–12/college partnerships, and to support the learning of the P–12 students in our partnership sites. Today, the Buffalo State PDS consortium has grown to include more than 100 schools and community partners with approximately 45 signed agreements each semester (del Prado Hill & Garas-York, 2020; Garas-York et al., 2018). Partnerships have grown from local schools to multiple schools within the state as well as international partners in Chile, Colombia, Costa Rica, Dominican Republic, Germany, Honduras, Italy, Rwanda, and Zambia.

There are many important contributing stakeholders who are a part of the PDS consortium. The consortium includes teacher education faculty who instruct teacher candidates in various subject areas from early childhood to high school. The faculty use their designated expertise to provide professional development, workshops, and presentations when it adds to the educational growth of stakeholders. The faculty also serve as liaisons between the university and individual school partner sites. Further, they guide teacher candidates at the site as well as receive and respond to feedback from the school and community partners.

Teacher candidates progress through their programs in a cohort model with field placements at partner schools. Throughout their preparation, candidates have the opportunity for experiences in a range of schools. Their experiences are scaffolded to provide support and build confidence beginning with shadowing and service-learning activities, then moving to one-on-one tutoring, and eventually taking responsibility for small group and large group instruction. For these teacher candidates, the PDS consortium provides an orientation and workshop to prepare them before their first experience at a partner school. During the course of their preparation, teacher candidates receive opportunities to enhance their pedagogical knowledge in education. Furthermore, they are provided with support for developing connections to secure jobs, including building their understanding of creating a resumé and interviewing tips.

The partner schools constitute an essential component of the consortium. Via the PDSs, teacher candidates gain valuable experience and education faculty ground their instruction in real world experiences. P–12 school partners also have opportunities to work with faculty to engage in action research and scholarship. The schools include public, charter, and private schools in urban, first ring suburban, suburban, and rural settings where children and adolescents of all backgrounds are enrolled. Moreover, the consortium partners with community agencies that host service-learning experiences for teacher candidates.

The PDS consortium is embedded and supported by the School of Education (SOE) and Teacher Education Unit (TEU) at Buffalo State. There are over 65 certification programs including early childhood, elementary, middle, and secondary as well as P–12 programs such as special education, TESOL, music and art. With this support, there are two PDS codirectors who lead and organize each component. Additionally, there are multiple leadership committees within the organization to represent the distinct stakeholders.

Structure

The Buffalo State PDS consortium adheres to the National Association of Professional Development Schools (NAPDS) 9 Essentials (2021). Buffalo State uses this framework to provide an organizational structure but builds in a great deal of flexibility to meet each school/community partner's unique needs and interests (del Prado Hill & Garas-York, 2020; Garas-York et al., 2018). The 9 Essentials allow the Buffalo State PDS consortium to foster strong relationships and close communication with stakeholders for more meaningful and responsive initiatives (Kindzierski et al., 2021).

Policies and Procedure

Leadership. The Buffalo State PDS consortium has two codirectors who are faculty members from the TEU who teach some college classes while also providing leadership for the consortium. The PDS consortium supports the entire TEU at the college. This includes elementary and secondary programs that are often housed in the departments of the disciplines to which they most closely align. For instance, social studies education resides in the history department. The PDS codirectors work to unite the varying programs and meet their distinct needs as part of the efforts of the consortium.

The PDS codirectors convene a PDS Leadership Team biweekly that includes a department chair of the largest program within the TEU and the PDS graduate assistant. These meetings are used to map out the work of the PDS consortium, address immediate needs, and discuss stakeholder perspectives. Careful notes are maintained for each meeting.

The PDS codirectors are also members of and convene a clinically rich practice group that includes the SOE dean, who is also the head of TEU, representatives from different programs across the unit and student teaching office. This is where information from the state level is conveyed and news from school partners is shared. This group helps to make decisions related to the TEU and compiles information to be shared with the PDS consortium and the college's Teacher Education Council (TEC).

The PDS budget comes from the office of the dean. The dean's support is essential for communication with the college administration to explain how the PDS mission aligns with and supports the college mission. The dean also assists with communication with state entities. The dean provides advice and approves all PDS activities. The PDS codirectors maintain close ties with the dean through meetings and emails and provide information through annual reports and maintenance of the PDS website (see https://pds.buffalostate.edu/international-pds). The dean's administrative assistants work with the PDS codirectors to manage the PDS budget, develop school agreements, implement PDS events, and manage the PDS website and online professional development for all partners.

PDS partnerships are created in a multitude of ways. Typically, they are formed from personal relationships. The college hires course instructors who have taught in area school districts and these P–12 teachers often form PDS relationships with their current or former schools. PDS codirectors and faculty members often connect with former students who are open to building relationships with the college. In addition, district administrators frequently hear of the benefits of being part of the PDS consortium and seek out school-university partnerships.

Partnerships are often formed to accommodate the need for more teacher candidate placements or give longtime partners a break from the partnership when necessary. Districts and schools are invited to participate in PDS partnerships in a variety of ways. Interested schools are invited to PDS events and provided with access to PDS-generated materials and professional development sessions. Schools or districts can enter PDS agreements at different levels of participation for a small stipend that increases with each level of participation. PDS codirectors visit interested schools and talk with potential liaisons and administrators to explain PDS concepts and the levels of participation. If all parties agree and the partnership will benefit teacher candidates and P–12 learners, a formal agreement is developed. Levels range from Initial, Beginning, Developing, and At-Standard as well as a special International PDS agreement (see resources).

Committees. Creating partnerships is an important aspect of PDS mission, however, maintaining those partnerships is equally important to sustaining the organization. At each partner site, at least three stakeholders in the partnership (such as school administrators, lead mentor teachers, and college faculty), form a liaison committee that meets several times per semester. This group makes decisions about the partnership, helps with teacher candidate placements, evaluates the partnership, and determines how the stipend from the college is spent. The liaison committee can apply for grants and develop projects that impact all stakeholders.

While liaison committees include the school-based stakeholders, PDS faculty meetings are also held to bring together college faculty members from across the TEU to discuss issues pertinent to teacher education and share ideas. These meetings are an opportunity to identify the successes and areas for improvement in their work as liaisons to partner schools. Faculty share and use one another's ideas to help guide and further their relationships with their schools. Moreover, the PDS consortium has a TEU Faculty Taskforce comprised of a smaller intersection of instructors from varying university programs (e.g., literacy, math, and art education) who brainstorm ideas for events, professional development, and other opportunities based on feedback from these various meetings.

Faculty members and members of the PDS liaison committees can also participate in the Teacher Education Unit Professional Advisory Council (TEUPAC), or the PDS advisory board. This stakeholder input helps to ensure that the PDS codirectors and college faculty are aware of the needs of schools and districts. School partners on TEUPAC often suggest helpful and relevant initiatives for the PDS leadership to direct resources. TEUPAC meets approximately four times annually to guide the direction of the PDS consortium. Members of TEUPAC represent all stakeholders across the PDSs including district/building leaders, classroom teachers, teacher candidates, and teacher education faculty. Meetings are an opportunity to identify stakeholder needs and ideas for how to leverage resources for collaborative professional development and to address common challenges.

Collaborative Partners on Campus. The PDS consortium works to leverage valuable resources such as time, space, expertise, and money. Through structures afforded by PDSs the consortium serves as a hub of information and communication across the organization. PDSs rely heavily on collaborative efforts with other campus offices and P–12 programs to provide distinctive programming and meet the strategic goals of the college and fulfill the mission of the PDS consortium.

Buffalo State has an extensive International Professional Development School (IPDS) program. Through the international contacts of the college faculty, IPDS program was established in 2012 with two short-term, faculty-led study away programs. IPDS program now includes P–12 school partnerships across five continents. To maintain and expand this programming, collaborative relationships with the campus's Center for Global Engagement and International Graduate Programs for Educators (IGPE). IGPE coordinates on-site, accredited, high-quality graduate coursework and professional development for teachers and administrators in international schools. Together, the PDS and IGPE programs help support international travel and remote programs to strengthen and sustain global learning.

PDSs also partners with the campus's Teacher Certification Office to guide teacher candidates and provide credit for professional development. Similarly, PDS partners with the Career Development Center to prepare teacher candidates to work in schools and apply for teaching positions. These offices also work with PDSs to address issues in the field of education such as the substitute teaching crisis and teacher shortage.

In addition, PDSs collaborates with student groups on campus, such as the Future Teachers Club and Kappa Delta Pi. These collaborations afford the teacher candidates input into programming and leadership opportunities. The partnerships often involve other PDS stakeholders, such as school administrators, who assist in the preparation of teacher candidates for professional activities such as substitute teaching and interviewing for teaching positions.

These collaborative endeavors enhance the entire PDS consortium by sharing resources and preparing teachers who are knowledgeable global citizens capable of working effectively in any classroom.

PDS Components

The overarching mission of PDSs does not change but the NAPDS 9 Essentials (2021) provide structures that allow the Buffalo State PDS consortium to be responsive to the immediate and growing needs of stakeholders while leveraging resources available at the time; therefore, the PDS components can differ. For instance, prior to the COVID-19 pandemic, the Buffalo State PDS consortium was focused on research as professional development and examining the impact of PDSs on all stakeholders, social-emotional learning, and resilience, and helping some partner schools develop future teachers as Buffalo State teacher candidates worked in the schools one day a week as substitute teachers. At the onset of the pandemic and as it dragged on, the components of the work of the consortium had to be revised. The emphasis on social-emotional learning increased as teacher candidates, school partners, and P–12 learners suffered from the isolation of remote learning. Professional development on the technology and techniques involved in remote learning became a necessity for all PDS stakeholders. A shortage of substitute teachers in a few partners' schools became a more widespread issue along with an overall teacher shortage.

The structures of PDSs allow the Buffalo State PDSs to pivot and grow to meet the changing needs of stakeholders and the current educational climate. Although components of the PDS, availability of resources, and methods of meeting stakeholder needs are everchanging, PDS are continuously committed to the following central principles: mentoring teacher candidates in authentic settings, offering shared professional development, impacting student learning, conducting research on innovative and best educational practices.

Support

By design, PDS relationships are reciprocal, but as with all relationships, the dynamics change based on the educational climate, available resources, and countless other variables. There are times when college faculty are relying heavily on schools to find appropriate placements for additional teacher candidates or there are times when the school administrators need the help of college faculty and teacher candidates to implement an event or initiative at the school. Together, the end goal is well-prepared teachers who have positive impacts on P–12 learners. These give and take relationships are nurtured over time and the amount of support and the nature of the support is different depending on the school, stakeholders, grade levels, etc. The type of support needed and offered is usually communicated through each liaison committee, the advisory council or through program evaluation surveys that are completed by PDS stakeholders after each professional development session.

Professional Development

One general area of support provided across stakeholders is professional development. The college often provides professional development for teacher candidates and any other interested stakeholders based on what PDS partners communicate as an area of need for new teachers, such as social-emotional learning or trauma-informed practices. At times, partner schools will invite the PDS consortium to school PDS meetings to share new initiatives across the entire organization.

Professional development needs can be different for each stakeholder group. For example, PDS school partners have a need for substitute teachers. The PDS consortium collaborated with the college's Career Development Center to record a three-session series on successful substitute teaching that was made available to teacher candidates. This professional development was especially designed for teacher candidates, but it also impacted school partners by providing them with better prepared substitute teachers.

More widespread use of remote technologies has allowed the Buffalo State PDS consortium to have a wider impact regarding professional development. Recorded professional development sessions are stored on the PDS website and accessible to all stakeholders for free. This has provided increased access for stakeholders who are not able to attend synchronous and/or in-person professional development. International partners and stakeholders who cannot be on campus for PD at a specified time take advantage of the resources provided by the PDS consortium.

Challenges

Clearly, the field of education faces many challenges. PDSs may be the answer to some of these challenges. The Buffalo State PDS consortium is viewed locally and by international partners as an organizing body to problem solve in alignment with the mission and goals of the PDS consortium. The consortium will continue to work together as a team to address the many issues that impact teacher preparation and P–12 learning. In general, there are some challenges that can hinder the consortium's work: resources, communication, and relationships.

A lack of resources, such as money, space, time, and expertise, can make PDS work challenging. The PDS consortium must collaborate and look for creative ways to leverage resources. In difficult times, such as the COVID-19 pandemic, the Buffalo State PDS consortium had to change its typical professional development options and reallocate money to fund more remote PD sessions. Based on the needs of stakeholders, the PDS consortium began an "All Hands On Deck" initiative to provide online professional development prior to the return of school. Professional development topics included: social-emotional learning, equity, learning acceleration, classroom management, tutoring, coteaching, and specific sessions on math and literacy. The PDS structures and relationships were already in place, so the PDS consortium was able to make this happen fairly easily (Kindzierski et al., 2021).

At times, communication is challenging. To address the needs of all PDS stakeholders, communication is crucial. The PDS consortium maintains a website and social media platform, publishes newsletters, sends emails, and distributes surveys. The PDS consortium also meets with different groups of stakeholders throughout the year. Video conferencing has helped to increase attendance at remote events and meetings, but the consortium is always challenged to find the best ways to communicate with members.

Maintaining relationships and fostering new PDS relationships is a constant challenge. For instance, during the COVID-19 pandemic the enrollment in education courses that rely on school partners for school experiences and placements increased. Many long-time partners needed a break from placing teacher candidates at various times throughout the pandemic as determined by school-based liaison committees. New relationships were forged to accommodate teacher candidate placements.

The consortium also relied on partners to speak up about the importance and benefits of having teacher candidates in schools even during challenging times.

Opportunities

PDS Student Representatives

Teacher candidates are a very important stakeholder group in the Buffalo State PDS consortium. For teacher candidate voices to be heard, the consortium has student representatives (reps) who share the perspectives of their peers. They participate on the PDS Leadership Committee and the TEUPAC. The reps are often leaders in their individual programs and in organizations across campus. They assist with PDS events, advertising, social media, newsletter writing, and other forms of communication and relationship building with other stakeholders.

The PDS Student Representative program provides a distinctive experience for teacher candidates interested in the PDS consortium. Candidates apply to be reps at the end of their freshman or sophomore years. There is an application and interview process (See resources). Each rep identifies a research area of interest. They are assigned a faculty mentor and begin to read and collect data on their topic. Along with a mentor and the PDS codirectors, the reps submit proposals to present their research at the NAPDS. They develop posters/presentations of their research and practice for presenting before a national audience. The reps travel with faculty members, present their research, attend sessions, and network at the NAPDS annual conference.

Minigrants

The Buffalo State PDS consortium provides two types of minigrants for its stakeholders. The PDS Action Research Mini-Grant actively promotes action research and collaboration throughout the consortium. A guiding principle of this minigrant is to demystify the action research process, to encourage collaboration between faculty, teacher candidates, and PDS P–12 partners for the purpose of using inquiry to meet needs of schools, instruction, and further education-based scholarship. Action research is a powerful tool to study what is working pedagogically and what can be enhanced in the classroom (Calhoun, 2002).

The consortium has designed a standardized process that takes the fear out of conducting research. The application for a minigrant (see resources) includes identification of the participants in conducting the research, a description of the project with expected outcomes, an assessment plan to measure the outcomes, and a breakdown of the how the expected budget would be used. The application is evaluated by the PDS codirectors for approval. Examples of past projects include conducting book clubs with teachers as a form of professional development, implementing a Saturday book club for students, and instituting a math night for families to provide information and resources regarding the new state standards.

The collaborative model pools the strengths of mentoring teachers, principals, college faculty, and teacher candidates to help meet the needs of the prekindergarten through 12th grade learners. All partner schools are encouraged to apply for mini grants from the PDS consortium to conduct action research on a topic of their choice based on school or classroom needs. The research projects are shared at Buffalo State's annual PDS Conference that brings together about 250 consortium members for a free event that also includes a keynote address by the New York State Teacher of the Year.

A newer initiative is a smaller minigrant opportunity to support the study of coteaching between a PDS mentor teacher and a student teacher (see resources). These pairs may apply for this grant to implement teaching models or activities. Minigrant funds are awarded for supplies, substitute teacher pay, instructional materials, literature, software, technology, and for support of the research process in the school.

Day of Scholarship

Many PDS initiatives afford stakeholders opportunities to participate in teaching, service, and scholarship. The Buffalo State PDS consortium views research as professional development and works to foster action research with school partners and teacher candidate research in the form of publications and presentations. Days are set aside each year for college faculty and PDS partners to engage in scholarly activities. Each "Day of Scholarship" offers time for participants to work collaboratively or independently. There is a morning discussion about goals for the day. There are people on hand to discuss research ideas or read drafts and give feedback. The coffee is flowing all day and lunch is served. Brown bag and wrap up sessions have been provided as needed over the years. Pre- and post surveys provide information that guide the planning of subsequent days of scholarship and any necessary professional development. Opportunities for presenting and publishing are shared with stakeholders and success stories are published in Buffalo State PDS newsletters and on the Buffalo State PDS website.

Next Steps/Summary

Now more than ever, stakeholders in the field of education need to stand together. By pooling resources, being colearners, and collaborating professionally, stakeholders can continue to foster quality teacher preparation and positive impacts on P–12 learners. A PDS consortium and its structures can be the organizing body to bring all stakeholders together to meet the current and future challenges in education. The Buffalo State PDS consortium endeavors to be responsive to the needs of all its stakeholders. The consortium will rely on PDS structures, such as the NAPDS 9 Essentials to guide the growth of the organization and make decisions about future initiatives.

REFERENCES

Buffalo State—The State University of New York. (n.d.). *Professional development schools*. https://pds.buffalostate.edu/

Calhoun, E. J. (2002). Action research for school improvement. *Educational Leadership, 59*(6), 18–24.

del Prado Hill, P., & Garas-York, K. (Eds.). (2020). *The impact of PDS partnerships in challenging times*. Information Age.

Garas-York, K., del Prado Hill, P., Day, L. K., Truesdell, K., & Keller-Mathers, S. (Eds.). (2018). *Doing PDS: Stories and strategies from successful clinically rich practice*. Information Age.

Kindzierski, C., del Prado Hill, P., & Garas-York, K. (2021). PDS bends but doesn't break: How PDS structures and processes can help schools and universities respond effectively during a crisis. *School-University Partnerships, 14*(2), 83–97.

National Association for Professional Development Schools. (2021). *What it means to be a professional development school: The nine essentials* (2nd ed.). [Policy statement].

CHAPTER 4

CALIFORNIA LUTHERAN UNIVERSITY PDS NETWORK

Sustaining Successful Partnerships

Michael N. Cosenza

Context

California Lutheran University (CLU) is a private liberal arts university founded in 1959. CLU is located in Ventura County, just north of Los Angeles, in Thousand Oaks, California. The university serves 3,700 undergraduate and graduate students from 40 states and 59 countries. CLU has been designated by the United States Department of Education as a Hispanic serving institution (HSI) with 39% of students identifying as Latinx (California Lutheran University, 2022).

The Graduate School of Education offers certification and masters programs in teacher preparation (general education, special education and deaf and hard of hearing), counselor preparation, and educational leadership (administrative). Additionally, there are two doctoral programs, one in P–12 Educational Leadership and the other in College and University Educational Leadership.

The program highlighted in this chapter is The Professional Development School (PDS) - Residency program. This is a full-year program where clinical practice and methods courses are concurrent. The program is based on the Holmes Group (2007) concept for PDSs. The CLU program and uses the relationship between a medical school and teaching hospital as its foundational model.

Rationale for Starting PDS

CLU first began embracing the PDS concept in 2002, through a partnership with the Simi Valley Unified School District (SVUSD). The Dean of the School of Education at that time was a former colleague of Dr. John Goodlad, a former Dean of the UCLA Graduate School of Education, who is a highly regarded scholar and educational researcher in the field of school university partnerships. Goodlad's many publications focused on educational renewal and new teacher preparation. The dean of CLU embraced Goodlad's ideas regarding the importance of developing strong school university partnerships and the concept that these partnerships can result in simultaneous renewal for both universities and P–12 faculty (Goodlad, 1994). The dean believed the PDS concept was the direction he wanted CLU's teacher education programs to go (Cosenza et al., 2021).

In 2002, CLU was making clinical field placements for teacher candidates at more than 50 different schools. Oftentimes only one candidate was assigned to a school. The dean was concerned about the quality of placements when using so many schools and the lack of peer support teacher candidates had when they were the solo placement at a P–12 school. He believed that PDSs would improve the quality of clinical fieldwork through deliberate and beneficial collaboration and by having the P–12 schools and universities be equal partners sharing the responsibility of preparing new teachers (Cosenza, 2018).

Partners and Demographics

Though the very first partner school is no longer part of the network, the experiences of that partnership have contributed greatly to the success of the current PDS network.

There are five schools across three school districts that make up the CLU PDS Network with varying demographics:

- Flory Academy of Sciences and Technology
    - Moorpark Unified School District, Moorpark, California
    - Grades Transitional Kindergarten (TK) -5
    - Partnership began 2007

- 37% English Learners (CA Dept. of Education, 2022)
- 17% Special Education (CA Dept. of Education, 2022)
- Los Cerritos Middle School
  - Conejo Valley Unified School District, Thousand Oaks, California
  - Grades 6–8
  - Partnership began 2008
  - 7% English Learners (CA Dept. of Education, 2022)
  - 10.6% Special Education (CA Dept. of Education, 2022)
- Campus Canyon College Preparatory Academy
  - Moorpark Unified School District, Moorpark, California
  - Grades TK–8
  - Partnership began 2011
  - 22.6% English Learners (CA Dept. of Education, 2022)
  - 12.1% Special Education (CA Dept. of Education, 2022)
- Royal High School
  - Simi Valley Unified School District, Simi Valley, California
  - Grades 9–12
  - Partnership began 2018
  - 8% English Learners (CA Dept. of Education, 2022)
  - 10.6% Special Education (CA Dept. of Education, 2022)
- Walnut Canyon Arts and Technology Magnet School
  - Moorpark Unified School District, Moorpark, California
  - Grades TK–5
  - Partnership began 2021
  - 25% English Learners (CA Dept. of Education, 2022)
  - 12.4% Special Education (CA Dept. of Education, 2022)

Network Description

The CLU PDS Network collaboratively developed a mission statement using the acronym PREPARE. This statement was developed with NAPDS Essential #1: *A Comprehensive Mission* in mind to demonstrate that the partners are greater than the sum of their units. NAPDS Essential #1 states: "A PDS is a learning community guided by a comprehensive, articulated mission that is broader than the goals of any single partner, and that aims to advance equity, antiracism and social justice within and among schools, colleges/universities, and their respective community and professional partners" (NAPDS, 2021 p. 5).

PREPARE (California Lutheran University, 2022)

- **P – Prepare.** Prepare aspiring teachers in an environment that is collaborative, reflective and utilize best practices grounded in research. Prepare young P–12 students to be college/career ready, critical thinkers and productive citizens. Prepare P–12 faculty and university faculty to be lifelong learners in a collaborative professional learning community.
- **R – Reciprocate.** Classroom teachers receive reciprocal professional development through mentoring of teacher candidates and collaborating with university professors. University professors receive reciprocal professional development by reconnecting with young students and working in classrooms with practicing teachers.
- **E – Engage.** All stakeholders are engaged in the partnership: P–12 students are more engaged through use of research-based practices and better adult to student ratios. All other stakeholders are engaged through collaboration and the development of a professional learning community.
- **P – Practice.** The partnership provides an environment for both P–12 teachers and university professors to use and share best practices to maximize student achievement. Teacher candidates can conduct fieldwork concurrently with coursework giving them an opportunity to make immediate connections between theory and practice.
- **A – Access**. The partnership provides access to equal opportunities. P–12 students from subpopulations benefit from increased adult to student ratios and use of best practices. Teacher candidates have access to students from diverse backgrounds, providing them with opportunities to become proficient in designing lessons to meet all needs.
- **R – Reflect**. Through reflective inquiry, stakeholders improve practice to meet the goals of the partnership.
- **E – Empower**. The partnership empowers P–12 students to become more successful, be critical thinkers and increase achievement. Teacher candidates are empowered to be competent professionals, leaders and more confident in their teaching practice. University professors are empowered to positively influence the future of education. P–12 teachers are empowered as mentors and new roles of teacher leadership.

Description of the Teacher Preparation Program

In the State of California, the majority of teacher preparation programs are post baccalaureate. Aspiring secondary teachers typically earn a bachelor's degree in a subject area (math, science, English, etc.), while aspiring elementary teachers typically earn a degree in educational liberal studies or integrated educational studies. Teacher candidates demonstrate subject matter competency either by earning a state approved degree or by earning a passing score on the California Subject Exam for Teachers (CSET) which is a subject matter competency exam. Teacher candidates who are eligible may then enter a teacher preparation program (typically referred to as the fifth year) which includes foundational courses, methods courses and clinical fieldwork.

The CLU Graduate School of Education offers three pathways to becoming a teacher: the PDS-Residency Program, the Community Collaborative Schools program, and the Blended Program. Candidates choose the pathway when they apply to the program. There are information sessions offered throughout the year that explain the differences of each pathway and the reasons for choosing one over another.

The PDS-Residency Program uses the relationships between teaching hospitals and medical schools as its foundational model. The teaching hospital model provides medical students with specific and detailed field work giving them an opportunity to practice theory in a realistic environment. Similarly, in a Professional Development School (PDS), teacher candidates work alongside veteran cooperating teachers for an entire academic year, giving them the same opportunity to connect theory to practice.

This program's coursework is taken concurrently with a year-long field placement at one of the university's PDS partner schools. Candidates choosing this program commit to be at the school placement for the entire academic year following the school district's calendar. Candidates begin in August on the first day their cooperating teacher reports to work and stay until the P–12 students' last day of school in June. The year-long residency allows candidates to fully become a member of the school community by participating in staff meetings, grade level meetings, parent/teacher conferences, professional learning communities and evening events.

In the Community Collaborative Schools Program model, candidates take in person courses in the evenings while concurrently placed at P–12 schools in Ventura or Los Angeles Counties. This model offers the teacher candidates two different placements at two different school districts/schools. Many teacher candidates use their methods and full-time/clinical instruction experiences to explore for future employment opportunities within these school districts. Community Collaborative Schools moving toward a K–8 STEM theme/focus model have expressed support for teacher candidate placement in their schools that serve underrepresented populations. This aligns with the Cal Lutheran Hispanic Serving Institution (HSI) designation.

The Blended Program offers method courses in a 60/40 hybrid format. Sixty percent of the class meetings are face to face and 40% of the classes are online. The online classes are asynchronous modules. The modules typically consist of online video, voiced over PowerPoint, blogs, discussion boards, online quizzes, and other assignments completed in BlackBoard and other web-based platforms. The program is taken concurrently with a field placement at a P–12 school in Ventura County. In this placement, teacher candidates work alongside a veteran cooperating teacher, giving them the same opportunity to connect theory to practice. The blended model requires the candidate to have a high comfort level of using technology.

Teacher candidates who choose the PDS-Residency pathway are making a commitment to spend over 1,000 hours in the field which is significantly more than the 600 hour commitment in the other pathways.

Oversight of the PDS Network

There are various personnel from both CLU and the P–12 Schools who are principle stakeholders in the PDS network. The administrators and faculty of all partners collaborate to support the learning of P–12 students and the preparation of preservice teacher candidates. They also support the professional development of their respective faculties through mentoring and participating in collegial activities. These principle stakeholders are involved in the daily management and maintenance of the PDS partnership through the various committees responsible for PDS oversight. Facilitating oversight includes key personnel serving in specific roles. They include: the PDS-Residency Director, PDS University Liaisons, and a P–12 Site Liaison.

The PDS-Residency Director serves as CLU's representative within the PDS partnership supervising the program and working collaboratively to achieve the goals of the program. The Director works closely with the site P–12 Liaisons and University Liaisons to provide leadership for the PDS. The Director visits school sites regularly and is available to provide support for all stakeholders of the PDS network. The Director oversees the continual evaluation and assessment of the goals of the PDS and chairs the leadership committee and cochairs the steering committee with the site PDS liaisons (Cosenza, 2018).

Two individuals serve the PDS University Liaisons role, one for elementary school partners and one for secondary school partners. The University Liaison acts as the primary contact to schools in the PDS network maintaining critical relationships among the stakeholders. The liaison works directly with teacher candidates, university field supervisors, school principals, and cooperating teachers to provide support and guidance for growth and development. The University Liaison meets weekly with the P–12 Site Liaisons to discuss any issues or concerns that may arise. The University Liaison serves on both the PDS Leadership Committee and the PDS Steering Committee (Cosenza, 2018).

There is one lead teacher who serves as the P–12 Site Liaison at each P–12 school. The P–12 Site Liaison serves as the P–12 school's representative within the PDS partnership. This P–12 Liaison works closely with the university PDS Liaison and PDS Director to provide leadership for the PDS. They have frequent, consistent, and equitable interaction with all the stakeholders and are the primary contact for cooperating teachers and teacher candidates at their school site. The P–12 Liaisons ensure ongoing and clear communication to all participants and assist with continual evaluation of the program (Cosenza, 2018).

Structure

Creation of Partnerships

A suburban school district near CLU planned to reopen a school in August 2002 that had been closed for many years due to low enrollment. Through discussions with leaders from both the district and university, it was agreed to reopen the school as a PDS. A 5-year memorandum of understanding (MOU) was drafted outlining the expectations of the partnership and the goals of the PDS (Cosenza, 2018). The MOU specified requirements for oversight, professional development expectations, and PDS principles to be followed. The MOU specified the partners were to use the Standards for Professional Development Schools published by the National Council for the Accreditation of Teacher Education (NCATE, 2001).

A few years into the agreement the partnership began to struggle. It was discovered that the university professors were not always in sync with the practices of the P–12 teachers at the school. This resulted in a disconnect between theory and practice regarding teaching methodology and classroom management strategies. Eventually each partner began to assume that the other disapproved of individual teaching ability and philosophy (Cosenza, 2018).

At the end of the 5-year MOU, it was evident that the partners had entered an agreement before they fully understood what it meant to be a PDS. CLU and the school district decided to part ways and end the PDS partnership. Even though this was a great disappointment, CLU was still committed to the PDS concept and took to heart the lessons learned from this unsuccessful PDS to create more collaborative and transparent partnerships in the future.

Five major lessons were learned from this experience (Cosenza, 2018, p. 29):

1. Lack of familiarity with the teachers: Although all the teachers at the site were veteran educators, they were all new to this school site, and most had never worked together before. Very little was known about their teaching styles and teaching philosophies. Even the principal was new and not familiar with the majority of the teaching staff. As time went on, it was discovered that not all teachers shared the same philosophy about how new teachers should be prepared and how P–12 students should be taught. This included differences in viewpoint regarding teaching strategies, classroom discipline, and how engaged in actual teaching a teacher candidate should be.

2. Communication: Though the MOU outlined the parameters for collaboration, this never happened at the level necessary to sustain the partnership. It was discovered that most university professors in the teacher education program were not included in the planning phase of the PDS, which diminished the level of buy-in to the overall program. Because of this, the professors never fully understood the model and what was expected of them. This contributed to poor relations between the P–12 faculty and the university faculty.

3. Steering committee: Though the MOU outlined the requirements of a governing body, a commitment to a steering committee that met regularly was never made. During the first 2 years, a group met with some frequency, but this began to wane as time went on. During the final 2 years of the partnership, the site principal and the director of student teaching at the university made most decisions regarding the PDS. This resulted in most of the elementary teachers feeling alienated and voiceless.

4. Professional development: A PDS is intended to be a learning community where teacher candidates, veteran teachers, and university professors, through collaboration, are all renewed in their practice. As a result of not involving key stakeholders in the initial planning and the lack of collaboration after the partnership began, none of the stakeholders felt they were truly gaining professional development from the experience. During the first few years of the partnership, the site teachers acknowledged that they experienced professional renewal through coaching aspiring teachers. Unfortu-

nately, other ways of gaining professional development were not taking place for any of the stakeholders.

5. Demographics: As a newly reopened school, there were only predictions regarding the eventual demographic diversity of the student population. It was initially believed that the school would have sufficient diversity to give teacher candidates experience in working with students with varying needs. The school did not achieve a demographically diverse population and had very low numbers of English learners, students with special needs, and those from lower socioeconomic backgrounds. This did not fully comply with the fieldwork standards for the university. These standards were developed to ensure that candidates had opportunities to work with a variety of subpopulations to gain experience in adapting instruction to meet all students' needs.

Policies and Procedures

One of the greater lessons learned from the unsuccessful PDS was you cannot begin something as complex as a PDS without first fully understanding each partner. It is almost impossible for stakeholders to make commitments in writing before they understand what a PDS is and the common goals to be achieved. Each partner needs to understand the other partner's teaching philosophy, discipline strategies, and overall approach to working with students with special needs and the English learning population. Likewise, it is also necessary to explore logistical issues such as parking for a cohort of teacher candidates, access to Wi-Fi, and space in the lunchroom for additional people. Though these issues appear trivial, they can be important factors regarding the success of a partnership.

The book, *A Pathway to PDS Partnership: Using the PDSEA Protocol* (Shoemaker et al., 2020), provides a series of guidelines and surveys to help ascertain answers to the questions that often are not asked prior to beginning partnerships. These protocols are key to discovering the matches and mismatches regarding the qualities, characteristics, and perceptions of the partners. Matches and mismatches are neither positive nor negative. Instead, they allow issues to be put on the table for discussion to maximize the potential for a successful partnership. These guidelines combined with a 1-year pilot are the manner in which new partnerships are created today. During the pilot, the results of the PDSEA Protocols are reviewed and discussed. At the end of the pilot year, if both partners agree, a new MOU for a longer period of time, typically 3 years, is created and signed. During the pilot year, discussions can take place that result in a well-constructed MOU that truly represents the common goals and expectations of both parties. The combination of the PDSEA data and 1-year pilot greatly increases the chances of long-term success.

Financial and In-Kind Contributions. There are no fees or exchange of funds between the university and the school districts to set up a PDS partnership. The University funds a few items with the majority of the partnership relying on in-kind contributions. The items that bear a cost to the university include:

- A nominal stipend of $300 is paid by the university to each cooperating teacher who hosts a candidate
- Payments to the school district to fund substitute teachers to release the P–12 Liaisons up to 6 half days per year. This release time is provided so the P–12 Liaisons can attend meetings and collaborate with the PDS Director and University Liaisons
- Provide a university-based PDS Director and 2 University Liaisons. The PDS director receives a course release each semester and the liaisons receive a stipend of $1000
- CLU's in-kind contributions include:
- Additional programs and grant opportunities as they become available and as agreed by both parties
- Annual professional development for Cooperating Teachers (up to 10 hours)
- 1.5 hours annually of Staff Development for teachers on a topic to be determined
- collaboratively by the partners through the steering committee.
- Invitations to P–12 partners to attend university workshops, events and lectures.
- The school district's in-kind contributions include:
- Access to copying and supplies
- Parking for teacher candidates, field supervisors and site-based instructors
- A classroom for CLU courses to be taught on-site in the PDS or in a nearby location
- Access to wireless technology for teacher candidates
- Access to educator resources for teacher candidates as needed to plan and implement lessons
- Inclusion of teacher candidates in school-based professional development

PDS Components

Governance Structure. The CLU PDS Network relies on strong collaboration among the university PDS Director, University PDS Liaisons, and PDS Site Liaisons for successful governance. Additionally, two distinct but equally important committees have been developed to serve important roles in PDS governance. The first is the PDS Leadership Committee and the second is the PDS Steering Committee. A figure in the resource chapter (see resources) illustrates the collaboration of the CLU PDS Network Governance system.

PDS Leadership Committee. This committee is made up of the university PDS Director, University PDS Liaisons, PDS Site Liaisons, university field supervisors, and methods course instructors. The team collaborates so that coursework and fieldwork complement each other to ensure that expectations of candidates and cooperating teachers are consistent. The committee discusses course syllabi, assessments, and overall curriculum to be certain that teacher preparation goals are met. Additionally, the committee discusses teacher candidate progress and evaluations. This allows the group to collaboratively determine whether some candidates require additional support from the team (Cosenza, 2020).

PDS Steering Committee. The CLU PDS Network has two steering committees that extend representation to multiple stakeholder groups including university administration and faculty, school administration and faculty, teacher candidates, union representatives, and parents. One steering committee is devoted to the elementary schools and the other to the secondary schools. Each committee meets 4 times per year to develop, implement and evaluate all aspects of the PDS including resource sharing and identifying professional learning needs. Having all stakeholder groups represented is key to collaborative dialogue and being certain all voices are heard. At least one teacher candidate from each school site represents their colleagues because their perspective has great value and must be considered in decision-making. These committees also review data for program improvement and plan recognition events to celebrate the successes of the partnership. The Steering Committee is formed each year by sending an invitation to all stakeholders. Everyone who volunteers to be on the committee makes a commitment to attend all four meetings. Bringing the same people back to the table each meeting ensures continuity in conversations and planning (Cosenza, 2020).

Residency. The National Center for Teacher Residencies (2022) describes a residency as a rigorous year-long field experience similar to an apprenticeship for teacher candidates with academic coursework that is closely aligned with classroom practices. The CLU PDS Network blends the year-long residency model with the PDS concept. Teacher candidates commit to a year-long placement following the school district's calendar.

In May of each year, candidates are identified and assigned to cooperating teachers at each of the five P–12 schools. This early application date allows the teacher candidates time to develop rapport with their cooperating teachers over the summer and fosters opportunities to assist with classroom set-up and planning prior to the first day of school.

During the year-long residency, each teacher candidate works with two teachers so they can gain experience working with children in two different age groups. In elementary placements one cooperating teacher will be in the primary grades (K–2), and the other in an upper elementary grade level (3–5). Secondary candidates work between both the middle school and high school so that they can gain experience in both settings. Teacher candidates are immersed in the school setting and participate in all activities that take place such as: staff meetings, grade level meetings, department meetings, evening events, parent conferences, Individual Education Plan (IEP) meetings, response to intervention (RtI) rotations, and professional development days.

In the CLU PDS-Residency program, teacher candidates begin their placement when the cooperating teachers return to work in the fall of the P–12 school's academic year. This generally begins with two pupil-free days of professional development, classroom preparation, and staff meetings. Typically, on the third day, P–12 students return for the first day of school and the candidates experience all that occurs on that important day. Being present on that first day of school gives teacher candidates equal status as the cooperating teacher in the eyes of the P–12 students. Another benefit of being present on the first days of school is that teacher candidates are full partners in creating the classroom management model and overall classroom environment.

The teacher candidates stay through the last day in June, well beyond the university's semester end date, so they can witness the year-long growth that takes place in each child with whom they worked. Coursework and fieldwork are balanced during the first half of the year with mornings spent with the cooperating teacher and afternoons spent with an instructor in methods courses. During the second half of the year the teacher candidates transition to spending the entire school day with their cooperating teacher and take only one advanced pedagogy course in the evening while also preparing the state certification assessment, edTPA. edTPA serves as the capstone for program completion. Tables 4.1 and 4.2 illustrate the teacher candidates' schedule during the program. Candidates are observed by their university-based supervisors a total of 12 times during the year-long placement and are provided reflective feedback both verbally and in writing (Cosenza et al., 2021).

Teacher candidates are also permitted to work as substitutes during the program. Elementary candidates may substitute teach for their cooperat-

Table 4.1. First Half Year Elementary Schedule

Monday	Tuesday	Wednesday	Thursday	Friday
8:00–2:50 pm Fieldwork	8:00–11:50 am AM Fieldwork	9am–11:50 am Course EDTP 521-02	9am–11:50 am Course EDTP 522-02	8:00–11:50 am AM Fieldwork
3:00–4:50 pm Course EDTP 511-02	1:00–3:50 pm Course EDTP 520-02	1:00–3:50 pm PM Fieldwork	1:00–3:50 pm PM Fieldwork	1:00–3:50 pm PM Fieldwork

Table 4.2. First Half Year Secondary Schedule

Monday	Tuesday	Wednesday	Thursday	Friday
8:00 am–12:30 pm Fieldwork	8:00 am–12:30 pm Fieldwork	8:00 am–12:30 pm Fieldwork	8:00 am–12:30 pm Fieldwork	8:00 am–3:10 pm Fieldwork
1:40–4:40 pm Course EDTP 532-02	1:40–3:30 pm Course EDTP 513-02	1:40–4:30 pm Course EDTP 530-02	1:40–4:30 pm Course EDTP 531-02	

ing teacher or any other teacher in the same grade level. Secondary candidates may substitute teach for their cooperating teachers and any other teacher in the department with the same subject matter. Substitute teaching gives the candidate the ability to develop confidence working unaccompanied in a safe environment in which they are already familiar. It also provides greater continuity to the young children in the classroom as opposed to an arbitrary substitute teacher who is likely to be unfamiliar with the students, the curriculum, and established classroom management routines. This is a great benefit to the school and the P–12 students. The partners also agree that the primary purpose for clinical fieldwork is for candidates to be working with a mentor, therefore, substitute teaching for teacher candidates is capped at a total of 20 days for the entire academic year. Opportunities are also available for candidates to work as coaches in before and after school programs (Cosenza et al., 2021).

Placement Process. Most field placement coordinators will likely state that making placements is one of the most difficult parts of the job because you never know whether a candidate and cooperating teacher will be compatible with each other. The CLU PDS Residency is a 1-year commitment and asking two people to work side by side for that period of time makes compatibility very important.

Once a candidate has applied to participate in the PDS-Residency, they are invited to a placement orientation meeting which is held in the month of June prior to the beginning of the fall semester. The timing is deliberate so that placements are made early and candidates and cooperating teachers have the summer to communicate with each other and develop rapport. It also permits the candidate to join the cooperating teacher in a classroom set up prior to the first day of school (Cosenza, 2020).

The placement orientation is an event attended by teacher candidates, cooperating teachers, principals, and the university supervisors. The goal is for everyone to get to know each other through a series of icebreaker activities and questions. Principals briefly discuss their school and its curriculum focus. Supervisors briefly discuss their role in the program. Cooperating teachers discuss what they are teaching and what they are hoping to achieve with a teacher candidate as coteacher in their classroom. The candidates introduce themselves and relate their academic background, experience with children, and other interests or talents they may have. The additional activities may have relevance regarding coaching, club mentoring or some other extracurricular opportunity.

The teacher candidates are also asked unusual questions to provide some insight about how they think or tackle a problem. One such question is, *"Do you view teaching as an archeological dig or the building of a future city and why?"* (California Lutheran University, 2009). At the end of the orientation, a short presentation is made about the program and important dates and next steps. The candidates are then dismissed. Cooperating teachers remain and complete a form indicating their top three choices for a teacher candidate who they believe they will be compatible with for an entire year. The PDS Director, University Liaisons, and P–12 Site Liaisons remain to review the choices. Upon review and discussion, the Director and Liaisons make the final decision for placements. Candidates are notified and directed to reach out to their cooperating teacher.

This process has proven over time to minimize the incompatibility issues that are common when people are partnered randomly. This process truly provides insight on personalities and interests which have minimized the need to change placements later on.

Boundary Spanning. In its policy statement, *What it Means to be a PDS: The Nine Essentials* (2nd edition), NAPDS defines Boundary Spanning as "engaging in and understanding professional life in both P–12 and college/university contexts or cultures" (NAPDS, 2021, p. 17). Boundary spanning can provide leadership opportunities for both university faculty and P–12 teachers that are not normally available absent a PDS partnership.

The P–12 teachers who serve as PDS liaisons at each school site are one example of boundary spanners as they also serve a dual role of teacher educators. Their role as a P–12 teacher is expanded by the work they do to serve the PDS. They collaborate with university faculty and administrators and serve as a primary resource for teacher candidates at their school site.

Another example is the opportunities afforded to P–12 teachers to guest lecture or teach methods courses as adjunct faculty members of the university. This is a true boundary spanning position that also validates their expertise as an educator.

A final example includes university faculty who go into P–12 classrooms to demonstrate lessons and strategies. University faculty are too often long removed from practical experience in P–12 classrooms. This opportunity to model pedagogy with real P–12 children reconnects them to the field, improving their connections between theory and practice (Cosenza, 2018).

Orientation. During the first week of the academic year, an annual kick-off dinner takes place for all the teacher candidates, cooperating teachers, liaisons, instructors, and field supervisors. The purpose of this dinner is twofold. First, it serves as an orientation for everyone to hear important information about the program. Having all the stakeholders together at the same time minimizes confusion and misunderstandings. Second, it serves as a time to recognize and celebrate the commitment everyone is making by sharing a meal together and developing community. Over time, this event has developed into one that all the stakeholders look forward to because it sets the tone for the year ahead (Cosenza, 2020).

Cooperating Teacher Training. New cooperating teachers are provided 10 hours of professional development in mentoring by the university. The training focuses on coaching adult learners, teaching strategies for all learners, and inclusive education. This training is online and can be done by the cooperating teacher at a pacing schedule that is convenient for them. Cooperating teachers can also get waivers for the three modules if they have evidence of recent equivalent professional development in the same areas of concentration. The 10 hours of professional development are only for a brand new cooperating teacher. Returning cooperating teachers receive 2 hours of professional development to keep them current about teacher preparation program policy and curriculum.

Acknowledgments. At the entrance of each school, there is a sign or banner that identifies it as a PDS in partnership with the university. Signage makes it clear that being a PDS is part of the school's identity. In California, many districts have schools with specific academic themes and parents are permitted to apply to enroll their children in schools outside their immediate neighborhood school. For example, some focus more on technology, STEM or performing arts. The principals of the CLU PDS Network schools certainly make use of the PDS partnership as a positive element of the school's distinctiveness when parents take school tours and are choosing a school that best meets their family's needs.

Additionally, cooperating teachers are individually recognized by a sign on their classroom door indicating that they are a Mentor Teacher for the University. This personal recognition is particularly important because it confirms the teacher's professionalism and their dual role as a classroom teacher and a teacher educator (Cosenza, 2020).

Celebrations. Each year during teacher appreciation week, the PDS Director and University Liaisons plan something special for each of the schools. This has varied over the years and has included the distribution of appreciation pins to treats in the teachers' lounge. Though these acknowledgments are modest, the point is to continually acknowledge and celebrate the work of P–12 teachers and teacher candidates.

As a way of recognizing the hard work that goes into sustaining a PDS, the university's PDS Director hosts an annual dinner for the leadership team. The dinner begins with a simple announcement that expresses gratitude for the commitment to PDS partnership and the collaboration that takes place to keep the partnership strong and viable. The remainder of the evening is purposefully without any other PDS business. It is an evening where the team can simply enjoy a meal and each other's company. It has become a well-attended event and one that the team looks forward to each year (Cosenza, 2020).

Resources

MOUs. Through a MOU, the goals, and objectives of the partnership, along with the expectations of each partner are outlined. After the pilot year, the MOU typically cover a 3-year time period. This allows the partners to revisit the terms and conditions frequently and make adjustments to future MOUs.

Support

University Support

Though most of the support to run the program is through in-kind contributions from the partners, the university has made financial commitment to the program by providing funding for the University PDS Director and the University Liaisons. The PDS Director receives a course release each semester to provide oversight of the program. The University Liaisons receive a stipend which is the equivalent of 1.5 course credits each semester to serve in their roles. Lastly, the university gives a small budget to the PDS Director to fund items that include substitute teachers for the P–12 site liaisons, the orientation kick-off dinner, supplies and refreshments for leadership and steering committee meetings and small gifts for teacher appreciation week.

School District Support

The primary support from the school districts is their treatment of teacher candidates as if they were employees of the school. All schools have totally embraced the candidates as part of their community and include them in meetings and other school and districtwide activities. Candidates at all five schools are given access to the school's curriculum resources, email system and course platforms (if there are online components). Additionally, the schools provide the candidates with photo identification cards further making them feel that they are part of the community. Lastly, all three districts guarantee the candidates interviews for potential jobs when they complete their residency.

Challenges

The primary challenge to managing successful PDSs is the tendency to become complacent. When things run well, there is a temptation to just sit back and let the program run itself. Unfortunately, as witnessed from the first PDS in 2002, complacency can cause partnerships to unravel. Maintaining a long-term sustainable relationship requires constant collaboration and transparent communication. The CLU PDS Network accomplishes this by having multiple opportunities for stakeholders to communicate and meet. Fidelity to the MOU's goals and expectations and the NAPDS Nine Essentials (NAPDS, 2021) are also key to long-term success as well as the recognition and celebrations.

The second challenge is the importance of making certain that both partners have equal opportunities in the decision-making process. Too often, universities take a lead role when partnering with a P–12 school. This is not possible in PDSs. A true partnership requires both the university and P–12 school to have equal voice. P–12 schools have not been in the habit of making decisions about teacher preparation. PDSs provide the platform for P–12 schools to have equal responsibility in the preparation of the next generation of teachers.

It is important to note that the COVID-19 pandemic placed a great deal of stress on many school districts and universities alike. While many teacher preparation programs experienced challenges related to clinical field placements during the pandemic, the CLU PDS network was able to continue its work without any pause. While many programs experienced trouble making field placements, there was never a question about whether teacher candidates would be permitted to do fieldwork at the

PDS partner schools. The leadership team of this PDS network believes this was due to the collaborative and trusting relationship that has been built over the years.

Opportunities

There are always opportunities to improve a PDS. Since 2002, the program has evolved and grown because of collaborative brainstorming. An example is the incorporation of the year-long residency into the program. Initially, candidates spent one semester at the PDS site and went off and had another experience at another school. Through deliberate discussion and review of data, the steering committee put forward the idea of how wonderful it would be if the candidates did not have to leave midyear, or for that matter, begin midyear. Midyear entrances or departures were awkward and made it difficult for candidates to feel fully integrated into the classroom community. The year-long residency, on the other hand, gives candidates the chance to be part of the community from the very first day. By staying the whole year, candidates can also experience the growth and achievement of the children they are working with over the course of time.

Opportunities currently being pursued include grant applications to diversify the teacher workforce and address the teacher shortage. A National Science Foundation grant has been funded to help with the teacher shortage by recruiting individuals and providing scholarships to become teachers of math and science, areas where the shortage has hit hard.

Conclusion

Every PDS is different, and there is not one formula to guarantee success. Through the sharing of our best practices, we hope that additional knowledge empowers others to make decisions that help their partnership become successful. We believe that using the PDSEA Protocol (Shoemaker et al., 2020) and piloting a partnership for 1 year have been the key contributors to the success of developing a strong network. There are always challenges to maintaining relationships and complacency is a key factor that can cause PDSs to unravel. Collaboration and communication are key factors to long term sustainability. Acknowledgment by NAPDS in 2021 with the Exemplary PDS Achievement Award further motivates the CLU PDS Network to continue the work it does. The network flourishes because of the dedication of the stakeholders who truly believe in the work. The fact that P–12 teachers can also call themselves teacher educators is an important step in sharing the responsibility of teacher preparation between universities and school districts.

REFERENCES

California Department of Education. (2022). *School accountability report card.* https://sarconline.org/public/findASarc

California Lutheran University. (2009). *Internal PDS Operations Manual.*

California Lutheran University. (2022). *Facts at a Glance.* https://www.callutheran.edu/about/quick-facts.html

Cosenza, M. (2020). California Lutheran University PDS residency: Resource sharing and recognition. In E. Garin & R. Burns (Eds.), *Clinically based teacher education in action: Cases in professional development schools* (pp. 224–230). Information Age.

Cosenza, M. (2018). From courtship to marriage. In M. Buchanan & M. Cosenza (Eds.), *Vision from professional development school partners: Connecting professional development and clinical practice* (pp. 27–37). Information Age.

Cosenza, M., Brown, E., Coler, C., Derrick, K., Nardo, J., Silva, R., & Wagler, K. (2021). A thriving third space: California Lutheran University PDS network. *PDS Partners Bridging Research to Practice*, *16*(4), 25–29.

Goodlad, J. (1994). *Educational renewal, better teachers better schools.* Jossey Bass.

Holmes Group. (2007). *The Holmes partnership trilogy.* Peter Lang.

National Association for Professional Development Schools. (2021). *What it means to be a professional development school: The nine essentials* (2nd ed.) [Policy statement].

National Center for Teacher Residencies. (2023). What is a teacher residency? https://nctresidencies.org/

National Council for Accreditation of Teacher Education. (2001). *Standards for professional development schools* [Policy statement].

Shoemaker, E., Cosenza, M., Kolpin, T., & Allen J. (2020). *A pathway to PDS partnership: Using the PDSEA Protocol.* Information Age.

CHAPTER 5

MASON'S ELEMENTARY PDS PROGRAM

Leveraging a History of Collaboration to Grow and Sustain School/University Partnerships

Audra Parker

Context

George Mason University (Mason) is a large, public research university (RU/H) serving the greater Washington, DC metro region. As part of the School of Education in the College of Education and Human Development, the Elementary Education (ELED) program provides undergraduate and postbaccalaureate teacher preparation that leads to P–6 licensure and either a Bachelor's in Elementary Education, a Bachelor's to Accelerated Master's in Curriculum and Instruction-Elementary Education or a Postbaccalaureate Master's in Curriculum and Instruction-Elementary Education Concentration. The framework for all three program licensure routes is rooted in research on effective teacher preparation and clinical practice (AACTE, 2018; Council of Chief State School Officers, 2012; Darling-Hammond, et al., 2005; NCATE, 2010); guided by national

A Practical Guide to Exemplary Professional Development Schools
pp. 73–87
www.infoagepub.com
Copyright © 2024 by Information Age Publishing
All rights of reproduction in any form reserved.

teacher education standards (Council of Chief State School Officers, 2011); and embedded within a context of inquiry, collaboration, and reflection among all stakeholders.

Rationale for Starting the PDS

Mason's Elementary Education Program, created in 1991, has a long history of collaboration through Professional Development School (PDS) partnerships in local schools. Guided by a core belief in partnerships with school-based teacher educators and situated in one of the largest, most diverse, and most progressive regions in the United States (US), Mason, Elementary Education faculty sought to capitalize on these assets to strengthen their program delivery. Over time, the Mason Elementary Education program and its PDS Network have enacted four substantial revisions to their shared work referred to as 'generations' (Parsons et al., 2017).

In each program iteration, the PDS model afforded a framework for (re)designing structures and roles as well as a philosophy for (re)orienting programmatic efforts around intensive field work. Mason Elementary Education faculty, along with school partners in surrounding districts, purposefully ground program revisions and (re)design in the literature on PDSs (Holmes Group, 1990; NAPDS, 2008; NAPDS, 2021) and specifically on the Nine Essentials (NAPDS, 2021). The Nine Essentials for PDSs are listed in the Introduction Chapter of this book.

The Nine Essentials have played and continue to play a critical role in sustaining our school/university partnerships and specific Essentials will be noted throughout to explicitly highlight their role. In the Elementary Education Program, a long-standing adherence to the Nine Essentials generally, and mutually beneficial partnerships and shared roles and governance structures specifically, has sustained the PDS partnerships between the Mason Elementary Education program and its school district partners. This dedication to an overall comprehensive and mutually beneficial mission by stakeholders is evidence of Essential 1: A Comprehensive Mission (NAPDS, 2021) in action. That along with strong reputations among faculty, school-based leaders, mentors, and PDS graduates also contribute to the stability and longevity of the Mason Elementary PDS Network.

Demographics of Mason and P–12 Schools

As the largest public university in Virginia, Mason serves over 38,000 students. Nestled just outside of Washington, D.C. in the Northern Virginia region, Mason is situated in one of the most diverse, progressive, and well-funded regions of the United States. Just fifty years old, Mason's motto 'Where Innovation is Tradition' contributed to both its rise in the

Table 5.1. Demographic Information for Mason ELED PDS Partnership Districts

	ACS	FCPS	LCPS	MCS	MPCS	PWCS
Total number of students	26,833	180,076	81,326	7,607	3.500	89,577
White	44%	36.8%	43.9%	13.3%	13.1%	28%
Hispanic	28.9%	27.1%	18.3%	68.3%	66.9%	35.7%
Asian	8.9%	19.8%	24.4%	3.6%	5.8%	9.7%
Black	10.3%	10%	7.1%	9.4%	8.3%	20.3%
2+ races	7.7%	5.9%	5.7%	5.1%	5.9%	5.9%
English learners	25.5%	26.8%	18.1%	47.1%	47.2%	27.7%
Students with disabilities	14.1%	14.4%	11.4%	11.8%	13.3%	12.8%
Economically disadvantaged	22.7%	27.8%	21.3%	48.2%	60.1%	39.7%

state and national landscape and its rapid growth. Residents of the Northern Virginia region are largely government-related and private sector employees, which contributes to a high degree of educational attainment. Northern Virginia is also home to a large number of immigrants from around the globe. The combination of highly rated public schools and an accessible 2-year community college system (Northern Virginia Community College) provides a pathway for many of the diverse and first-generation students in the Northern Virginia region to pursue higher education at Mason. The enrolled student population at Mason is approximately 43% White, 19% Asian, 13% Hispanic, 11% Black, 5% two or more races.

According to data gathered from the 2021–22 Virginia Department of Education's School Quality Profiles (Virginia Department of Education, 2022), the size and demographics of our six partnering school districts varies tremendously (see Table 5.1). For example, the school district in which Mason is situated, Fairfax County, has over 180,000 students speaking over 200 languages. In contrast, our smallest district is just over 3,500 students, has a large primarily Latinx population, and over 60% of students classified as economically disadvantaged.

Network Description

In alignment with Essential 6: Articulated Agreements (NAPDS, 2021), all six partnering districts have broad formal Memoranda of Understanding (MOUs) with the College of Education and Human Development , and three of the five have specific agreements with the Elementary Education program to support the structures of the PDS network. The remaining districts are supported with residual funds within the Elementary Education budget. Given the varied size and proximity of the districts to Mason, there are also differences in the number of schools engaged with the ELED PDS program. For example, Manassas Park City Schools (MPCS) has one school in the PDS network, whereas Fairfax County Public Schools (FCPS) has over 25 schools.

The Mason Elementary PDS Network is organized using our 'pathways to partnership' model (Parker et al., 2016) (see Appendix A). The multiple pathways provide flexibility for both the school partners and the ELED program and include three options: partner schools, clinical practice schools, or collaborative inquiry schools. Faculty and school partners created the pathways when they recognized a need for reorganizing and clarifying the partnership structures which aligns with Essential 4: Reflection and Innovation (NAPDS, 2021). Together we defined three pathways to partnership as follows:

- *Partner schools* in the Mason Elementary PDS Network host teacher candidates for their required clinical hours and engage with faculty to host innovative field experiences. The partner school route provides an entry point for schools new to the PDS concept and flexibility for long-standing partners who experience shifts in their capacity to sustain more robust partnership activities. This pathway provides an avenue to partnership for schools who have a large cadre of teachers with less than three years of experience. Through this gradual and flexible engagement with the Mason Elementary PDS Network, partner sites participate in professional development with us, growing a stable, experienced cadre of teachers in their school site. Currently, our network includes 17 partner schools, and one university faculty member serves as a support for all partner sites, although other faculty may engage with specific sites for course-based activities.
- The *Clinical Practice sites* and pathways work collaboratively with all Mason Elementary PDS Network stakeholders to support candidates in their final internship. Each clinical faculty and collaborative inquiry site has assigned University Facilitators, adjunct faculty members at our Clinical Practice sites and full-time Mason faculty members at four Collaborative Inquiry sites.
- *Collaborative Inquiry sites and pathways* are structured the same as the Clinical Practices sites. At Collaborative Inquiry sites, faculty purposefully engage in organic, inquiry-based research and grant projects emerging from the shared work of Mason and school-based faculty.

Regardless of route, there remains a shared commitment to improving P–12 education and impacting teacher preparation and the broader community. This is reflective of enacting Essential 1: Comprehensive Mission (NAPDS, 2021). Our partners move in and out of these three pathways in response to readiness, school context, and capacity. This flexibility allows stakeholders in the Mason Elementary PDS Network to work towards the NAPDS Nine Essentials at developmentally appropriate rates and honors the diverse, evolving, and specific needs of schools and Mason.

Number of PDSs in Mason ELED PDS Network

The Mason Elementary PDS Network provides a context for the field-based learning of all teacher candidates in the ELED program. In the 2022–23 school year, this included 30 elementary school sites in the five school districts across the Northern Virginia region: 24 in Fairfax County Public Schools, seven in Loudoun County Public Schools, six in Prince William County Schools, one elementary school in Arlington County Schools, two in Manassas City Schools, and one in Manassas Park City Schools.

Description of the Mason ELED Teacher Preparation Program

Students pursuing careers in elementary education at Mason can choose from three routes. The Bachelor's in Elementary Education opened in 2020 and culminates in a Bachelor's of Science in Elementary Education (BSEd). The Master's degree can be earned through two options: a 5-year Bachelor's degree to Accelerated Master's degree in Curriculum and Instruction-Elementary Education and a Postbaccalaureate Master's degree in Curriculum and Instruction-Elementary Education Concentration. Prior to program entry, all students must meet the Virginia Department of Education (VDOE) requirements for content knowledge (21 credit hours). Regardless of route, teacher candidates in elementary education have similar coursework, program structures, PDS-based field experiences and capstone student teaching internships.

Coursework emphasizes the knowledge and theory teachers need for effective instruction (Darling-Hammond, et.al, 2005) and is sequenced to scaffold teacher candidates' pedagogical and content knowledge. Beginning with courses in foundations, child development, and elementary methods and management, teacher candidates develop a framework for understanding the child, school, community, and families with whom they will work. Content-specific methods courses develop teacher candidates' understanding of research-based best practices in math, literacy, science and social studies. These are supported by an additional elementary methods course in differentiation and assessment. Each semester, teacher candidates complete 15 hours of clinical field work per course in one of the PDS partner sites. These placements are intentionally varied by age and school context each semester. All programs culminate with a capstone internship and action research course in one of our PDS clinical practice or collaborative inquiry partnership sites.

Within the program tracks there are some slight differences. For example, the undergraduate students complete 60 credit hours of coursework towards licensure, plus predegree work in children's literature, technology integration, and working with diverse learners, whereas graduate students complete 39 credits hours. The additional credit hours in the undergraduate track include electives in special education and working with English learners, as well as additional literacy, general methods, and science, technology, engineering and mathematics (STEM) courses. For their capstone internship experience, undergraduate students complete a practicum in the fall semester and their internship in the spring. Both of these experiences are in the same classroom, creating a year-long capstone student teaching with one mentor and one group of students. The nature of the final internships for graduate students varies from 16-week semester-long internships to academic calendar yearlong internships to increasingly frequent 'on the job' internships. The yearlong experience runs the span of the P–6 school year. In this route, students are provided a substitute teaching stipend to sub for up to 45 days across the school year in their placement site.

Oversight

Oversight of the Mason ELED PDS program is the responsibility of two program faculty members. The Academic Program Coordinator is responsible for the curriculum, admissions process, accreditation, scheduling and hiring within the network, and coordinating PDS network efforts more broadly. This includes leading the PDS Advisory group, the University Facilitators monthly meetings, maintaining district office relationships necessary for running the PDS network. The PDS Program Liaison is responsible for the placement process within the network. In addition to facilitating communication from Mason to school-based partners, the PDS Program Liaison coordinates the placement process within the network among teacher candidates, mentor teachers, and university faculty.

Structure

Policies and Procedures

Partnership Development and Maintenance. Because of the extensive history of the Mason Elementary PDS network, many partnerships have been in existence for 15+ years. As a result, all elementary PDS sites reflect on their engagement with the network and their commitment to continued partnership annually. Reflection for partnership sites is conducted through a series of written prompts that are emailed near the end of the academic year. Reflection for clinical practice and collaborative inquiry sites is conducted by the university facilitator and includes administrators, site facilitators, and mentor teachers. Discussions are guided by a 'Glows and Grows' (Missi, n.d.) protocol with notes gathered and shared with ELED program coordinators. In addition, every 5 years, the Mason ELED program engages in an application cycle. This process allows for existing partners to reapply for continued engagement and new partners to join the work. Recruitment for the application process varies from district to district. In some instances, the ELED faculty can communicate directly with school administrators to discuss their interest in or commitment to the PDS network. In others, school district leaders determine which schools can partner with the Mason ELED program.

Application Process. As a part of the application process, school administrators must first establish buy-in from school staff. This is evidence of whole-school commitment to four overarching tenets of PDSs and school/university partnerships: mutually beneficial partnerships; commitment to teacher preparation, ongoing professional development for all stakeholders, and shared inquiry (Holmes Group, 1990). This is a core component of the PDS application (see resources). Additionally, school administrators must describe each of the following in the application: preferred partnership pathway, student demographics, areas of pride (e.g., research-based best practices in mathematics, Responsive Classroom, Positivity Project, literacy instruction), inquiry-based initiatives, and coherence with the university's teacher education program. Upon application review, accepted applicants are organized into one of three ranges of engagement in our network: partner schools, clinical practice, or collaborative inquiry sites. It should be noted that prior experience in PDS partnerships often leads new administrators to seek out opportunities to engage with our program when they receive a promotion or change school locations.

Vetting Process. A review of applications is conducted by the Academic Program Coordinator and PDS liaison. It is important to note that we have accepted all applicants into the PDS network. This is largely due to the requirements of the application process and vetting at the district level in most of our school district partners.

Participation Guidelines. The Mason Elementary PDS Network is funded through grant proposals submitted to our large district partners each year (see Appendix C). These formal articulated agreements are examples of Essential 6: Articulated Agreements (NAPDS, 2021) in action. The proposal funds school-based teacher educators to serve in boundary-spanning roles as site facilitators and provides a stipend to students in the Master's in Education (MEd) in ELED program who are completing a yearlong internship. The stipend pays MEd teacher candidates $4500 a year to substitute teach for up to 45 days in their internship site from August–June. The yearlong subbing stipend is described in more detail in the PDS components section. In return, Mason provides payment to mentor teachers and university facilitators who support teacher candidates from all ELED program tracks during their practicum/internship experiences.

Governance. The oversight roles of Academic Program Coordinator and PDS Liaison described above interact within a shared governance structure to support the work of the Mason ELED PDS Network. These structures, which align with Essential 7: Shared Governance (NAPDS, 2021), include but are not limited to: an advisory group, regular meetings with school-based site facilitators and university facilitators, school leader meetings, and university facilitator monthly meetings located at rotating PDS sites.

The Advisory Group is composed of university faculty, school system administrators, school administrators, practicing school-based teachers, teacher candidates, and community/business partner representatives. The Advisory Group meets twice a year and provides feedback on program initiatives and annual goals. For example, the Advisory Group recently provided key insights on the design and development of the newly created BSEd in Elementary Education program.

Additionally, the network includes biannual meetings of site facilitators and mentor teachers and monthly meetings of the university facilitators. These meetings provide opportunities to share an overview of the year, collaborate around effective practices, cooperatively address challenges, and plan for program enhancement. Similarly, the network hosts an annual principals' meeting. The purpose of this gathering is to bring together the PDSs' school leaders to reflect on the mission and progress of the network, share effective practices and successes, address any concerns or issues, and plan for continuous improvement. Finally, all university facilitators meet monthly to discuss their work within their PDS sites. Lastly, the PDS has school-based PDS meetings at clinical practice and collaborative inquiry sites that include the principal, the site facilitator, the university facilitator, an advanced mentor teacher member representative, a teacher candidate representative, and others as determined by the PDS. Bringing together stakeholders from across the network capitalizes on the expertise of school-based teacher educators to address challenges and celebrate successes.

Leadership Roles. Specific, formal roles and responsibilities for both school-based and university-based teacher educators are key supporting structures within the Mason ELED PDS Network (see resources) and align with Essential 8: Boundary Spanning Roles (NAPDS, 2021). These responsibilities include the following:

Academic Program Coordinator. The network is led by the Elementary Education Academic Program Coordinator, who organizes and facilitates all aspects of the MEd and BSEd elementary education programs and oversees the PDS network.

PDS Liaison. The PDS Liaison coordinates the field and internship placement process and associated communications with site facilitators, mentor teachers, administrators, and university facilitators.

University Facilitators (UFs). ELED faculty members and adjuncts serve as University Facilitators. Faculty members serving as UFs receive a 3-hour course credit for every 5 interns supervised. For clinical practice and collaborative inquiry sites hosting interns, the UF spends one day a week at the school supervising teacher candidates, cultivating relationships with school faculty, participating in professional development activities, and engaging in inquiry. During their time at the school, the UF conducts weekly informal observations for semester-long internship students and fall biweekly/weekly informal observations for year-long students. In addition, UFs conduct two formal observations of each teacher candidate in their final semester of internship regardless of semester-long or year-long format.

Site Facilitator. Each PDS has a school-based Site Facilitator. The Site Facilitator serves as the liaison between the school and university and is a school-based teacher or instructional coach. Along with the UF, the Site Facilitator organizes placements for teacher candidates and is a point of contact for teachers and teacher candidates for information regarding the PDS partnership. Site Facilitators receive a small stipend for serving in this role.

Advanced Mentor Teacher (AMTs). AMTs are school-based teachers who host and mentor teacher candidates. All AMTs complete both an initial mentor teacher training and an advanced teacher mentor training developed to prepare teachers for supervising teacher candidates or mentoring new teachers. AMTs provide ongoing informal feedback to teacher candidates in myriad forms, and they conduct 4 formal observations across the final semester of internship regardless of semester-long or year-long format.

Mentor Teachers (MTs). MTs are school-based teachers who host and mentor teacher candidates. These teachers may have completed the initial training. In addition, mentors must have at least 3 years of teaching experience to support teacher candidates in their internship experience. MTs provide ongoing informal feedback to teacher candidates in myriad forms, and they conduct 4 formal observations across the final semester of internship regardless of semester-long or year-long format.

PDS Components

While the Mason ELED PDS Network incorporates a multitude of PDS components (inquiry orientation, educator preparation, intentional mentor/candidate matching), two specific activities best exemplify the essence of mutually beneficial partnerships in action: 1) Mentoring Va Essentials (Mentoring Virginia, n.d.) and Advanced Mentor Training, which aligns with Essential 2: Professional Learning and Leading (NAPDS, 2021) and 2) the year-long internship/substitute teaching program, which aligns with Essential 4: Reflection and Innovation (NAPDS, 2021).

MentoringVA (Mentoring Virginia, n.d.) began as a Virginia Department of Education grant funded activity for the Mason Elementary and Secondary program to build a sustainable model for mentor teacher preparation. The overarching philosophy of Mentoring Va from its inception has been to put the design and implementation of mentor training in the hands of the experts: exceptional school-based teacher educators/mentor teachers in our school/university partnerships. As university-based teacher educators, we provided the framework, the space, and the funding. Then we supported the mentor experts in designing the content and format and in leading the implementation of mentor training.

Currently Mentoring VA (Mentoring Virginia, n.d.) is comprised of five asynchronous training modules addressing the following topics: the current context of mentoring, characteristics of effective mentoring, coplanning and coteaching, giving feedback, and navigating difficult conversations. The modules are intentionally designed to address mentors serving in varied roles including supporting teacher candidates, on-the-job candidates and new teachers. Mentors may also participate in synchronous 'advanced' training sessions. Addressing the same topics in more depth, the 'advanced' training is conducted by the team of advanced mentors who designed the training. The format and structure of the modules evolved across the project based on emerging knowledge of online teaching and learning during COVID-19. MentorVA is currently funded for introduction across the state via site-based sessions. Advanced Mentor Teachers from our partnership will collaborate with university based-teacher educators to lead this rollout initiative. By honoring the expertise of mentors, the MentoringVA training has provided school-based teacher educators opportunities to learn and lead within our partnership networks, and now as part of a statewide initiative.

The yearlong substitute teaching option is historically rooted in the work of the Mason Elementary PDS program. However, it has also been a source of ongoing innovations in response to the needs of our students and school partners. Teacher candidates in the yearlong substitute teaching option are placed in a PDS school site for one year. During that time, they are paid a stipend of $4500 to substitute teach in that site for up to 45 days across the year. Funding for the substitute teaching stipend is provided by our school district partners through our annual Mason Elementary PDS grants (See Appendix C). Using a scaffolded model, the teacher candidates begin by subbing in their mentor teacher's classroom, then can sub across their grade level teams. At two points in the year, coinciding with breaks in the Mason calendar at the end of the fall semester and again at the end of the spring semester through the start of summer break, candidates can sub throughout the building. This structured foray into subbing allows candidates opportunities to be 'on their own' but in a context that is familiar. Because teacher candidates are placed in groups of 4–5 at a given site, administrators in buildings with yearlong subs can use the teacher candidates in a variety of ways, particularly during open subbing. Some groups have filled in for whole grade level teams to provide teachers long range planning time. Others have supported remediation and/or preparation for end of year assessments.

In recent years, the need for substitutes in our schools has increased significantly, and yet the supply has not kept up with demand. Because of our partnership, the Mason ELED program faculty, along with our school-based and district-based partners, brainstormed strategies for addressing this subbing crisis. Numerous outcomes emerged from these discussions. First, we collaborated with administrators to revise the typical yearlong scaffolding model for subbing, moving up the timeline for subbing on grade level teams and increasing the number of 'open subbing' hours. And while our sites supporting yearlong subbing candidates had a built-in cadre of building subs, our partners working with field hours or semester long interns also needed support. Together we changed the requirement to allow semester-long interns to substitute for up to 5 days in their mentor's classroom. We worked with several district human resource leads to clear the hurdles for all students to be included on substitute teaching lists once cleared for field placements. Looking ahead to the upcoming academic year, the clearance for teacher candidates to complete field hours will double as approval for the district subbing list in several of our partnerships. This is just one of many ways in which our long-standing partnership facilitates reflection and innovation.

Resources (see resources)

- Pathways to Partnership Model
- Sample PDS Application (includes budget model for PDS Network, and roles and responsibilities description)

- Sample Grant Proposal

Support

A key premise to PDS partnerships is the notion of reciprocal, mutually beneficial relationships (Holmes Group, 1990). As such, opportunities for the Mason ELED Program to support the work of our PDS partners and vice versa are numerous. First and foremost, program faculty work to prepare exceptional teacher candidates well versed in research-based best practices, reflective and responsive to diverse students' needs, and ready for diverse 21st century classrooms. PDS sites have early access to teacher candidates and an inside track on hiring. In addition, because of the PDS partnership, school partners have opportunities to engage as teacher leaders through boundary spanning 'site facilitator roles.' Similarly, through school-based activities associated with internship, teachers in a PDS site have opportunities to engage in inquiry, share their expertise through biweekly site-based seminars, and serve as model teachers, regardless of whether or not they are supporting a teacher candidate. Engagement with the PDS program affords ongoing professional development opportunities through m training, conference presentations and publications. With the advent of the BSEd in Elementary Education, exceptional school-based teacher educators are increasingly teaching courses in the undergraduate program. Each of these supports for PDS sites engages teachers in authentic professional development opportunities.

Similarly, our school and district partners support the Mason ELED PDS program in myriad ways. Because of the clear and consistent communication and ongoing engagement of our school partners with program faculty, we are able to tap into exemplary mentor teachers, coaches, and administrators for campus-based activities such as program and internship orientations, program feedback and revision, and service in governance roles. For the last seven years, district human resource leaders provided a program-specific job preparation session for our PDS students. Our school partners are eager and open to brainstorm 'outside the box' thinking about field hours structures and experiences. With an eye towards how to best support learning for all stakeholders, Mason PDS partners are willing to try unique structures (e.g., site based course instruction, guided observations, GoReact video coding). They support grant funded initiatives such as Mentoring VA and encourage their teachers to leverage training opportunities. Because of a history of collaboration and innovation, school partners are supportive and flexible in their work in the Mason ELED PDS program.

Challenges

While the Mason Elementary PDS Program certainly benefits from its proximity to a large number of exceptional schools and districts serving an incredibly diverse student population, one of the biggest challenges to our PDS partnership work is the sheer size of the region within which we are located. Mason has a history of students living off-campus and the Northern Virginia region is plagued by traffic issues. Engaging in extensive site-based coursework or mediated field experiences can be challenging when balancing commute times for students.

Another challenge for our PDS work is navigating the structures of the university that are often in conflict with the structures of our school partners. Calendars that are not aligned, rigidity in the time blocks of a university-schedule, early and late start times for school, and traditional course credit hour structures are all challenges when attempting to engage in robust clinically based teacher preparation. Last but not least, the teacher shortage is presenting a new challenge to our PDS work. Because of the incredible need for teachers, a newish phenomenon for the Northern Virginia region in Elementary Education, our PDS teacher candidates are being hired for on the job provisionally licensed positions. As a result, field work and internship experiences that have been hallmarks of our PDS partnership are not sustainable when teacher candidates are also working as full-time teachers.

Opportunities

Ongoing reflection and an orientation towards innovation reveal numerous future opportunities for the Mason ELED PDS program. First and foremost, the addition of a BSEd pr ogram creates a multitude of new opportunities. For example, school-based teacher educators with a master's degree are now eligible to teach in our program. In addition, coursework can now be situated during the day which increases opportunities for innovative, scaffolded field opportunities such as mediated field experiences and site-based course instruction. As comfort levels with online technologies such as Zoom have increased across the pandemic, so have opportunities to engage PDS stakeholders in PDS activities without requiring a trip to campus. In a large metropolitan area, organizing meetings has always presented challenges. Most recently we are learning how to leverage online platforms to improve communication, collaboration, and engagement across the PDS network.

Next Steps/Summary

The Mason ELED PDS program has an extensive history of school-university partnerships rooted in a belief in the power of mutually beneficial relationships and a valuing of the expertise of all stakeholders. The onset of the COVID-19 pandemic best highlights the philosophical orientation of school and university-based teacher educators in our PDS network (Brown et al., 2022; Parker et al., 2020). While many schools and universities retreated to their silos in March 2020, the Mason ELED faculty and our PDS school partners came together in search of support for navigating the unprecedented shift to online learning. Our school partners needed our field work candidates and teacher candidates to support online instruction. Whether through their technology skills or their willingness to support 'breakout' rooms and small group instructions, Mason teacher candidates played a vital role in our partnership sites. At the same time, our ELED faculty had limited knowledge about the pedagogies of online teaching and learning for P–6 learners. Our PDS partnership facilitated faculty learning by opening their 'online doors' and sharing their resources so that we could all learn together. While the pandemic certainly presented incredible challenges in teaching and learning, the tenets of PDS partnerships helped the Mason ELED program and our school partners sustain teaching and teacher education efforts within our PDS network.

REFERENCES

American Association of Colleges for Teacher Education. (2018). *A pivot toward clinical practice, its lexicon, and the renewal of educator preparation: A report of the AACTE Clinical Practice Commission.*

Brown, E. L., Groth, L. A., Parker, O'Brien, C., Laurits, E., Latham, C., Berman, R., Casablanca, F., & Douds, J. (2022). Pathways to partnership: How a differentiated approach sustained PDS efforts during times of uncertainty. *School University Partnerships*, *15*(1), 14–26. https://napds.org/wp-content/uploads/2022/01/SUPSpecialIssue01.04.2022.pdf

Council of Chief State School Officers. (2011). *Interstate Teacher Assessment and Support Consortium (InTASC) Model Core Teaching Standards: A Resource for State Dialogue.* https://ccsso.org/sites/default/files/2017-12/2013_INTASC_Learning_Progressions_for_Teachers.pdf

Council of Chief State School Officers. (2012). *Our responsibility, our promise: Transforming educator preparation and entry into the profession.*

Darling-Hammond, L. Hammerness, K, Grossman, P., Rust, F., & Shulman, L. (2005). The design of teacher education programs. In L. Darling-Hammond

& J. Bransford (Eds.), *Preparing teachers for a changing world: What teachers should learn and be able to do* (pp. 390–441). Jossey-Bass.

Holmes Group. (1990). *Tomorrow's schools: Principles for the design of professional development schools.*

Mentoring Virginia. (n.d.). https://www.mentoringvirginia.com/

Missi. (n.d.). *61 Inspiring Glow and Grow Sentence Starters for Feedback.* Elementary Assessments. https://elementaryassessments.com/glow-and-grow-sentence-starters/

National Association for Professional Development Schools. (2008). *What it means to be a Professional Development School.* [Policy statement].

National Association for Professional Development Schools. (2021). *What it means to be a professional development school: The nine essentials* (2nd ed.). [Policy statement].

National Council for the Accreditation of Teacher Education. (2010). Transforming teacher education through clinical practice: A national strategy to prepare effective teachers. [Policy statement]. http://caepnet.org/~/media/Files/caep/accreditation-resources/blue-ribbon-panel.pdf

Parker, A. K., Parsons, S. A., Groth, L., & Levine-Brown, E. (2016). Pathways to partnership: A developmental framework for building PDS relationships. *School-University Partnerships 9*(3), 34–48. https://napds.org/sup-2016-themed/

Parker, A. K., Sprague, D., Brown, E., & Casablanca, F. (2020). Leveraging school-university partnerships to support the transition to online learning. In R. E. Ferdig, E. Baumgartner, R. Hartshorne, R. Rakowski & C. Mouza (Eds.), *Teaching, technology, and teacher education during the COVID-19 pandemic: Stories from the field* (pp. 197–202). Association for the Advancement of Computing in Education (AACE). https://www.learntechlib.org/d/216903

Parsons, S. A., Groth, L. A., Parker, A. K., Brown, E. L., Sell, C., & Sprague, D. (2017). Elementary teacher preparation at George Mason University: Evolution of our program. In R. Flessner & D. Lecklider (Eds.), *Case studies of clinical preparation in teacher education* (pp. 109–124). Rowman & Littlefield.

Virginia Department of Education. (2022). *School Quality Profiles.* https://schoolquality.virginia.gov/

CHAPTER 6

ROOTED IN A COMMITMENT TO CHANGE

How a PDS Network Renews and Rebuilds Its Implementation of Best Practices

Stacey Leftwich, Cathy Brant,
Michelle Damiani, and Robert Eisberg

Context

Rationale

The Rowan University (RU) Professional Development School's (PDS) network was created to foster school-university partnerships that reflected a commitment to nurture and sustain close connections between P–12 schools and higher education with a focus on teacher preparation, ongoing professional development of pre- and in-service teachers, student learning and research. (National Council for the Accreditation of Teacher Education, 2001).

Demographics

RU's College of Education (CED)

RU, formerly Glassboro State College, is located in southern New Jersey (NJ) and is a comprehensive public research university with an R2 Carnegie Research Classification. Glassboro State College, founded in 1923, was initially established as a Normal School. RU has grown to 14 colleges and schools with both undergraduate and graduate programs, and has a student body of over 19,000, which is predominately White (63%). The College of Education (CED) at RU has stayed true to its beginnings as a Normal School with the CED remaining one of the largest colleges in the university.

P–12 Partners

The current 11 P–12 partners joined the RU PDS network between 2010 and 2019. Historically, the majority of the PDSs partnered with the CED mirrored the demographics of the university in both student population and P–12 teachers and administration. Although ethno racial diversity is lacking among educational professionals, the P–12 learners served in the network are racially and ethnically diverse as well as diverse across other identities and lived experiences such as linguistic, dis/ability, religion, and sexual orientation. As the need to diversify the teacher workforce is being addressed, the network is diligent in assuring that the NAPDS revised Nine Essentials (NAPDS, 2021), with antiracism at the core of this work, are adhered to, which requires professional development (PD) for all so that the diverse learners being served are supported.

Network Description

The CED has held a long and continuing commitment to the tenets of the National Association for Professional Development Schools' (NAPDS) Nine Essentials. In alignment with the mission of the college, the CED established a partnership in 1991 at Cooper's Poynt Family School in Camden, NJ, and at one point the college partnered with thirteen P–12 schools. These partnerships and the work were supported by external grant funds. However, in 2013, the grant funding expired causing the college to restructure the partnerships' requirements. Partners had to decide whether they would remain a PDS without grant funding support or choose to partner with the college in other ways, such as hosting early field placements, teacher candidates, or a combination of both. The impact of this new alignment and the new requirements reduced the number of partnerships from thirteen schools to two. This reduction resulted in the creation of the Rowan PDS network, requiring partner schools to align their work with the original NAPDS Nine Essentials (2008) and to do this without the support of external funding.

In 2016 a new position was created to oversee the network. The Executive Director for the Office of Educator Support and Partnerships (OESP) was charged with rebuilding the Rowan PDS Network and is currently the main point of contact for all schools and their respective academic staff. Since the creation of the Rowan PDS Network, the CED has partnered with 11 P–12 schools, and ten are currently partners in the network. The network consists of two early childhood schools, eight elementary/middle schools and one high school.

The mission of the Rowan PDS Network aligns with the vision of the CED; *to be a leading force in preparing and supporting reflective practitioners who use education to transform our global society* (Rowan University Website, 2022a). This mission also aligns with NAPDS Essential 1: A Comprehensive Mission (NAPDS, 2021). The CED's tagline is *access, success, and equity, turning research into practice* (Rowan University Website, 2022b). To ensure the vision and tagline are achieved, the work conducted with PDS partners is collaborative in nature to promote learning and the mental and physical health of diverse learners in all settings. The CED is fully committed to preparing and supporting all educational professionals, both preservice and in-service, through the development of knowledge, skills, and dispositions. Simultaneously, we are committed to continually improving practice in mutually beneficial and shared school-university partnerships. Efforts to establish a consistent framework for PDS work conducted in the Rowan Network were guided by the original Nine Essentials and the four pillars of PDS partnership articulated in the foundational work by the Holmes Partnership (2007). Leftwich et al. (2020) explained how these original four pillars were further adopted as the "four nonnegotiables" for the Rowan PDS Network. These four nonnegotiables are applied throughout the Rowan Network as the cornerstones that guide the work conducted at each PDS site. Specifically, the four nonnegotiables cover four aspects of school-university partnerships that further ensure attention to preparing and supporting reflective practitioners and connecting research to practice. The four nonnegotiables that PDSs in the Rowan Network must engage in include: professional development of preservice teachers, professional development of in-service teachers, research that focuses on teaching and learning through a PDS partnership, and measurable P–12 student achievement. The four components are intentionally broad. Each PDS site selects and engages in their work which is not prescriptive, thus allowing for each site to determine shared goals and agendas that meets their needs in a contextually relevant and responsive way. At the same time, these four nonnegotiables provide a consistent expectation and structural outline for all PDS sites to describe, report, and evaluate their Network activities and outcomes.

Description of Teacher Education Programs

The CED is organized into four academic divisions: Educational Services and Leadership, Interdisciplinary and Inclusive Education, Language, Literacy, and Sociocultural Education, and Science, Technology, Engineering, Arts, and Math Education. The college offers both undergraduate and graduate programs. Students prepare for careers in P–12 education (early childhood, elementary, and secondary), special education, inclusive education (dual certification program in elementary and special education), and physical education, as well as in school counseling, school psychology and educational leadership. The CED continues to grow its programs and now includes both full-time and part-time EdD and PhD programs in higher and postsecondary education, counselor education, literacy education, special education, and urban education and diverse learning environments.

Oversight

At Rowan, full-time, three-quarter time, and adjunct faculty are eligible to serve as Professors-In-Residence (PIRs). RU recognizes the importance and time involved with PDS work and allocates three credit hours to conduct work in this formal role. Full-time and three-quarter time faculty receive three credits of release time from their designated course load. Adjunct faculty receive the same credit hours, which equates to one three-credit course. Additionally, some Rowan doctoral students also serve as PIRs. They receive stipends as PIRs and use their assigned schools to create a platform to collect data for related doctoral research. All PIRs are required to work at least one day per week at the assigned partner school where they facilitate P–12 professional development opportunities that include workshops with qualified presenters as well as provide the resources and opportunities for professional learning collaborations among participants through school-based planning teams. PIRs also provide PD to clinical candidates and professional P–12 faculty and staff, establish a research agenda, and focus on increasing P–12 learners' academic achievements. PIRs further coordinate field and clinical experiences with school personnel and Rowan's Office of Clinical Experiences (OCE), as well as work with school partners to examine the effectiveness of the partnership as it relates to student achievement. Thus, the PIRs in each school work with their partners to ensure the four nonnegotiables are addressed at each site. These initiatives are integrated in their daily PDS work and are aligned to the NAPDS' Nine Essentials (NAPDS, 2021). Together the Nine Essentials and the four nonnegotiables are used to provide meaningful and rich experiences to all students, staff, and families in the partnerships, which is the ultimate goal of the Rowan PDS Network.

Structure

Partnership Creation

Becoming a PDS partner begins with a formal application of interest (see resources). Next, an initial meeting between the Executive Director of

OESP and the P–12 district's administrators takes place. Once a school becomes a formal partner in the network there is a meeting to define what a PDS is, how to use the NAPDS Nine Essentials to guide this definition, and to identify the goals, benefits, and expectations. The meeting also provides time to determine the shared commitment by aligning the district's goals with the expected PDS work. The Rowan PDS network prides itself on collaboration with the P–12 partners to prevent the belief that PDSs are "add-ons" to the work already being done in P–12 schools. Rather the PDS partnership is identified as an additional level of support towards the schools' and districts' goals.

After this thorough discussion, current PIRs and the university faculty assigned as a liaison to a PDS in the network are contacted to join the Executive Director of OESP and visit the school. Together they present information about PDS to the school's faculty/staff. The school's faculty/staff vote to become a PDS and only when there is a majority of "yes" votes will the university move forward in signing the PDS Memorandum of Understanding (MOU), making the partnership official (see resources).

As recognition and understanding the importance of the partnership goals and continued professional development, each P–12 school partner allocates funds, as articulated in the MOU, between $1,000 and $5,000 to support PD activities (e.g., guest speakers, events, data collection), materials/services (e.g., books for classroom libraries, research transcriptions) and travel (e.g., professional conferences, workshops, mileage reimbursement). Monies for the latter are specifically set aside for P–12 members' registration to attend the NAPDS conference each year. RU also recognizes the importance of attending the same conference, and the OESP provides monies for the PIRs and the district's yearly funding provides support for the P–12 faculty to attend the conference as well. Ideally this financial support also provides PDS teams an opportunity to present research and/or innovative practices happening at their schools. The state of NJ holds a free yearly NJ PDS conference. Partners are encouraged to attend and receive PD hours for their attendance which aligns with NAPDS Essential 9: Resources and Recognition, NAPDS, 2021).

The assigned PIR and school administrator identify a PDS Site Coordinator who is a P–12 staff member in the school. Together, the PIR and Site Coordinator work with a PDS Steering Committee to complete the PDS Initial School Report (see resources). The committee is made up of school and community representatives. Representatives include principals, teachers from each grade level and/or special areas, school staff as well as parents or other community members. When appropriate, students also serve on this committee. The Initial Report outlines the PDS goals and objectives for the year, promotes scholarship through local and national presentations and publications by Rowan faculty and PDS partners, and demonstrates a vision and mission that encompasses a fierce dedication to nurturing and sustaining close connections between P–12 schools and higher education.

PDS Components

Preparing Future Educators. All school partnerships in the Rowan PDS Network agree to accept/support a minimum of 10 educator preparation clinical candidates (both undergraduate and graduate) during the academic year based on the school capacity of mentor teachers. Partners also work to coordinate on-site CED courses before and/or after school hours. Courses include a field component, allowing candidates to implement coursework learning directly to an assigned classroom setting which meets NAPDS Essential 2: Clinical Preparation (NAPDS, 2021).

Clinical Placement Process/Structure. Clinical candidates at RU have opportunities to work in PDSs in multiple ways. Candidates may be selected to work in a PDS as part of the field component of an onsite course or select to be assigned to a PDS for their final clinical placement. The State of NJ requires a yearlong clinical practice (student teaching) placement, ideally in the same school and in the same classroom throughout the year. The OESP established a process for any teacher candidate interested in being placed at a PDS site for this two-semester experience.

Housed in the OESP, the OCE oversees the internal application process for clinical practice placements. Before applying online, teacher candidates can review a list of the school partners and their PDS video. The video shares information about not only what a PDS is, but also what is unique about each school in the network. Upon reviewing each video, applicants can identify a PDS site(s) where they are interested in being placed. Next, the OCE provides a preliminary list of candidates who have expressed interest in being placed in a PDS to the PIRs. The PIRs then meet to determine which students they plan to invite for interviews and visitations to the PDSs. After interviews and visits take place, a list of selected candidates is provided by each PIR to OCE, along with the name of the cooperating teacher to which each student will tentatively be matched. The clinical placement process meets NAPDS Essential 2: Clinical Preparation (NAPDS, 2021).

Accessing PDS Activities and Outcomes. The PDS Initial and End-of-the Year School Reports (see resources) provide an assessment process to support the continued development of the partnership. These collaboratively written reports, completed at the beginning and end of the year, provide a thorough analysis of the work of the partnership.

The Initial PDS Report requires the PDS's improvement plan, an explanation of baseline data to support the work identified, a list of PDS goals and objectives, a series of narratives describing the plan/focus of the

Rowan clinical interns assigned to the site, a list of the course(s) taught on-site, and a description of the expected outcome data (expected evidence that supports the PDS work described). The report ends with a tabled timeline of the activities to be implemented throughout the year.

At the end of the year, a final PDS End of Year School Report is submitted. Also collaborative in nature, this report provides evidence of the PDS work for the current year. The report summarizes how the PDS goals and objectives were achieved, an explanation of the impact on teacher professional development, clinical interns' plan/focus, and the course taught on-site. The report ends with explanations of the research conducted and student achievements as a result of implemented PD and research.

Both reports align with NAPDS Essential 3: Professional Learning and Leading (NAPDS, 2021). They are submitted to the OESP's Executive Director who reviews each site report, meets with PIRs when clarification is needed, and then shares the report(s) with the school district's superintendent. Typically, a representative of the building administrative team serves on the building's PDS Steering committee and is therefore a part of the report development and decision-making. This reciprocal process allows for all involved to be aware of the PDS work and provide opportunities for modifications if needed. Using both an initial and end-of-year PDS school report process, partners identify their PDS focus through actionable goals, and then following the year of PDS work partners report out on their progress toward those goals. At the end of each academic year the OESP's Executive Director meets with the PDS school districts' superintendents and principals to discuss the PDS End-of-Year school report. It is a time for partner administrators to talk about the accomplishments and/or challenges of PDS work so that the PDS can grow and evolve. The Executive Director meets with PIRs to share outcomes from the meetings and discuss ways any concerns, challenges or issues expressed by the administrators can be addressed.

At the end of each academic year, a full-day PIR/P–12 Partnership Retreat is held. Partners new to the network have an opportunity to learn about the PDS work within the network and formulate plans for the year while current partners share their year-long work and dialogue with their members on future plans. The retreat includes breakfast and lunch funded by the OESP, which is the university's expression of appreciation for all partners and their PDS work.

Support

PDS partnerships are developed to be mutually beneficial relationships in which each partner supports each other. All PDS work at RU revolves around the aforementioned four "nonnegotiables" in varied forms of preservice teacher preparation, such as clinical practice, field placements, and on-site coursework; multiple opportunities for in-service teachers/staff to engage in continuing PD by working with university faculty members; efforts to increase all students' achievement and promote scholarship in the form of research that focuses on teaching and learning to improve both.

Below are highlighted connections between Rowan's four nonnegotiables and the support that PDSs in the network and RU provide each other in each category.

Preservice Teachers

A robust PDS network helps both higher education and P–12 partners work with preservice teachers. PDSs provide placements for teacher candidates/early field experiences and the state of NJ's required yearlong clinical practices (student teaching). PDSs are also spaces for the university to hold on-site classes.

As a part of the MOU, the P–12 partner commits to provide placements for Rowan interns. The P–12 partners benefit from hosting preservice teachers in their buildings in a number of ways. First, it provides a pipeline of potential employment. Many of the Rowan preservice teachers ultimately gain employment in the PDS schools and/or school districts in which they conducted their placements. Additionally, having a PIR from Rowan assigned at the school provides preservice teachers an additional level of support and connection to the university during the clinical experiences. University PIRs have noted that their PDS work has benefited them in keeping in touch with the realities of P–12 schools, which benefits not only the preservice teachers placed in the P–12 school, but also the students in their other on-campus courses. For example, several PIRs have seen innovative teaching practices in their PDS placements and have shared these examples in their on-campus courses or have invited P–12 partners to come speak to their classes about these practices. Finally, Rowan interns (teacher candidates) often bring elements they have learned at the university to help enhance the curricula in the P–12 schools. Often mentor teachers have noted that they have learned from their preservice teachers as much as the preservice teachers have learned from them.

In-Service Teachers

Rowan PDS partnerships provide many benefits for the teachers in the P–12 schools. As with teacher candidates, mentors and in-service teachers in Rowan PDS sites benefit from the innovative teaching practices that preservice teachers bring from the university context, thus extending university access to current research and providing best practices to K–12 schools. With the pivot to online learning during COVID-19, Rowan interns were able to assist their mentor teachers with the rapid shifts and technology demands required for online, remote instruction. Several superintendents reached out to the OESP's Executive Director to express how helpful Rowan's interns were in assisting the mentor teachers with the technological transition. Rowan interns often entered their field placements with experience with diverse technologies, a skill set that proved valuable to intern's cooperating teachers during this unique time.

PIRs provide an extra level of support to mentor teachers at the PDS for both successful and struggling preservice teachers. For example, PIRs can meet with preservice teachers individually or as a group, and provide allowable support for course assignments for the state of NJ's mandated performance assessment, edTPA. For some of Rowan's PDS placement districts, edTPA can be a disincentive to host clinical interns because of the time, access, and work that it requires schools and districts to provide clinical interns. Having a PIR in the building provides in-service teachers an external resource for any challenges or questions that may arise regarding pedagogy, curriculum or practice in the school settings. For example, in the wake of COVID-19, in-service teachers reached out to PIRs for support in addressing student learning loss and to bridge the gap students have in their social emotional learning, due to online and hybrid schooling. The mentor teachers in the Rowan PDS network noted that they were grateful for the extra resource the PIRs provided.

When placing PIRs, the OESP's Executive Director strives to align the PDSs' interests and goals with the PIRs' areas of research interest or expertise. Recently, three of the schools in the PDS network have been working to make a more purposeful move from the use of self-contained special education classrooms to placement in inclusive general education classrooms. In one of the more established PDSs, the PIR's area of expertise is inclusive education, and the PIR has helped the school partner build teacher capacity, evaluate school structures for appropriate supports, and draft and enact plans for students to be educated in the least restrictive environment.

PIRs also provide in-service teachers hands-on assistance in the classroom and the teacher can ask PIRs for resources about a given issue. PIRs often coplan and/or coteach lessons with in-service teachers. They have recorded lessons taught by in-service teachers to help them reflect upon their practices in ways that differ from traditional administrative observations. Finally, PIRs become the facilitators for traditional PD for in-service teachers. The schools' PDS Steering Committees work with their PIRs and the administration to develop a list of PD workshop topics that would benefit the staff during the school year. The PIR may either run the PD themselves or tap the resources available at the university to invite a colleague to conduct workshops.

Student Learning

The nonnegotiables of preservice teacher preparation, in-service teacher professional development and research within the PDS setting are all aimed to support student learning. The support for preservice teachers, in-service teachers, and research that occurs in PDS sites ultimately helps increase P–12 student achievement. The increase in student learning and achievement occurs at both the microlevel, within any given classroom, and the macrolevel, within the school and beyond to district and national educational settings.

Research

PDS partnerships provide opportunities for research for both university faculty and school partners. At RU, several PIRs, who were also doctoral students, have conducted their dissertation research in their PDS settings. Full-time faculty members have been able to establish a robust research agenda from their work in PDS schools. Peer-reviewed journal articles, conference presentations, and book chapters, often coauthored or copresented with P–12 partners, are examples of how research from PDS sites are disseminated to the profession. Perhaps more importantly, P–12 faculty can use the PIR's expertise in research to engage in their own practitioner and action research in the classroom and greater school context. PIRs and P–12 faculty can collaborate to explore problems generated from within the school context rather than from outside. In-service teachers, with the support of the PIR, can learn more about the process of research, present research at academic conferences and publish research in refereed journals. PDS-based research can impact students' learning of students within the specific PDS, the larger Rowan PDS network, and ultimately PDS settings across the country.

Pepper Elementary School. A successful example of how PDS work can support student learning comes from Pepper Elementary School (PES). According to PES's 2018 state standardized test score (New Jersey Department of Education, n.d.), 29.9% of Hispanic students scored proficient on the English Language Arts (ELA) state examination. Furthermore, 81% of students classified as English language learners (ELLs) and who were enrolled in an English as a second language (ESL) program in Grades 4–8 were at the *developing* level (student knows and uses social English and some specific academic language with visual and graphic support) of English proficiency and were not ready to exit the program. For the fifth-grade level, which was a focus for the PES PDS research plan, 6.25% of ELLs were at or above the proficiency level necessary to exit the ESL program. With help from the PIR, PES engaged in PD, instructional improvement and school culture enhancement, resulting in an overall increase of student achievement. By the end of the year, 50% of Grade 5 students were at the developing level, and a significantly reduced 20% were below the developing level (New Jersey Department of Education, n.d.).

Challenges

As successful as Rowan has been in rebuilding its PDS network, its leadership and PIRs are cognizant of the challenges that remain in place. Any challenge can create stress at a PDS and a combination of them can threaten the sustainability of an individual partnership and, ultimately, the PDS network. In this section we highlight three challenges that have impacted our network: financial restraints, changes in leadership (both in the P–12 schools and the university), and the changing needs of university faculty and school partners.

Fiscal Challenges

One ongoing challenge in PDS work is the fiscal considerations related to supporting PDS work across multiple school districts, schools, and a larger network. Rowan recognizes this as an equity consideration and that PDSs have different resources available. Although partner schools commit to financial support, it varies based on school budgets. Schools are under continual pressure to reduce expenses, which could jeopardize allotting limited funds to PDS work. Additionally, as previously mentioned, RU offers a three-credit course release for faculty serving as PIRs to conduct PDS work. If at any time, university administration decides that it can no longer fiscally support that initiative, many faculty members may find it unmanageable to select yearlong sustained PDS work solely under the scope of service, particularly as demands on faculty continually increase in terms of research, teaching, and service.

Changes in Leadership

This is a time of tremendous transition throughout the field of education (Walker, 2022). The same can be true of PDSs and how partnerships are structured. Transitions in leadership at the district and school levels, as well as at the university, raise uncertainty for PDS partnerships. While there did not appear to be a mass exodus of administrators in the wake of the Covid pandemic, a national survey by the Rand Corporation in Fall 2021 found that half of the superintendents surveyed said they were likely to leave or undecided about their plans within the next five years (Schwartz & Diliberti, 2022). Nevertheless, superintendents, curriculum directors, principals, assistant principals, and others come and go, and the commitment to PDS work may be in jeopardy because of these changes. In addition, the university faculty members who serve as PIRs (tenure-track professors, nontenure track lecturers, adjunct professors, and doctoral students) may move into different roles, develop different research interests, or take jobs in other institutions, creating a need to continually recruit, hire and develop training for new PIRs.

Shifting Needs

The shifting needs of schools also can raise challenges. For example, while a PDS may have determined that inclusion or literacy instruction was their top priority when they joined the PDS network that may have shifted as it reassessed its needs. Social-emotional learning became more important in the wake of the pandemic, and many of the staff at both the PDSs and at the university expressed a belief that adults needed as much support as students in rebuilding the competencies that support learning. When priorities change, PIRs sometimes state that they can not be effective in addressing school needs as they were when they first accepted their PDS assignment.

A final challenge can be found in the NAPDS's revised Nine Essentials (NAPDS,2021), specifically in the first essential that states that PDSs aim to "advance equity, antiracism, and social justice within and among schools, colleges/universities, and their respective community and professional partners" (NAPDS, 2021, p.15). While equity and social justice have long been part of the stated mission of the RU COE, the terms antiracism and social justice have become emotionally charged across the country. When the revised essentials were presented to one partner P–12 school, they decided to discontinue their participation. Although not specifically stated, statements from the leadership alluded to a discomfort in meeting elements of the revised essentials. Rowan agreed not to resume a partnership when discomfort about this aspect of PDS work was expressed.

Opportunities

The foundations of the Rowan PDS Network have provided a strong base to reflect on practices and outcomes related to support and challenges that have emerged prior to, during, and as schools returned amidst the shifting trajectory of COVID-19. Both the supports and challenges discussed in this chapter have created opportunities and spaces to continue to grow, develop and improve as a PDS network. These possibilities, and partners' reflections on the ever-evolving practice may also be informative to the larger PDS community. This chapter closes with three specific opportunities for moving forward in the practices of engaged PDS work. Those opportunities are considerations related to shifting school partners, explicit efforts toward implementing the revised Nine Essentials (NAPDS, 2021), and revised documentation tools and procedures designed for efficiency, yielding usable data, and increasing school partners' participation and input.

Considerations Related to Shifting School Partners

As an established PDS network, Rowan has a combination of PDS districts and schools as partners. Rowan also maintains publicly available an online form for potential school partners (see resources). By providing PDS information and materials on an ongoing basis we are always welcoming new interest in PDS work. In other words, interested partners are not limited to a specific time frame to express interest, and they do not have to wait for postings to open. Even if we were not able to bring a new potential partner on board right away, the Executive Director makes contact with the interested school or faculty member at the time of their inquiry. Having a waiting list also allows a new potential school partner to be identified more readily when an opening becomes available. The Executive Director does have to limit participation based on resource availability, however this careful management also creates the opportunity to ensure that we are able to do and sustain high quality PDS work within the allocated resources.

Implementing the Revised Nine Essentials

With the revision of the Nine Essentials of PDS in 2021, the Rowan PDS Network felt that it was critical to reexamine the network's commitments to and applications of conducting antiracism work as an essential aspect of advancing equity and social justice. In an effort to solicit input from and understand partners' positions on the network's collective next steps, this question was presented at the biannual PDS Network meeting. This meeting includes intentional input from and dialogue between school, university, and community partners. In that meeting, the Executive Director posed the following question: Given that NAPDS aims to advance equity, antiracism, and social justice within and among schools, colleges/universities, and their respective community and professional partners, how committed was Rowan PDS Network?

Together, all partners reified that any PDS in the Rowan Network was expected to have an explicit commitment to antiracism. The revision of NAPDS Nine Essentials (NAPDS, 2021) presented a critical moment of opportunity for all partners, existing and new, to evaluate their commitments to antiracism and for Rowan to think about what kinds of deliverables or applications of antiracist work are expected in aspiring best practices. Likewise, it was explicitly shared with P–12 partners that NAPDS's and RU's commitments to antiracism must be evident in the work being done in P–12 PDSs. This resulted in an update to the Rowan Network's MOU, where the revised Nine Essentials and Rowan's revised mission statement are now listed in the MOU. In addition to writing this commitment into partnership agreements, the collective commitment to antiracism also resulted in new discussions about how to enact this commitment through action items, specific initiatives, and how to assess outcomes of these efforts in our practice.

Revised Documentation Tools and Procedures

Finally, a "one size fits all" approach does not work in education, nor in PDS work. Both are constantly changing and evolving. COVID-19 helped the OESP's Executive Director discover that some of the approaches within Rowan's own network were no longer serving the shifting context of education and the future of PDS work. For example, policies and procedures that had previously been used were not always practical or usable in the return to schools during the pandemic. The challenges faced in having PDS work formally paused and then resuming created spaces to examine the tools used within the network and highlighted the need for some revision. For example, the Initial and End of Year PDS Reports are being revised. The aim is to develop an Initial PDS Report template that is more streamlined and yields more readily usable information in the form of "school snapshots" based on information that is relevant to PDSs at the time of creation (early fall). In the End of Year PDS Report, more clearly identified activities and outcomes at each PDS site that address the mission of PDS work and the Revised Nine Essentials will be required. Each year, P–12 partners also complete initial and final evaluations of their PIRs. Revising written tools and documentation procedures creates an additional important opportunity for both P–12 partners and the PIRs to provide input into what kinds of information and goal planning should be included in the Initial and End of Year PDS Reports and the PIR evaluations. Lastly, an end-of-the year "exit" survey for P–12 partners is being considered. This would provide not only a space for the PDS partners to assess their own commitments to PDS work, but also a space for the PIR to provide the Executive Director of OESP feedback on their view of the partners' commitment to PDS work at large, including alignment to the Revised Nine Essentials and antiracism work.

Conclusion

In PDSs, and throughout the field of education, there is work to be done. The Rowan PDS Network is an established network, being rewarded twice for their work as NAPDS Exemplary Award recipients. Network members continue to learn, which is of critical importance to avoid stagnancy and develop new pathways to best practices. The Rowan PDS Network's purpose and commitment to sustained, engaged school-university partnerships has not changed. The four nonnegotiables still create the foundational structure for the Rowan network's work.

In addition, the NAPDS revised Nine Essentials have only strengthened partners' resolve and provided impetus to some of the challenging situations that we navigated as a PDS network. Putting these commitments into practice, especially amidst returning from a global pandemic, has illuminated the need to rebuild and reinforce the ways that PDS work is practiced. As a network, members have embraced these challenges in an effort to learn from them. What has been recognized first and foremost is the need to be fluid and responsive to the needs of all stakeholders (i.e., P–12 students, P–12 faculty and staff, P–12 administrators, clinical interns, University faculty, University administrators, and community partners).

Essentially, what has been most important is responding to the changing times, which involves simultaneously remaining steadfast in the PDS vision and mission while finding new, innovative, and shared ways to implement and assess those commitments in practice. The Rowan PDS Network is rooted in a commitment to change. Through a renewing and rebuilding of the network's purpose and goals, it is positioned to implement best practices for all stakeholders.

REFERENCES

Lang, P. (2007). *The Holmes partnership trilogy*.

Leftwich, S., Elder, B., Woodfield, C., LoCastro, A., & Rencher, L. (2020). It took decades to build: How four non-negotiables helped guide a PDS network to launch and sustain partnerships for close to 30 years. *School-University Partnerships, 13*(2), 8–17.

National Association for Professional Development Schools. (2008). *What it means to be a professional development school: The nine essentials*. [Policy statement].

National Association for Professional Development Schools. (2021). *What it means to be a professional development school: The nine essentials* (2nd ed.). [Policy statement].

National Council for the Accreditation of Teacher Education. (2001). *Standards for professional development schools*. [Policy Statement].

New Jersey Department of Education (n.d). Assessment. https://www.nj.gov/education/assessment/results/reports/

Rowan University. (2022a, March 10). *College of Education Vision Statement*. https://education.rowan.edu/about-the-college/mission-and-vision.html

Rowan University. (2022b, March 10). *College of Education Tagline.* https://education.rowan.edu/about-the-college/documents/coeannualreport13_141.pdf

Schwartz, H. L., & Diliberti, M. K. (2022, February 15). *Flux in the educator labor market: Acute staff shortages and projected superintendent departures.* Rand Corporation. https://www.rand.org/pubs/research_reports/RRA956-9.html

Walk, T. (2022, February 10). Survey: Alarming number of educators may soon leave the profession. https://www.nea.org/advocating-for-change/new-from-nea/survey-alarming-number-educators-may-soon-leave-profession

CHAPTER 7

ENGAGING AND IMPACTFUL PRACTICES IN AN AWARD-WINNING PDS NETWORK

Sara Elburn, Diallo Sessoms, and Ron Siers Jr.

Context

Professional Development Schools Network Rationale

The impetus for creating Professional Development Schools (PDSs) in partnership with Salisbury University (SU) was to comply with the State of Maryland's mandate that all interns complete their 100-day extended internships (capstone clinical practice experiences) in a PDS. coupled with the fact that SU is located in a predominantly rural region, the Seidel School of Education's Regional PDS Network spans seven Maryland counties and includes 39 schools.

The mission of SU's Regional PDS Network is to provide a learning community to improve practice and enhance student achievement in P–12 public schools. In conjunction with the University's rich history in preparing future teachers, its national reputation for its partnerships with public schools is exceptional. SU was honored with the NAPDS Spirit of Partnership Award in 2009, the Emerging PDS Leader Award in 2018 and 2021, and the NAPDS Award for Exemplary Professional Development School Achievement in 2011, 2015, 2017, and 2021.

A Practical Guide to Exemplary Professional Development Schools
pp. 105–121
www.infoagepub.com
Copyright © 2024 by Information Age Publishing
All rights of reproduction in any form reserved.

Demographics

SU is located in the city of Salisbury on the Delmarva Peninsula between the Atlantic Ocean and the Chesapeake Bay. The major cities of Washington, D.C., Baltimore, and Philadelphia can be reached in two hours from the region. The City of Salisbury is home to over 32,000 people. SU is a public institution and is part of the University System of Maryland. It began as the State Normal School for teacher preparation in 1925. Now, SU facilitates 46 undergraduate degree programs, 15 master's degree programs, and two doctoral degree programs for approximately 7,500 undergraduate and graduate students (MSDE, n.d.)

Within its undergraduate enrollment, SU had 44% males and 56% females in Fall 2021. 74% of undergraduate students were white, 11% African American, and 15% identified as "other minority." 93% of undergraduate students were 24 years of age and under, with 7% of undergraduates as nontraditional students 25 years and older (Salisbury University, n.d.)

Regional PDS Network

SU currently partners with 26 elementary schools, one elementary/middle school, four middle schools, one middle/high school, and five high schools. Thirty-three schools serve as PDSs, hosting teacher candidates and interns in clinical practice for preprogram and teacher preparation program courses. Six schools serve as partner school sites, hosting a handful of teacher candidates and interns when needed.

The largest number of PDSs and partner schools is found in Wicomico County, where SU is located. The University partners with 21 Wicomico County schools, 6 Worcester County schools, 5 Dorchester County schools; 2 Somerset County schools, 2 Caroline County schools, 2 Anne Arundel County schools, and 1 Talbot County school. All PDS and partner sites reflect diversity, racial and/or socioeconomic, and seventeen elementary schools within the network are Title One schools. More information regarding the counties with whom Salisbury University partners is included in Table 7.1.

Teacher Preparation Programs

The University's Seidel School of Education offers undergraduate programs in early childhood education and elementary education, as well as a combined dual early childhood/elementary education program. It also offers P–12 programs in music education, physical education and ESOL, and secondary education programs in English, mathematics, history, biology, chemistry, earth science, physics, French and Spanish. The Seidel

Table 7.1. PDS Partner Counties' Demographics

County	Enrollment	Attendance Rate	Graduation Rate	Students Receiving Free and Reduced Meals	Students With Special Needs	English Learners	Largest Student Group by Race/Ethnicity	Second-Largest Student Group by Race/Ethnicity
Anne Arundel	83,044	94%	90.23%	21.4%	10.6%	8%	50% White	22% African American
Caroline	5,553	90.9%	89.76%	58.5%	10.1%	7.8%	59% White	17% Hispanic
Dorchester	4,462	87.7%	80.06%	95%	9.2%	5%	41% White	42% African American
Somerset	2,818	93.2%	75%	72.8%	14.4%	5%	46% African American	38% White
Talbot	4,524	95%	95%	49.5%	11%	10.6%	54% White	22% Hispanic
Wicomico	14,354	91.7%	83.11%	63.1%	11.2%	8.3%	39% White	37% African American
Worcester	6,711	95%	91.71%	10.9%	5%	5%	65% White	19% African American

School also facilitates graduate and doctoral programs for practicing educators.

The Department of Early and Elementary Education (DEEE) is housed in the Seidel School of Education. DEEE offers a Bachelor of Science in elementary education (Grades 1–6), early childhood education (P–3), and dual certification in elementary/early childhood education. Programs are accredited by the Association for Advancing Quality in Educator Preparation (AAQEP) and the Maryland State Department of Education (MSDE). The mission statement of SU's Seidel School of Education's DEEE is: "We honor children by empowering teacher candidates to engage in creative, caring, and compassionate pedagogies (Salisbury University, n.d.)."

DEEE collaborates with the Seidel School's PDS network of 26 elementary and early childhood schools. Teacher candidates experience multiple opportunities to learn in local schools while engaging with professional educators, P–6 students, and other professionals in public schools such as technology specialists. Education majors are placed in clinical settings prior to entering an education program to gain early classroom experience in pre-K through Grade 3 and interact with professional educators as well as other professionals in education. The clinical setting experience increases as teacher candidates progress through prerequisite courses and methods courses, culminating in a full-time clinical experience with designated mentor teachers in PDS P–12 school sites. The senior year begins with an intensive clinical practice placement prior to the final clinical experiences. During the intensive clinical practice in the first part of the senior year, candidates are expected to have 20 full, consecutive days in the clinical placement. Candidates do not assume the lead-teacher role at this point; however, they are fully integrated into the process. After the 20 full days, candidates return to campus for class while continuing in the same placement. During the final clinical experiences, teacher candidates assume the lead-teacher role in the classroom while planning and coteaching with the mentor. The first part of the final clinical experience is with the same teacher from the previous semester which provides continuity with the mentor teacher and with the kids depending on the cycle of the school year. For example, if a candidate is in a placement during the fall semester, they will be with the same classroom in the spring for the first part of the final clinical experience.

DEEE programs provide education majors with a variety of innovative experiences. Methods courses focus on integrating course work with clinical experiences to reinforce, reflect, and continually revisit key pedagogical ideas. With an intense focus on preparing candidates to teach literacy, teacher candidates are well prepared to teach in this area. Additionally, teacher candidates are rigorously prepared to infuse technology into their teaching practice and to develop *a maker* mindset. A maker mindset encourages educators to allow students to make to learn (Bull et al., 2019).

The Secondary and Physical Education Department offers both undergraduate and graduate programs that lead to secondary education certification in a number of liberal arts and science disciplines, including biology, chemistry, earth science, English, French, health, history, mathematics, physics and Spanish. P–12 certification is available in music, English to speakers of other languages (ESOL) and physical education. Department faculty are committed to preparing classroom teachers and other educational personnel. The department's programs are designed with the following goals:

- provide for the individualization of instruction of teachers and prospective teachers during their professional training,
- encourage the emergence of a personal teaching style on the part of each teacher and prospective teacher,
- assist teachers and prospective teachers in developing as reflective persons who, when confronted with a teaching problem, carefully identify the problem, take steps to accurately and systematically assess the problem, generate alternative solutions to the problem and choose an appropriate resolution on the basis of its desirable implications and consequences,
- gather evidence that prospective teachers can bring about desired learning in students before they assume full responsibility for a classroom,
- help prospective teachers develop self-confidence and competence as effective learners and teachers,
- emphasize the importance of increasing interaction and collaboration among teachers, new and experienced, in resolving educational problems and
- prepare teachers who are responsible agents of educational change.

Teacher candidates in a secondary education program complete a rigorous program of study in the academic major and professional education courses. Secondary education programs are accredited by the AAQEP and approved by the MSDE for secondary school teacher certification (Grades 7–12). Persons already holding an undergraduate degree who wish to teach in their subject area at the P–12 level, apply to the Master of Arts in Teaching (M.A.T.) program. This collaborative degree program with the University of Maryland Eastern Shore is designed to prepare students for initial teacher certification and is approved by the MSDE for Initial Teacher Certification. Students are admitted by a joint admission process and take coursework on the campuses of both universities, taught by the faculties of both institutions.

Regional PDS Network Oversight

There are several key employees responsible for overseeing SU's Regional PDS Network, with roles and responsibilities outlined in the memoranda of understanding (MOU) with each of the seven partner school districts (See resources). In the spirit of NAPDS Essential 6: Articulated Agreements (NAPDS, 2021), the following individuals' roles are identified in each MOU, as they share a commitment to teacher preparation and P–12 student achievement.

- Dean of the Seidel School of Education is SU's leader in teacher preparation.
- School Partnerships Coordinator maintains partnerships with P–12 schools, ensuring that MSDE PDS Standards are met.
- Clinical Practice Coordinator works with principals and site coordinators to secure quality placements for interns and teacher candidates.

STRUCTURE

Policies and Procedures

PDS Partnership Creation and Vetting Process

SU began PDS partnerships with P–12 schools in 1996, with two elementary schools and one high school in two counties close in proximity to its campus. These schools were selected by district leadership in each county. As the need for additional school partners across the region has grown, SU has reached out to P–12 school leaders for guidance in identifying more PDS and partner sites. The School Partnerships Coordinator begins the conversation with the district level PDS liaison regarding the specific needs of the Regional PDS Network. These individuals determine what schools would be a best fit, and then obtain approval from the Dean and Superintendent of Schools. Following Maryland PDS guidelines, SU seeks school partners that possess a diverse student population, supportive administrators, collaborative (and tenured) mentor teachers, and above all, a desire to partner with SU (See resources).

Application Process and Fees

Since PDS and partner sites are selected by University and P–12 leaders, an application process is not necessary. Additionally, since PDS partnerships have been mandated by the MSDE, no fees are required in order to be a part of the Regional PDS Network. However, SU and its PDSs and partner schools make the most of their human resources, reflecting NAPDS Essential 9: Resources and Recognition (NAPDS, 2021). The individuals previously described collaborate in SU's Regional PDS Network, many serving in boundary-spanning roles, as described in NAPDS Essential 8: Boundary Spanning Roles (NAPDS, 2021). Faculty and staff from SU are members of P–12 advisory councils and steering committees. Several PDS administrators, site coordinators and mentor teachers are adjunct instructors at SU. This includes practicing mentor teachers serving as internship seminar instructors, guiding interns through their capstone experiences.

While the MSDE mandates the PDS framework for teacher preparation, there is not an allocation in the budget to implement PDS work. However, the SU Regional PDS Network seeks and secures financial resources. The University's May Literacy Center provides tutoring for local elementary school students each semester. Faculty members continuously secure grants to support teacher candidates' and mentor teachers' professional growth in areas such as cultural responsiveness, linguistically rich pedagogical skills, and restorative practice.

Governance and Leadership Roles

University-Based Roles. In addition to the aforementioned individuals involved in oversight of SU's Regional PDS Network (the Dean, School Partnerships Coordinator, and Clinical Practice Coordinator) there are many other key players supporting PDS efforts.

SU PDS Roles:
- Associate Dean supports the Dean of the Seidel School of Education, and its faculty. The Associate Dean leads accreditation efforts and serves on the Local School System.
- PDS Liaison Council serves as the program director for the Science/Secondary Education program, allowing connections with science teachers and supervisors throughout the network.
- Assistant Dean for Program Assessment is a faculty member in the DEEE who oversees schoolwide assessment data collection and decision-making. He often seeks feedback from principals and other P–12 school partners.

- Seidel School Faculty involved in teacher preparation, strive to make connections with school-based teacher educators. Department chairs and program directors also serve on the Regional PDSs Council. This group meets twice each academic year to seek P–12 partner input on schoolwide and PDS decisions.
- PDS liaisons are either full-time faculty members or adjunct faculty hired by SU. Liaisons serve as the main points of contact, often supervising interns at their PDS sites.
- Internship Supervisors support interns and mentor teachers by completing weekly visits of observing, reflecting, guiding, goal setting and cheerleading.
- Teacher Candidates and Interns amount to an average of 500 teacher candidates (university students in preprogram and methods courses) and interns (seniors completing 100-day extensive internships) who are placed in PDSs and partner schools each semester.

P–12 Public School PDS Roles. Salisbury University's Regional PDS Network relies on the dedication from these stakeholders in P–12 PDS and partner school sites:

- Local School System PDS Liaison Council: SU partners with seven school districts in Maryland, which are divided by county. A representative from each school district office serves as the point person for the PDS partnership districtwide. This group meets twice each academic year with individuals involved in PDS leadership at the University.
- School Administrators: All clinical practice placements are approved by building principals. Many principals attend orientation and exit conference opportunities, and often conduct observations and interviews with interns, reaping the benefits of hiring interns when they graduate and full-time positions become available.
- PDS Site Coordinators: These school-based teacher educators support SU teacher candidates and interns in their clinical practice experiences. They work with the PDS liaison to plan and implement intern orientations, check-in experiences, professional development opportunities and exit conferences.
- Mentor Teachers: Mentor teachers are the heart of the PDS network, collaborating and coteaching with SU teacher candidates and interns.

IPDS Components

Educator Preparation

SU teacher candidates and interns truly become a part of their P–12 school communities. Candidates participate in staff versus students sporting events, perform in school talent shows, grill hamburgers at back-to-school nights, dress up with fellow team members in group Halloween costumes, or take part in spirit week activities. PDS site coordinators and administrators share the belief that if teacher candidates and interns feel comfortable in their schools, their P–12 students will benefit.

A shared commitment to reflective practice, responsive innovation, and generative knowledge, as detailed in NAPDS Essential 4: Reflection and Innovation (NAPDS, 2021), is evident in SU PDS practices. For example, at Glen Avenue Elementary School, the PDS Site Coordinators and PDS liaisons collaborate to implement several experiences for interns to become familiar with key staff members in their building. Interns shadow, interview, and/or attend a panel discussion that includes support staff, student support educators, and behavior specialists. These opportunities provide the interns with an understanding of how each staff member can support them and their P–12 students throughout their internship experiences. Self-care and mental health are terms that emerged during the height of the pandemic as educators were tasked with learning new technological skills, more responsibility, and increased concerns about the safety and well-being of students. To help interns understand how to deal with unique challenges, the PDS liaison and site coordinators provided several learning opportunities for both interns and teacher candidates at all stages of the program.

One of these experiences was a session with a faculty member from the SU community in Conflict Analysis and Dispute Resolution (CADR). A presentation titled, "Potentials of Self-Examination for Deep Listening in the Workplace and Beyond" focused on self-examination as a tool for awakening the potential for peace within self because existential contradictions, such as work, can subject self to the wind of disharmony (Koko, 2018). Self-examination is a tool that allows educators to address the wars and conflicts within to help them deal with conflicts outside of us such as workplace stress, interactions with parents, and student concerns. Teacher candidates placed at Glen Avenue Elementary were exposed to a powerful message that caring for self means caring for others which is one of the many goals a teacher has to meet. The simplicity of the practice made it easy for teacher candidates, interns, and Glen Avenue Elementary staff members to understand and they were appreciative of being exposed to tools to help them cope with the mountain of stress faced by educators, especially in the current climate of public school education. The panel discussions with school social workers, guidance counselors, and special education teachers allowed interns to ask questions and get feedback related to real situations that they might experience. It also provided an example of the resources that are available as they begin their professional careers as educators.

Finally, interns attended a session with the technology specialist. The technology specialist is a critical part of teachers successfully implementing tools that address specific learning needs for their students as well as tools that help them manage classroom tasks. Technology can be intimidating with all that is required to facilitate student success in the classroom. The session provided teacher candidates and interns at Glen Avenue Elementary with tools that teachers integrate into their lessons. While technology has always been a critical tool for educators, the pandemic exposed teachers to the need for new skills, tools, and applications that allow them to be nimble practitioners who can successfully respond in a variety of situations.

SU's first prerequisite course for secondary and physical educators is taught on-site at Mardela Middle and High School (MMHS). This dual enrollment course is taught by the school's PDS liaison. The teacher candidates' experience includes a mentor/candidate joint orientation, participation in Back-to-School Night, course content delivered on-site, and immediate clinical practice visitations. A set of Core Values and Norms for Expectations for the on-site course was established (Ward, 2014) (See resources).

During the 2021–2022 school year, the practice of clinical instructional rounds was introduced. Clinical instructional rounds are primarily utilized by in-service professional educators. The process involves teacher candidates in the course held at MMHS, mentor teachers, and the course instructor in the following procedures:

- Weekly opportunities to visit additional mentor teachers' classrooms for ten to twelve minutes, beyond their assigned mentors and disciplines, in order to experience how other educators teach (Wilson, 2020).
- Application of course content within clinical instructional rounds sessions.
- "Hallway huddles" between each round allow for teacher candidates to have a positive dialogue and reflection about quality pedagogy and learning, facilitated by the on-site instructor (Wilson, 2020).

- Appreciation cards with positive feedback from each teacher candidate are given to each mentor teacher at the end of the clinical instructional round session (Wilson, 2020).
- A final reflection of the entire experience in all classrooms visited to summarize insights and learning by responding to reflective prompts is then facilitated by the course instructor (Wilson, 2020). Teacher candidates are asked to respond to the following prompts:
  - "As a result of what I saw and heard during our clinical instructional rounds, which aspects of my current teaching beliefs and their impact on student learning do I feel were validated" (Wilson, 2020)?
  - "As a result of what I saw and heard during our clinical instructional rounds, what questions do I have about my current teaching beliefs and their impact on learning? What new ideas did I learn that can help me in the future to promote high levels of student learning" (Wilson, 2020)?

The success of the on-site preprofessional course at Mardela Middle and High School prompted the principals of North Salisbury School and Prince Street Elementary School to offer space and staff support in their schools to provide similar opportunities to teacher candidates in early childhood, elementary and dual programs. All three on-site courses allow teacher candidates to become immersed in a P–12 school right from the start and give them the experience of immediately connecting course content to current practice in the field.

Supporting Mentor Teachers

In keeping with NAPDS Essential 3: Professional Learning and Leading (NAPDS, 2021), SU and its PDS partners seek one another's support in professional development (PD) opportunities for their stakeholders. SU faculty have visited local classrooms to support interns and their mentor teachers. They have also given demonstration lessons and facilitated after-school workshops guided by need. The University provides space on its campus each summer for its largest P–12 partner, Wicomico County's annual Leadership Academy. Wicomico County Public Schools asks SU faculty to share their expertise in PD sessions, but more importantly, they invite the University faculty members to learn from leaders in the school district. SU faculty are able to participate in the academy's keynote exercises and sessions, or can simply grab lunch to make connections with P–12 supervisors of instruction in their disciplines.

SU's Mentor Workshop provides mentor teachers with PD regarding their role and the University's coteaching model. To date, 1,373 mentor teachers have completed this voluntary workshop and are considered "clinical mentors," which allows them to receive an additional $50 added to their stipend each time they coteach with a full-time intern from SU.

The SU Mentor/Intern Forum is an additional PD opportunity offered to mentor teacher and intern pairs. The forum is delivered at the start of the internship in order to allow pairs to establish a positive relationship and share core values and communication strategies. The forum's format is constantly evolving to provide pairs with a rich, research-based experience.

The Regional PDS Coordinator, Clinical Practice Coordinator, PDS liaisons and site coordinators are in constant communication to support teacher candidates, interns and their mentor teachers. Most recently, SU faculty created an online course for mentor teachers detailing the edTPA performance assessment process and hosted a Zoom drop-in session for mentor teachers who needed additional clarification. SU also created mentor teacher one-sheets describing expectations for teacher candidates in preprogram and methods courses in all teacher preparation programs (See resources).

SUPPORT

SU Support for PDS Partners

Serving the Eastern Shore of Maryland and beyond, SU's Seidel School of Education makes countless efforts to support local teachers, administrators, and most importantly, P–12 students. A few examples of utilization of human, physical, and financial resources are as follows:

- SU education faculty seek, secure, and administer grants to support its P–12 partners' school initiatives. For example:
    - In 2018, SU secured a 3-year grant to partner with Wicomico County Public Schools to bring together teacher candidates and practicing teachers in an intensive, innovative, and collaborative model that emphasizes culturally responsive and linguistically rich pedagogical practices.
    - In 2019, one of the university's PDS liaisons worked with the elementary school's principal, to secure grant funding to provide restorative practice professional development for school staff and parents. Additional funds were utilized to purchase culturally and linguistically diverse books for the school library. The liaison also leveraged SU's AmeriCorps program to provide

teacher candidates with resources to assist teachers in the implementation of literacy intervention strategies.
- Two faculty members serve as codirectors of the Academy for Leadership in Education, which provides ongoing PD for aspiring school leaders.
- SU faculty and staff serve on multiple steering and advisory committees of Career and Technology Education and early childhood programs in several partner counties.
- As identified in its MOU with all partner counties, the University offers space on campus for educators and P–12 students to utilize throughout the school year and summer months. One example is that SU hosts 150 school leaders from Wicomico County Public Schools at its annual Leadership Academy each summer.

Faculty and staff in the Seidel School of Education at SU truly value their public-school partners for their commitment to teacher preparation and willingness to serve as school-based teacher educators. In keeping with NAPDS Essential 9: Resources and Recognition (NAPDS, 2021), SU hosts all PDS stakeholders at its annual Regional PDS Celebration. This event is designed to sincerely thank SU's P–12 partners for their dedication to its programs and recognize individuals for their contributions to the regional PDS network. SU interns proudly present the awards to their mentor teachers, university supervisors, PDS liaisons and site coordinators. The celebration is a themed event each year, such as sunshine, high-five, a 21st anniversary casino night, and a circus that was complete with juggling professors!

P–12 Partner Support for SU

The major contribution to SU's Seidel School of Education by its P–12 public school partners is providing quality clinical practice placements for teacher candidates and interns. Since the University is a regional institution, many of its mentor teachers, PDS site coordinators and administrators are graduates of its undergraduate and graduate programs. This experiential buy-in inspires stakeholders to provide additional support to SU teacher preparation endeavors, such as:

- Mentor teachers, PDS site coordinators and public-school administrators serve as adjunct instructors in all education departments at SU.
- Several P–12 partners serve on SU's May Literacy Center Advisory Council. The May Literacy Center provides tutoring to local stu-

dents by undergraduate and graduate students taking courses in reading intervention.
- Stakeholders from P–12 schools participate in schoolwide retreats, providing insight for what is needed in teacher preparation from their perspectives.

CHALLENGES

SU's Regional PDS Network is spread across seven counties; with six found on Maryland's Eastern Shore. Since the area is predominantly rural, securing quality clinical practice placements for specific disciplines can be difficult. For example, the State of Maryland allows the University to place interns outside of its Regional PDS Network for physical education placements when the intern cohort is large because of the limited number of physical education mentor teachers available.

Additionally, teacher preparation programs across the state of Maryland and the country are seeing drops in enrollment in teacher education programs. The benefits that P–12 partnerships provide can address recruitment and retention for all stakeholders. There are many challenges that exist for teachers. A challenge that many educators encounter is creating authentic learning experiences that engage students rooted in the ideas of Dewey, Piaget, and Montessori (Hsu et al., 2017) in the context of modern public education which does not empower teachers to be creative and innovative. The irony is that as modern tools and concepts allow more freedom to create and invent, school policies may restrict educators from being innovative in terms of trying new methods of teaching. Because innovation and creativity emerge with time, it may be difficult to allow this type of learning to develop in a nonlinear, low-stakes manner. An emerging concept that can address this challenge is *maker* education and its application in the classroom. Maker education "exist[s] at the intersection of the arts, crafts, engineering, mathematics, science, and technology, [and] making is made visible through the breadth and depth of what makers create" (UTeach, 2019, p. 2). To address this challenge, it is important to instill the idea of invention in new teachers so that they can innately create learning experiences. This challenge opens the door to opportunities that will be discussed in the next section.

OPPORTUNITIES

Education programs must encourage preservice teachers to develop an understanding of the philosophical and pedagogical roots that manifest in *maker*-centered learning in collaboration with PDS sites (UTeach,

2019). There are various approaches to accomplish this task; however, the most powerful and effective method is for an entire education program to adopt the concept. This means developing the knowledge and skills necessary to facilitate this experience within courses throughout the programs. Additionally, *makerspace* experiences within the PDS would be useful in reinforcing and providing real time experience with students. This can be a combination of media center experiences as well as classroom experiences. Some schools that have a *makerspace*, locate that space in the media center while some schools may have teachers that transform their classroom into a *makerspace*. A comprehensive, cross cutting approach within the program and across the PDS sites will help preservice teachers encode the values and principles of the maker education that will follow preservice teachers into the classroom. Developing an understanding of student-centered educational models, such as constructionism, allows preservice teachers to connect theory to practice through contextualized application of content knowledge. Continued enhancement of learning experiences might require building a coalition of key stakeholders such as site coordinators, liaisons, mentor teachers and principals to advance the idea of innovative practices within the PDS.

NAPDS Essential 8 states that "PDSs-figuratively spaces between schools and universities-are conceived of as places of discovery and experimentation…" (NAPDS, 2021, p. 16), which is similar to the concept of a *makerspace*. Maker education is both literal in terms of the space where learners "make to learn," and is figurative because the concept is rooted in a philosophical approach to learning that incorporates discovery, experimentation, failing, innovation, etc. Makerspaces are still emerging in both higher education as well as public schools. Incorporating the idea of a makerspace from the campus as well as the PDS can facilitate a new tradition in which the PDS model supports maker education as an essential part of the learning environment for all stakeholders. The DEEE program at SU has started a process of infusing maker education into the learning experience for preservice teachers and for PDSs. First, the university adopted the maker concept and opened a makerlab in the academic commons (library), which is situated in the middle of the campus. It is open to all faculty and students as well as the city of Salisbury communities, which includes public schools. The makerlab is unique in that the main focus is digital fabrication (3D printing and laser printing). Faculty encourage students to use the space to enhance the work they are required to do. In addition to the makerlab, the Perdue School of Business launched the Dave & Patsy Rommel Entrepreneurship Center in downtown Salisbury. The center offers a different focus for students because there is a focus on making in the context of invention and entrepreneurship. The center encourages and supports entrepreneurship, supporting students with experts to help bring ideas to fruition. Preservice teachers in DEEE participate in the center through unique coursework that encourages collaboration and invention.

NEXT STEPS

The maker education group in DEEE is developing a makerspace in the department that will be used to encourage faculty throughout programs to get involved as well as a space for professional development for in-service teachers in Salisbury's PDS network. The makerspace group is currently studying the infusion of digital fabrication with literacy in which additive manufacturing is used with children's literature to create a robust learning experience for pre-K—Grade 6 learners. The makerspace group and other maker-related projects will be pursued that will impact PDS stakeholders. Results from the research will be used to inform best practices (Bull et al., 2019).

The Department of Secondary and Physical Education plans to expand the on-site preprofessional course offerings at more secondary PDSs. This will provide teacher candidates more opportunities for immediate immersion into the P–12 classrooms. The Department of Secondary and Physical Education is also considering additional on-site offerings within methods courses for interns. This could help to foster a culture of clinical placement and practice from the first semester through the last.

At Mardela Middle and High School, plans are in motion to conduct a robust measurement of the impact teacher candidates are having on-site. The outcome variable could be a myriad of options: academic achievement, P–12 student efficacy, classroom learning environment, psychology, safety, grit, or aspirational views towards school.

SUMMARY

As a collective group of learners, P–12 schools and IHEs work to ensure the success of teacher education candidates while enhancing the community. This symbiotic relationship functions to improve outcomes for preservice teachers, enhance the knowledge and skills of in-service teachers, and support innovative practices that facilitate the continued growth of all stakeholders. Engaging and impactful practices are critical for the advancement of PDSs in SU's vast network as well as the development of the next generation of educators. This book will serve as a collective set of tools and ideas for others to borrow and improve as they create partnerships that enhance all stakeholders. SU's PDS network has been sustainable because of the collaborative efforts (Burns et al., 2021) of the role players.

The PDS is a living, learning community intended to close conceptual and practical separations that tend to exist between teacher education programs and the nation's schools.

All involved in the SU Regional PDS Network are proud of its reputation across the nation for its exemplary partnerships during its 26 years in existence. Each partnership plays a significant role in the identity of each individual institution. True collaboration is simply understood by all partnership stakeholders, no matter what their roles may be. This collaborative spirit will be evident in future endeavors to create engaging and impactful practices that benefit teacher candidates, practicing teachers, and most importantly, P–12 students.

REFERENCES

Bull, G., Garofolo, J., & Rutter, J. (2019). *Make to learn—An introduction to design through making*. Society for Information Technology & Teacher Education. https://www.learntechlib.org/primary/p/209811/

Hsu, Y. C., Baldwin, S., & Ching, Y. H. (2017). Learning through making and maker education. *TechTrends*, *61*(6), 589–594.

Koko, J. L. (2018). *Facing existential contradictions: Self-Examination as a tool for peace and happiness* (Vol. 1). Balboa Press.

Maryland State Dept. of Education. (n.d.). *Welcome to the Maryland Report Card*. Maryland State Department of Education. Retrieved https://reportcard.msde.maryland.gov/

National Association for Professional Development Schools. (2021). *What it means to be a professional development school: The nine essentials* (2nd ed.) [Policy statement]. https://napds.org/nine-essentials/

Salisbury University. (n.d.). *Factbook pages*. Salisbury University. Retrieved February 16, 2023, from https://www.salisbury.edu/administration/university-analysis-reporting-and-assessment/reporting/factbook-pages.aspx

Salisbury University. (n.d.). *Seidel School strategic plan*. https://www.salisbury.edu/academic-offices/education/strategic-plan.aspx

UTeach Maker Consortium. (2019). *Incorporating Maker-centered Learning into Preservice STEM Teacher Education: A Model from UTeach Maker*. https://makered.org/wp-content/uploads/2019/07/UTeach-Maker-Consortium-White-Paper-FINAL.pdf

Ward, M. (2014). Top ten tips for university partners of professional development school teaching. *PDS Partners*, *10*(1), 11.

Wilson, V. (2020). *Lead with instructional rounds: Creating a culture of professional learning*. Dave Burgess Consulting.

CHAPTER 8

SCHOOL-UNIVERSITY PARTNERSHIPS

Lessons Learned From the UNC Charlotte-Kannapolis City Schools Initiative

S. Michael Putman and Drew Polly

Context

In 2018, the American Association of Colleges for Teacher Education Clinical Practice Commission released a report that advocated for the "incorporation of innovative, rigorous partnerships" to "prepare high-quality teacher candidates to practice in a dynamic landscape" (AACTE, 2018, p. 22). Within this context, school-university partnerships have been viewed as opportunities for educator preparation programs (EPPs) and P–12 schools to craft a common vision of effective teaching, thereby supporting the development and growth of teacher education candidates (Cosenza, 2018; Gutierrez & Kostogriz, 2020). When school-based clinical educators (CEs) and university faculty engage in ongoing and substantive dialogue, they can collaborate to create opportunities that maximize candidates' preparation to enter the classroom. Further, these types of Professional Development Schools (PDS) or school-university partnerships serve as a rich opportunity for professional learning for CEs who work fre-

A Practical Guide to Exemplary Professional Development Schools
pp. 123–140
www.infoagepub.com
Copyright © 2024 by Information Age Publishing
All rights of reproduction in any form reserved.

quently with teacher candidates and university faculty (Putman, 2012; Polly, 2016; Polly, 2017).

Systematic, intentionally designed clinical experiences are also an essential component of these partnerships (AACTE, 2018; Garin et al., 2018; Putman & Polly, 2021). Research has clearly shown the positive impact on teacher candidates' (TCs) understanding of theory and its connections to practice when opportunities for application occur directly with K–12 students in school settings (Darling-Hammond, 2014; Goodson et al., 2019; Snow et al., 2016). Subsequently, through jointly planned clinical experiences where both the EPP and partner school leaders and CEs share ownership, collaboratively designed activities can scaffold TCs development through feedback and joint guidance that originate within the same guiding principles and pedagogy (Snow et al., 2016). This approach also increases the likelihood of diminishing the historically recorded dissonance between coursework, observations, and enactment of pedagogies (Bartanen & Kwok, 2021; Dunst el al., 2020). These opportunities should be sustained over time and characterized by the application of knowledge in increasingly complex situations (Brownell et al., 2019).

Rationale

The impetus for our partnership between UNC Charlotte and Kannapolis City Schools was to expand our knowledge of partnerships and clinical experiences through an examination of the embedded, multisemester internship. Leveraging previous research on clinical experiences and successful partnerships (Burns & Badiali, 2018; Polly, 2016), we created a structure that provided opportunities for coordination and coherence between practices observed in clinical experiences and information presented in coursework, while deliberately focusing on increasing the amount of time TCs spent in authentic contexts. Subsequently, the latter was intended to provide TCs with opportunities: 1) to participate in activities that occur during the first weeks of school; 2) to build deeper relationships with various stakeholders, including school staff, CEs, students, and families; 3) to teach weekly small group lessons prior to student teaching; and 4) to be observed and receive extensive feedback from faculty and CEs using a common protocol. Simultaneously, we sought to determine the structures and supports necessary for the delivery of experiences through partnerships between universities and P–12 schools as a programmatic feature that could be replicated and grown to encompass all aspects of the EPP.

Network Description

This school-university partnership included UNC Charlotte, located in the southeast United States, and the partner school district, Kannapolis

City Schools, located approximately 20 miles from the university. The partnership was built upon an existing relationship between the EPP and district, with a focus on formalizing structures and processes to incorporate elements of effective teacher education, including the Nine Essentials for a strong school-university partnership (National Association for Professional Development Schools, 2008, 2021). The partnership emphasized creating coherence between coursework and clinical experiences and the development of a community of practice among stakeholders. See Table 8.1 for a summary of the features of the program across the years of the partnership, to date.

Demographics

University of North Carolina at Charlotte

The EPP has an undergraduate elementary education program with an average enrollment of slightly more than 270 students across the 2019–2021 academic years, which represent the initial years of development and implementation for the partnership. During this time period, 70% or more of these TCs identified as white, with the next largest demographic groups represented by African American (~9%) and Hispanic (~8%). Six percent of the students identified as two or more races. Enrollment was largely composed of females (94%) (UNC Charlotte, 2022).

Kannapolis City Schools

According to the North Carolina School Report Card (2020), in 2019–2020, the partner district served approximately 5,459 students across eight schools, including six elementary schools. The district has a diverse student population, with a racial distribution of 30% white, 27% African American, 35% Hispanic, and 1% Asian, Native American, Native Hawaiian. Five percent of the students identify as two or more races. Furthermore, the majority of the students in the district (~70%) are eligible to receive free or reduced lunch and 13% are categorized as English language learners. All six elementary schools were included in the partnership activities, although in the first year, only five schools elected to be included. Racial demographics for the schools were similar to the district with ranges for the largest three categories as follows: white, 33%–43%; African American, 23%–32%; and Hispanic, 22%–35%. Furthermore, free and reduced lunch status at the schools ranged from 64%–93%. Four of the participating schools were neighborhood schools, (e.g., students were from communities proximal to the schools), while two were partial magnets, including students who lived near the school and students who

Table 8.1. Partnership Features Across Years

Partnership Features	Year 1 (2017–18)	Year 2 (2018–19)	Year 3 (2019–20)
Funding	• Small, university-funded grant, which was used to provide a stipend for CEs and to purchase books for Year 1 PD	• Grant was used to purchase books for Year 2 PD	• No funding
Teacher candidates	• 20	• 19	• 18
Clinical educators	• 20	• 19 (6 returning for second year, 13 new)	• 18 (10 returning for second year, 2 returning for third year, 6 new)
Faculty	• 4	• 4 (3 returning from first year)	• 4 (all four returning)
University courses	• Classroom management and the learning environment • Instructional design and pedagogy • Assessment • Students with exceptionalities • Equity and diversity in the elementary classroom (n = 14)	• Classroom management and the learning environment • Instructional design and pedagogy • Assessment • Students with exceptionalities • Assessment, design, and implementation of classroom reading instruction (n = 18)	• Classroom management and the learning environment • Instructional design and pedagogy • Assessment • Students with exceptionalities • Assessment, design, and implementation of classroom reading instruction
TC activities in elementary classrooms	• TCs taught 3 edTPA Literacy lessons • Some TCs taught math small groups weekly • Some TCs led morning meetings and noninstructional roles (taking students to specials, lunch, etc.)	• TCs taught 3 edTPA Literacy lessons • TCs taught at least 3 individual or small group reading lessons • TCs taught math small groups weekly • Some TCs led morning meetings and noninstructional roles (taking students to specials, lunch, etc.)	• TCs taught 3 edTPA Literacy lessons • TCs taught at least 3 small group reading lessons • TCs taught math small groups weekly • Some TCs led morning meetings and noninstructional roles (taking students to specials, lunch, etc.)

Partnership Features	Year 1 (2017–18)	Year 2 (2018–19)	Year 3 (2019–20)
Communication and coordination	• Monthly meetings among all stakeholders prior to Year 1 launch • Ongoing communication between university and district administrator • University faculty provided instructions to TCs during courses and visited schools to observe and interact with TCs, CEs, and building-level administrators • University faculty provided regular updates to university administrator • University team participated in monthly meetings	• University faculty provided instructions to TCs during courses and visited schools to observe and interact with TCs, CEs, and building-level administrators • University faculty provided regular updates to university administrator • University faculty created and shared newsletters that contained information relevant to all stakeholders • University faculty created and shared tools to support communication between TCs and CEs about sharing instructional roles and responsibilities in the classroom	• University faculty and administrator provided orientation to CEs over Zoom • University faculty only entered schools to complete observations and feedback. Supervision during student teaching was virtual for the entire spring semester • University faculty provided TCs with course activities and suggestions during virtual synchronous courses to address any concerns
Professional development (PD)	• Focus: Effectively teaching children from low-income backgrounds, grounded in Paul Gorski's (2018) *Reaching and Teaching Students in Poverty: Strategies for Erasing the Opportunity Gap* • Format: Book study, in which TCs summarized portions of the book and the group engaged in discussion focused on classroom application	• Focus: Instructional practices to engage students in active learning, grounded in Himmele and Himmele's (2017) *Total Participation Techniques: Making Every Student and Active Learner* • Format: Book study, in which TCs led sessions by targeting specific instructional techniques described in the book	• None

Source: Reprinted with permission from Putman et al. (2022).

opted to attend the school for the arts integration and Spanish immersion programs, respectively.

Description of Educator Preparation Program

The elementary education program consists of 60 credit hours of coursework completed during TCs' junior and senior years. Clinical experiences are incorporated within each semester and increase in complexity and time spent in the field as candidates progress within the program, per legislative mandate. Furthermore, state licensure requirements stipulate all students enrolled in an EPP must participate in at least one clinical experience in a high poverty school during their course of study. The state defines high poverty schools as those which are categorized as Title I, are categorized as low performing, or serve a student population of which at least 60% is eligible for free and reduced meals. At the time of this writing, 75% of the candidates within this EPP were placed in schools across 17 different districts meeting at least one of these three criteria. All six of the participating schools within the district met this designation. Educational equity is a foundational principle within the program, as aligned with the vision of the College. Thus, attention toward diversity and inclusion is foundational and represented within coursework in each semester of the program.

During the first semester of the program, which typically begins in the first semester of TCs' junior year, TCs enroll in courses focused on instructional design and assessment, child development, and primary grades (K–Grade 2) reading and math instruction. Within the clinical experiences associated with this semester, candidates spend time working with individuals and small groups of students, with an emphasis on developing proficiency in instructional planning and assessment and delivering instructional segments in mathematics and literacy. Clinical experiences have not traditionally been linked to any specific school sites; yet, the program has collaborated with a local nonprofit to deliver tutoring in mathematics at specific school sites identified by the organization. TCs typically spend between 30 and 40 hours in clinical experiences during this semester within the tutoring and course-level requirements.

Referred to as the Methods Block, the second semester is focused upon the development of knowledge and pedagogies associated with specific content areas, including social studies, science, language arts, and math (Grades 3–5). Teacher candidates also enroll in a course focused on applied practices in reading, which serves to demonstrate methods to integrate literacy into content area instruction. Clinical experiences are held at various partner schools in the region where faculty teaching in the Methods Block typically have relationships with teachers and administrators; yet, there are no systematic structures in place to coordinate content and instruction between coursework and clinical sites. While some of the clinical placements in this Methods Block occur in the partnership district described in this chapter, the large number of TCs in our program necessitates that we place students in multiple schools across multiple districts.

Candidates are encouraged to spend one day per week at a clinical site, beginning in the fourth week of the semester. Additionally, candidates are required to participate in a 2-week period where they spend 10 consecutive days in a classroom, observing instruction and delivering lessons in each content area to small groups of students. Students spend an average of 60–70 hours in a classroom, with 40–45 hours accumulated during the aforementioned 2-week period.

Next, TCs progress to their senior year, which is referred to as the Year-Long Internship (YLI). In the first semester of their senior year TCs complete five courses and spend at least 1 full day per week in the same classroom that they will complete their full-time student teaching semester during the following semester. Coursework in the first semester of the YLI is focused upon advanced instructional design, assessment, classroom management, and instructional differentiation. There is an emphasis across all coursework on supporting children from diverse backgrounds, with specific attention to race/ethnicity and exceptionalities. Given the length of the placements, clinical experiences are arranged through the UNC Charlotte's Office of School and Community Partnerships and communicated to candidates at or near the beginning of the relevant semester. While there is some coordination that occurs between university faculty and the clinical educators supervising the candidates in the YLI, it is generalized in nature and there are no programmatic requirements regarding direct collaboration to ensure coherence between content presented in coursework and teaching experience. Candidates are expected to spend 6–8 hours in the classroom each week during the first semester of the YLI, accumulating 70–80 hours over the course of the semester. Within these clinical experiences, students teach a minimum of three lessons, delivered to small groups and the whole class, and examine facets of the classroom associated with concepts introduced in coursework, including assessment and classroom management.

During the second semester of the YLI, TCs complete full-time student teaching, gradually assuming all teaching responsibilities. Guidance and support within student teaching are provided by the CE and a field supervisor associated with the Office of Field Experiences. Supervisors are full-time site coordinators from the Office of Field Experiences or adjunct faculty, who are typically current or former master level teachers or administrators. University faculty are typically not active within the supervision of student teachers. During the student teaching semester, teacher candidates complete a summative edTPA assessment to address state licensure requirements.

Partnership Attributes

The partnership included a modified version of the traditional YLI component of the EPP, delivered through a partnership with Kannapolis City Schools. Several modifications were made within the YLI, especially the first semester of TCs' senior year, to introduce attributes enabled through the longstanding relationship between the EPP and district. First, there were deliberate efforts to plan and coordinate aspects of the clinical experiences between various stakeholders, including university and district administrators, university faculty, and clinical educators. This included communicating clinical placement information to TCs 2–3 months prior to commencement of the YLI. Subsequently, this enabled the TCs to meet and develop a relationship with their CE before school started and attend beginning of the year events, including district-level professional development, team planning meetings, and the first day of school. This also contributed to the development of relationships between TCs and various stakeholders, including children and families, and provided familiarity with the school context. Second, the number of clinical hours required per week during the first semester of the YLI while candidates were engaged in university coursework was increased to a minimum of 10 hours over two separate days each week. Finally, and directly associated with the increased time in classrooms, TCs were required to teach each week, beginning around week 4. Candidates' teaching was supported through informal and formal feedback by CEs. In addition, a university faculty member and the CE jointly observed two lessons using a faculty-developed protocol that focused on specific facets of instruction aligned with coursework. The faculty member and CE provided feedback after these lessons.

Oversight of Partnership

This partnership was initiated when the department chair from the EPP approached the district's elementary education director and proposed the idea of developing structured internship opportunities, providing the district with opportunities for classroom teachers to mentor and work with teacher candidates and, in turn, increasing the number of teacher candidates who could be hired to work in the school district. Initial meetings between the administrators established the parameters and the organizational details of the partnership, including the identification of the clinical sites and mentor teachers as well as the formative feedback mechanisms to identify and facilitate improvements in processes and outcomes. With an inherent goal of ensuring the initiative was mutually beneficial, it was also determined within these initial meetings that the EPP would facilitate professional development on a mutually agreed upon topic for participating CEs and TCs.

Ongoing oversight was provided by the two identified administrators. Within the EPP, the department chair led all recruiting efforts for teacher candidates, oversaw the candidate application process, and served as a liaison to the faculty for planning purposes. The district's elementary education director served as the liaison to all school principals, coordinating and establishing all of the placements with clinical educators, while providing access to district-level resources associated with delivery of the professional development activities.

Oversight at the EPP course level was jointly distributed, with faculty meeting informally and at regular intervals to discuss organizational facets, candidate outcomes, and ongoing course-based assignments and adjustments. To provide an element of consistency around communication, one faculty member was designated to disseminate email as well as a monthly newsletter to participating CEs. While emails served the purpose of conveying information that necessitated immediate dissemination, the newsletter included reminders of dates, major clinical practice assignments, and photos and updates from partnership activities. The same faculty member also oversaw the processes associated with internship reflections and evaluations. The former is a requirement of all candidates and includes descriptions of their activities in their classroom and self-reflections about successes and potential areas of growth. The latter is associated with midsemester and end-of-semester evaluations of teacher candidates by clinical educators, which were used to ensure that the teacher candidates were performing at the level necessary to begin full-time student teaching in the following semester.

Structure of the Partnership

Policies and Procedures

As noted, this partnership was created through an existing relationship between the EPP and the district. Given this structure, there was not a formal vetting process for inclusion. The district's elementary school director reported the names of participating schools and the number of placements at each site to the department chair. Principals at each of the elementary schools chose the participating CEs, all of whom had to meet the state's minimum requirements for supervision. This includes holding a professional license in elementary education, a minimum of 3 years of experience in a teaching role, and a rating of "proficient" or higher as part of the state's Teacher Evaluation System. TCs expressed an interest to participate in the initiative through a communication process overseen by the department chair. As part of this process, the TCs acknowledged the increased expectations and identified selections for possible grade levels for the clinical experience. When the number of candidates exceeded the number of placements, the department chair and faculty reviewed applicants, using information such as instructor feedback and prior academic performance, to identify the participants.

While there is a Memorandum of Understanding between the College and the district, there are no fees required from the university or the partnership district. There are also no specific resources identified or allocated to support the initiative. At the partnership's inception, the first author (Putman) submitted and received an internally funded grant, which was primarily used to provide a small stipend for the CEs to attend professional development activities and to purchase books for the professional development experience. In the second year, Putman and the district's elementary education director were able to locate internal sources of funds to pay for the book for the professional development. The professional development component of the partnership was discontinued after the second year due to lack of funding.

Partnership Components

This school-university partnership focused explicitly on the effective preparation and mentorship of the next generation of elementary education teachers. Importantly, it sought to include mutually beneficial outcomes with the district including an expansion in the number of applicants seeking employment as part of a "grow your own" initiative, the development of clinical educators' capacity for mentorship and leadership, and improvements in K–6 student learning through augmented classroom support.

As shared above and within previous publications (see Putman & Polly, 2021; Putman et al., in press-a; Putman et al., in press-b), there were also unique aspects of this partnership compared to the typical experience for elementary education teacher candidates from the EPP. This included increased time in their clinical placement, more opportunities to teach students directly in classroom settings, with related opportunities to receive feedback from both faculty and clinical educators during the first semester of their year-long placement, and participation in jointly delivered professional development.

Professional development was deemed to be an important mechanism that could jointly support clinical educators' and candidates' growth simultaneously. For the purposes of this partnership, the professional development involved after-school meetings that included teacher candidates, clinical educators, faculty, and administrators. In the first year, participants read Gorski's *Effectively Teaching Children from Low-Income Backgrounds* (2018). Candidates were directly involved in the delivery of the sessions, sharing responsibility with a faculty member for the presenting of aspects of the book and facilitating discussions about those aspects with a focus on classroom application of the content. In Year 2, the district advocated for the use of Himmele and Himmele's *Total Participation Techniques: Making Every Student an Active Learner* (2017) to guide the professional development activities. Instead of formal presentations, the format for the book study this year focused on providing space for conversations among small groups of paired TCs and CEs about specific teaching strategies highlighted in the book, with an emphasis on how these strategies have been used by both groups as part of the current experience and how the strategies could be used in the future.

Support

Clinical Educators

At the onset of the partnership, meetings between the team of university faculty and participating clinical educators were held. The goal of the meetings was twofold: to develop shared goals and understandings around pedagogical strategies and principles (e.g., high leverage practices, classroom management) between the stakeholder groups and to discuss methods to link course content and assignments deliberately and systematically. These experiences in the clinical setting would enhance candidates' classroom teaching and learning opportunities. Furthermore, instructional design requirements for the university were presented and plans were made to ensure the candidates could develop instructional plans under joint guidance of the university faculty member and clinical educator. To ensure the CEs were familiar with the requirements for the teacher education candidates, university faculty presented information on programmatic assessment, such as, edTPA. As part of a broader, college-level initiative, the partnership provided professional development opportunities for clinical educators to develop techniques related to coaching and to giving feedback to candidates. Notably, participation in the various meetings and professional development was voluntary, thus attendance varied and never reached 100%.

As the partnership continued to evolve through feedback and observations from CEs and university faculty, it was noted that CEs needed methods to support TCs who were reluctant to teach and be actively involved while their CEs were teaching or managing the learning environment. As a result, the faculty created a checklist of potential instructional activities

Table 8.2. Possible Responsibilities During the YLI Semester

Activity	How many times has the candidate led this activity? How is it going so far?	When are there opportunities for the candidate to lead this activity, this fall?
Facilitated a morning meeting		
Facilitated an individual or small group lesson in literacy		
Facilitated a small group lesson in mathematics		
Facilitated a whole class mini lesson in literacy		
Facilitated a number talk or math routine		
Facilitated a whole class mathematics activity		
Facilitated the launch of an activity where directions were given and students were going to move or work together in groups		
Led movement or rotation of students during class (e.g., centers, small groups, transitions)		

that TCs could complete to gain more experiences in the first semester of their internship (see Table 8.2).

This checklist was provided to the CEs and TCs. Further, in an effort to provide more opportunities for active involvement, the second author required each candidate to teach small group math lessons to the same group of students weekly with materials provided by the classroom teacher. This teaching requirement provided a venue for CEs to discuss planning with TCs, while simultaneously providing valuable teaching experience for TCs and opportunities for CEs to provide them with feedback.

The partnership was intentionally designed to create active and equal ownership among partners. For example, monthly meetings among all stakeholders commenced six months prior to the first semester of implementation to ensure coordination and joint input, with the intended goal of engaging TCs in high-quality learning opportunities. Subsequently, the department chair of the EPP and the district administrator, the Director of Elementary Education, regularly communicated between the scheduled meetings to discuss ongoing organizational facets and to ensure continuity within participation among the stakeholders. The latter proved especially important at various times as unforeseen circumstances necessitated prompt action. For example, during several years, CEs changed roles in their school or moved out of the district, requiring last minute placement changes.

Support and development were enhanced as the course instructors adopted more active roles within these processes once the semester started. For example, several instructors regularly visited school sites to observe and interact with candidates, which provided direct opportunities to hold formal and informal conversations with building-level administrators and CEs. Information was then shared with the university administrator, who could follow up with the district administrator as necessary. These visits also enabled the instructors to provide detailed and explicit directions to TCs within course-based interactions, facilitating opportunities for TCs to quickly respond to circumstances. Subsequently, the university faculty team met formally and informally to discuss ongoing developments, with the instructors making ongoing adaptations at the course level, which often went unnoticed by other stakeholders, to address contextual elements.

Challenges

Research has shown that despite the many benefits of partnerships, there are also inherent challenges, including the need for considerable planning and coordination by university faculty with CEs and local education agencies (Brownell et al., 2019). Despite the variety of efforts made within the partnership to address various logistics and to maximize coherence, at various points within the partnership, communication was identified as an area that needed continued attention. For example, during the first year, candidates felt the university faculty did not communicate and coordinate with each other regarding assignments and due dates, thus creating challenges in meeting expectations associated with the assignments and clinical requirements. CEs also felt additional communication from university faculty was warranted to ensure they were aware of due dates for assignments, thereby allowing them to proactively support TCs within the completion of various assignments.

A second challenge was associated with the varying types and amount of feedback provided to TCs by both university faculty and CEs after observations. Despite direct attention towards this area, including the development of a protocol that was used across the observations, feedback from university faculty and CEs on mutually observed lessons was not always aligned. This may be attributed to the need for time and space to debrief. Specifically, the regular school day did not provide sufficient time to have conversations intended to maximize TC growth. University faculty, for example, were able to hold conversations immediately following observations by meeting with TCs in the media center or a different location, while CEs reported that they nearly always had to wait to give feedback until a suitable period of free time for the discussion, which sometimes was later that day or the next day. Subsequently, the observation process would have been more effective through jointly facilitated meetings between TCs, CEs, and university faculty.

The initial phases of the partnership were focused on jointly planning facets of the partnership at the classroom and course-level, for example, ensuring assignments had direct relevance in the classroom, and opportunities were present for TCs to teach regularly. However, the necessity of involving P–12 teachers in planning and delivering professional development became readily apparent through the subsequent delivery of the individual sessions. While the faculty and administrators agreed upon the topics for the professional development, noting the perceived relevance to the CEs and TCs, CEs' participation was largely constrained to simple attendance at the meetings. Engagement with the books and materials that formed the basis of the professional development was less than optimal. Time and other commitments may have contributed to this; yet, in hindsight, a significant factor was that CEs did not have a voice or ownership in the topic, materials, timing of the meetings, or delivery format. While Year 2 provided improvement through conversations between TCs and CEs about the teaching strategies provided in the book selected by the administrators, future professional development should incorporate participating TCs in the initial planning processes.

Another challenge reported by TCs was the focus on the high-stakes assessment edTPA during the courses in the first semester of the partnership. TCs had opportunities to interact with students and teach during their clinical practice experiences, and they reported that they wished they had more opportunities to debrief and discuss those in courses, but most class sessions, especially early in the semester, focused on edTPA and the multiple components of that project. In later years of the partnership, university-based faculty intentionally made room for opportunities to debrief about TCs clinical experiences, but most TCs reported on course evaluations that clinical experience debriefing could have been more of a priority.

Opportunities

One benefit from this partnership was the opportunity for TCs to commence their clinical experience much earlier and spend much more time in that setting compared to the traditional program. During focus groups and surveys, candidates cited that the early experiences with their CEs on the workdays before the school year started as well as the large amount of time that they spent in their placement at the beginning of school year led to some powerful relationships with CEs, which, in turn, was one of the most significant factors that contributed to their growth. Notably, the relationships enabled candidates and CEs to develop a mutual trust of each other as they came to know each other's teaching styles and collaboratively worked toward enabling student learning. TCs reported that the strong relationships between TCs and CEs made them feel comfortable receiving feedback from clinical educators as it was viewed as an opportunity for growth.

TCs also reported that they felt that the increased amount of time spent during clinical practice as well as being present for parent open house and the first day of school, and teaching relatively early in the semester contributed to strong relationships with students where students viewed them more as a teacher instead of as a college student that will later be a teacher. Some TCs cited that being seen as a teacher gave them more opportunity to develop trusting relationships with their students which in turn led to more of a seamless transition during the second semester of the YLI internship when TCs spent 16 weeks full-time in the setting and completed their 5 weeks as the full-time classroom teacher. A few TCs also mentioned that classroom management was easy and attributed that to being around the students for most of the school year.

Summary

The initial implementation of the partnership between the EPP and the district was for 3 years. Despite this seemingly short period of time, it was inherently clear that sustaining the partnership was challenging given the commitments of personnel, time, and resources. While the university faculty stayed consistent, the participation of CEs in the district has varied, with most teachers participating for a maximum of 2 years. This resulted in the need for university-based faculty and district leaders to orient and develop new CEs each year.

While this partnership has led to a number of insights associated with effectively delivering clinical experiences within school-university partnerships, there are questions that arose during the delivery of the program that remain unanswered. Extending what was learned regarding sustainability, there is a need to consider how to expand planning and recruitment to maximize the participation of experienced CEs, while also having some form of rotational system in place to avoid overtaxing those most willing to participate. This is especially critical when partnering with a small district. Similarly, within the university, there is the immediate need to consider mechanisms to ensure the sustainability of the program beyond the primary administrator and faculty involved, while also determining ways to expand the model to other schools and districts. This means examining resource allocation as well as incentives to participate.

In addition to the logistical questions of the broader partnership, further examination of the individual benefits is necessary. For example, how has supervision of TCs within the partnership contributed to the leadership and development of the participating CEs? Information from CEs as well as a more detailed reporting and analysis of mentorship activity would be helpful to document the impact of the partnership and could be used to inform others implementing similar programs. Finally, while early data analysis has revealed positive effects of participation in the partnership on candidate development (Putman et al., 2022), the long-term impact of the program on practices and effectiveness of participants is not yet known. Given the potential for candidates to be hired within the partner district, which is a specific goal of the partnership, there is a high probability for the investigation of outcomes using metrics such as teacher effectiveness ratings and student outcomes across multiple years after participation to gauge success.

This partnership provided TCs with an intensive, structured field experience that was created and delivered through a school-university partnership. Based on the initial data shared among the stakeholders, the partnership facilitated candidates' ability to connect theoretical constructs related to effective teaching practices to application in the classroom. These results were attributed to the active efforts of the faculty members to work directly with the clinical educators within the planning process of the courses, facilitating the alignment of information introduced within coursework with the curriculum, content, and instructional strategies observed within the clinical experience. Examining the various facets associated with the partnership revealed the importance of communication and collaboration within the partnership to maximize the benefits for all stakeholders. Yet, there are questions that remain unanswered to ensure the long-term success of the partnership in producing teachers who can engage students in high quality learning opportunities.

REFERENCES

American Association of Colleges for Teacher Education. Clinical Practice Commission. (2018). *A pivot toward clinical practice, its lexicon, and the renewal of teacher preparation*. American Association of Colleges for Teacher Education.

Bartanen, B., & Kwok, A. (2021). Examining clinical teaching observation scores as a measure of preservice teacher quality. *American Educational Research Journal, 58*(5), 887–920. https://doi.org/10.3102/0002831221990359

Brownell, M. T., Benedict, A. E., Leko, M. M., Peyton, D., Pua, D., & Richards-Tutor, C. (2019). A continuum of pedagogies for preparing teachers to use high-leverage practices. *Remedial and Special Education, 40*(6), 338–355. https://doi.org/10.1177/0741932518824990

Burns, R. W., & Badiali, B. J. (2018). Clinical pedagogy and pathways of clinical pedagogical practice: A conceptual framework for teaching about teaching in clinical experiences. *Action in Teacher Education, 40*(4), 428-446. https://doi.org/10.1080/01626620.2018.1503978

Cosenza, M. (2018). PDS governance. In M. Buchanan & M. Cosenza (Eds.), *Visions from professional development schools: Connecting professional development and clinical practice* (pp. 131–142). Information Age.

Darling-Hammond, L. (2014). Strengthening clinical preparation: The holy grail of teacher education. *Peabody Journal of Education, 89*(4), 547–561. https://doi.org/10.1080/0161956x.2014.939009

Dunst, C. J., Hamby, D. W., Howse, R. B., Wilkie, H., & Annas, K. (2020). Research synthesis of meta-analyses of preservice teacher preparation practices in higher education. *Higher Education Studies, 10*, 29–47. https://doi.org/10.5539/hes.v10n1p29

Garin, E., Burns, R. W., & Polly, D. (2018). The intersection of the AACTE clinical practice report and the NAPDS nine essentials. *PDS Partners: Bridging Research to Practice, 13*(3), 5–7.

Goodson, B., Caswell, L., Price, C., Litwok, D., Dynarski, M., Crowe, E., Meyer, R., & Rice, A. (2019). *Teacher preparation experiences and early teaching effectiveness*. National Center for Education Evaluation and Regional Assistance.

Gorski, P. C. (2018). *Reaching and teaching students in poverty: Strategies for erasing the opportunity gap*. Teachers College Press.

Gutierrez, A., & Kostogriz, A. (2020). The influence of chronotopes on pre-service teachers' professional becoming in a school-university partnership. *Teachers and Teaching, 26*(5), 475-489. https://doi.org/10.1080/13540602.2021.1873761

Himmele, P., & Himmele, W. (2017). *Total participation techniques: Making every student an active learner* (2nd ed.). ASCD.

National Association for Professional Development Schools. (2021). *What it means to be a professional development school: The nine essentials* (2nd ed.). https://napds.org/nine-essentials/

North Carolina School Report Card. (2020). Kannapolis City Schools. https://ncreports.ondemand.sas.com/src/

Polly, D. (2016). Considering professional development school partnerships in light of CAEP standard two. *School-University Partnerships: The Journal of the National Association for Professional Development Schools, 9*(3), 96–110.

Polly, D. (2017). Providing school-based learning in elementary school mathematics: The case of a professional development school partnership. *Teacher Development: An International Journal of Teachers' Professional Development, 21*(5), 668–686. https://doi.org/10.1080/13664530.2017.1308427

Putman, S. M. (2012). Investigating teacher efficacy; Comparing preservice and inservice teachers with different levels of experience. *Action in Teacher Education*, *34*(1), 26–40.

Putman, S. M., Cash, A. H., & Polly, D. (2022). Examining the impact of an embedded, multi-semester internship on teacher education candidates teacher self-efficacy. *Teacher Educator Quarterly*, *49*(4), 28–48.

Putman, S. M., Cash, A. H., & Polly, D. (in press-b). Examining the impact of structured clinical experiences within a school-university partnership on student-teacher candidate instructional interactions. *The Teacher Educator. 57*(3), 325-342. https://doi.org/10.1080/08878730.2021.2014006

Putman, S. M., & Polly, D. (2021). Examining the development and implementation of an embedded, multi-semester internship: Preliminary perceptions of teacher education candidates, clinical educators, and university faculty. *Peabody Journal of Education*, *96*(1), 99-111. https://doi.org/10.1080/0161956X.2020.1864250

Putman, S. M., Polly, D., & Fitzgerald, M. (2022). Innovative School-University Partnerships: Insights and understandings from a year-long internship. *PDS Partners: Bridging Research to Practice*, *17*(1), 31–37.

Snow, D., Flynn, S., Whisenand, K., & Mohr, E. (2016). Evidence sensitive synthesis of Professional Development School outcomes. *School-University Partnerships*, *9*(3), 11–33.

UNC Charlotte. (2022). UNC Charlotte Data Dashboard. https://sites.google.com/uncc.edu/initialteachereducation/home

CHAPTER 9

COMMON CHARACTERISTICS AND CHALLENGES OF SUCCESSFUL SCHOOL-UNIVERSITY PARTNERSHIPS

Michael N. Cosenza

COMMONALITIES

The stories of the eight awarding winning partnerships presented in this book revealed several themes across institutions. This suggests that these commonalities may be key characteristics for successful and sustainable school-university partnerships and PDSs. The commonalities are presented here as a resource for those who would like to start or expand their partnership work.

Governing Boards—Steering Committees

It is clear throughout the chapters that some type of leadership team exists to provide guidance and oversight of the partnership work. These go by different names in different institutions, such as leadership team, governing board or steering committee. Regardless of the name, these groups assure that the partnership is mutually beneficial with shared decision making among all stakeholder groups.

These governing groups are assembled differently in the partnership stories of this book. Sometimes they are between the university and one partner P–12 school and sometimes they span across multiple partner P–12 schools. Regardless of their makeup, these committees work to identify the needs of the P–12 school, P–12 students, teacher candidates and university faculty and to subsequently address those needs through collaborative goal setting. It is through shared visions and goals that these partnerships prioritize the work being done.

Several stories in this book point out the importance of having steering committees meet on a regular basis to ensure that communication and collaboration take place consistently throughout the academic year. Documenting the frequency of meetings in a Memorandum of Understanding (MOU) provides accountability, further assuring the meetings take place as promised. Another key factor is the inclusion of all stakeholder groups such as, P–12 teachers and administrators, university faculty and administrators, teacher candidates, parents, union representatives, and paraprofessionals. Having all stakeholders represented creates an atmosphere of collaboration and supports the premise that all groups have a voice in the partnership. Lastly, there is evidence that these committees make use of program data, survey data and anecdotal information to make informed decisions about the partnership and program.

Professional Development

Another emergent theme is the concept that continuous professional development is important not only to the teacher candidates being prepared for the profession, but for veteran P–12 teachers and university faculty as well. A key role of the steering committee (described above) is to assess and identify the areas of expertise that exist at both the P–12 school and the university. Once individuals with expertise are identified and a needs assessment finalized, decisions can be made about providing professional learning opportunities to the stakeholders in the partnership.

Several of these partnerships describe instances where the university provides professional development to the P–12 school and vice versa. Several school districts that are featured in the book regularly extend their professional development sessions to the university's faculty and the teacher candidates. Similarly, universities regularly invite P–12 teachers and teacher candidates to participate in their workshops and seminars.

Several chapters include a discussion about the use of Instructional Rounds, which like PDSs, is a model borrowed from the relationship between a medical school and a teaching hospital. Instructional Rounds is a program where educators visit classrooms seeking specific information regarding teaching and learning. The data gathered is not intended to be judgmental or evaluative. Instead, the information is used to foster collaboration about teaching practices and to inform educators of issues that can be improved to meet the needs of all learners (Buchanan et al., 2018; Darling-Hammond & McLaughlin, 2011; Teitel, 2009).

Capacity and Compatibility

Oftentimes, school university partnerships struggle or even fail because elements of capacity and compatibility are overlooked. Determining each partner's philosophy of education, work cultures, structural differences, resources, and teaching ideology is important at the onset of partnership work. Questions about policy regarding diversity, equity, inclusion, and social justice must also be answered. Engaging in discussion about the matches and mismatches that are discovered is key to long-term success of partnerships (Shoemaker, et al., 2020).

There is evidence in the chapters of this book that some institutions take time to conduct analyses of capacity and compatibility. The partners must share their positions about curriculum, classroom management strategies, methods for teaching students with special needs, and those whose first language is not English. It is key to the success of the partnership to discover whether there is a shared vision regarding research-based pedagogy and culturally responsive teaching practices. The stories in this book suggest that long term success of these partnerships is owed to the discussion and transparency surrounding these issues at the onset of a partnership and during steering committee meetings once the partnership is in motion.

Compatibility and capacity also extend to logistical issues. Many logistical questions that can impact the work of the partnership are often neglected. These questions surround issues about whether a school has sufficient parking, lunchroom space, and technology capacity for a cohort of teacher candidates and their accompanying university instructors and supervisors. The availability of a classroom, office or conference room should be considered to be sure there is a place for the work of the partnership to take place. These issues may seem inconsequential, but they can quickly derail a partnership if not agreed upon ahead of time. Working these details out in advance can avoid the grief, hurt feelings, and possible collapse of the partnership which may occur if discovered too late.

Stakeholder Buy-in

Several stories point out the importance of assuring everyone is supportive of the partnership. The cases suggest that partnerships should not be decided by administrators alone. Instead, work is put into educating the stakeholders about the PDS model, the Nine Essentials, and the importance of collaboration. Time is spent making certain everyone has common understandings of the desired outcomes and the commitment needed to be part of a school-university partnership or PDS. This can be accomplished by meeting with small groups in department meetings or doing presentations in large group meetings. It is important that the stakeholders have opportunities to ask questions and be assured that communication will be transparent. Too often universities take the lead in these types of partnerships. It is key to make clear, in advance, that both partners have an equal voice as well as equal accountability. This commitment helps build support and trust between the partners.

A common theme among the cases includes the use of an MOU. Several samples of these were submitted by the chapters' authors and are found in this book's resource section. These documents are used to declare the scope of the work including common goals and any legal language that may be required by the state or local government. MOUs also help hold each partner accountable which further supports the partners' commitment to each other. Several of the cases also mentioned that MOUs were reviewed collaboratively when approaching their expiration date. This is typically done with the steering committee so that all stakeholders can review the current language and make recommendations for any changes when the document is submitted for renewal.

Some partnerships reported use of a one-year pilot model, which gives the partners additional time to discover compatibility while beginning the work of the program. A pilot year gives each partner active experience working together, which helps uncover issues that may not have been considered at the beginning of the relationship. During the pilot, additional items may be placed in a revised MOU which may include revised goals, changes in commitments to space and resources and updated professional development needs.

Teacher Residency

Year-long teacher residencies appeared in several partnership stories. Some of the programs described in the chapters were designed to be residencies, while others evolved into one over time. The National Center for Teacher Residencies describes it as a partnership between a P–12 school and a teacher preparation program where teacher candidates work as apprentices alongside an exemplary mentor for an entire academic year (NCTR, 2023).

As the U.S. grapples with a nation-wide teacher shortage, the residency model has gained a great deal of support as a preferred model for new teacher preparation. Funding in the form of grants are widely available from the federal government, many state governments, and nonprofit organizations. The fact that several of the stories in this book combine the residency model with the PDS model suggests that they are highly compatible and create an excellent foundation for teacher preparation.

Boundary Spanning

The National Association for Professional Development Schools (NAPDS, 2021) describes boundary spanners as, "PDS participants span boundaries between university and P–12 settings; thus, their work is situated in the *third space*, which distinguishes it from work occurring solely in school or only in university organizations. PDS participants assume a variety of boundary-spanning roles, defined by each respective PDS. These boundary-spanning roles incorporate necessary functions and are integral to the operations of each PDS" (p. 16).

The chapters refer to many individuals who work across settings and discuss the importance of being able to navigate the cultures of both partners. Some examples of boundary spanners include:

- P–12 educators serving as instructors of university courses
- P–12 teachers serving as teacher educators through seminar presentations, supervision of teacher candidates and serving as liaisons between the school and university
- University faculty co-teaching in P–12 classrooms
- Stakeholders serving on leadership teams or steering committees to provide oversight of the work

The concept of *third space* mentioned in the NAPDS definition above also comes through in various chapters. Though a university in its entirety is partnered with a P–12 school (or district), not every individual employed in these partnering institutions is directly involved in the work of the partnership. Consider a Venn Diagram where one circle represents the university and the other represents the P–12 School. The overlap is the *third space* where the work of the partnerhsip takes place. *Third space* is "the space between schools and universities—are conceived of as places of discovery and experimentation, governed by ideas and ideals and not bound by the traditions of any one institution" (NAPDS, 2020, p. 13). The cases in this book revere the concept and go the great lengths to protect the concept.

Recognitions and Celebrations

Honoring and celebrating the work of the program is another common theme across the stories presented in this book. Value is placed on recognition of individuals and groups from all stakeholder groups. Certain events that are described have grown into traditions that take place regularly and are not only expected but looked forward to by the partners. Some examples of recognition and celebrations include:

- Kick off dinners
- End of year celebrations
- Credentialing ceremonies
- Events for sharing student work and results of research and inquiry projects
- Signs and banners on schools
- Pins and signs identifying individuals as mentors, coaches or cooperating teachers
- Awards for exemplary teacher candidate, exemplary mentor, and other similar recognition

Whether a partnership engages in some or all of the items mentioned above, it is clear that this is an important component for long-term success and sustainability of school-university partnerships.

CHALLENGES

In addition the commonalities that contribute in a positive way, the stories of the eight awarding winning partnerships presented in this book revealed several common challenges. These challenges likely exist in all partnerships and can be used as learning experiences to improve future work. The existence of these common challenges suggests that addressing them in advance, or at least being prepared for them to crop up, may be a good practice for successful and sustainable school-university partnerships and PDSs.

Complacency

When complacency was discussed, it commonly referred to the high risk of paying less attention to a partnership that seems to be running well. In other words, sitting back and letting the program run itself. Complacency can lead to a breakdown in policy and procedure and the risk of losing sight of the common goals that the partnership originally set for itself. This can undermine its effectiveness and overall sustainability over time.

The issue of complacency also took into consideration the fact that universities tend to take the lead in this type of partnership work. It is important that P–12 schools not allow that to happen and both partners stay true to their commitment to be equal partners in both decision making and accountability.

Communication

Similar to complacency, it is very easy to become lax in engaging in regular communication. Too often assumptions are made that all stakeholders are fully informed all the time about program requirements and other issues at hand. Partners must commit to transparent and regular communications. Communication can be accomplished through meetings (in person or virtual), phone calls, emails, newsletters, and through the circulation of meeting minutes. It is important to develop regular means of communication so that trust is not compromised. Misunderstandings can lead to suspicion and misgivings which can endanger the health and sustainability of the partnership

COVID-19

Several of the chapters discussed the angst that was experienced during the COVID-19 pandemic. During this time, many teacher preparation programs found it increasingly difficult to secure fieldwork placements for teacher candidates. School districts were reticent to add additional people into their school sites. Many teacher preparation programs have fieldwork placements at both structured partnership schools' sites, and other schools where the relationship is less formal.

The stories in this book discussed how candidate placements were never a concern with the schools where they had structured and long-term partnerships. They suggest that the rapport that was built between the partners and the level of trust that was attained over the long term, negated the placement issues that were otherwise common during the pandemic. This suggests that the work has become part of the both the culture and identity of the partnership. When this is achieved, there is a greater likelihood for long-term success. It further implies that these partners can overcome future obstacles together because of the solid foundation upon which their work rests.

Final Thoughts

The cases in this book clearly outline the benefits of school-university partnerships and PDSs, and how they are beneficial for all stakeholders. Despite the challenges described in each chapter, and the additional work required for long term sustainability, these partnerships often become an impetus for growth and revitalization. It is clear from reading each story that the common policies and protocols seen across institutions are foundational to partnership work. Though each partnership is unique, the practices described can easily be adapted or replicated to meet the individual needs of other partnership work. This implies that this book and its resources can be beneficial for the creation of new partnerships and the reinvigoration of existing partnerships.

REFERENCES

Buchanan, M., Helmstedter, C., & Freidman, L. (2018). Teachers doing the rounds. In M. Buchanan & M. Cosenza (Eds.), *Visions from professional development school partners: Connecting professional development and clinical practice* (pp. 311–334). Information Age.

National Association for Professional Development Schools. (2021). *What it means to be a professional development school: The nine essentials* (2nd ed.) [Policy statement].

National Center for Teacher Residencies. (2023). *What is a teacher residency?* https://nctresidencies.org/

Shoemaker, E., Cosenza, M., Kolpin, K., & Allen, J. (2020). A pathway to PDS partnership: *Using the pdsea protocol*. Information Age.

Teitel, L (2009). Improving teaching and learning through instructional rounds. *Harvard Education Letter, 25*(3), 1–3.

RESOURCES

RESOURCE I

Memoranda of Understanding

SAMPLE A

Professional Development School Partnership Agreement
Between
XXX University and Sample Public Schools ("SPS"),
(known legally as The Board of Education of Sample)

The mission of the Professional Development School (PDS) Partnership is to employ the collaborative resources of pre-K–12 and higher education to:

- Create a collaborative culture and governance structure to guide the placement and support for XXX University preservice teacher candidates in field placement/internship assignments in Sample Public Schools (SPS).
- Provide enhanced clinical practice experiences for XXX University candidates through the integration of theory and practice in a clinically based teacher education program.
- Promote collaborative practices that support the inquiry into and refinement of effective practices in teaching and learning by XXX University candidates, XXX University faculty and professional staff, and SPS teachers and administrators.
- Contribute to the professional development of instructional staff at collaborating PDS sites.

- Support efforts to enhance SPS pre-K–12 student achievement.
- Disseminate research-supported practices and structures to the education community.
- Encourage the coteaching model.

A Professional Development School ("PDS"), as defined in the XXX State Department of Education Standards, is a collaboratively planned and implemented partnership for the academic and clinical preparation of preservice teacher candidates and continuous professional development for professional personnel from both the partnering school and the institution of higher education. The foci of the PDS partnerships are: excellence in preservice teacher preparation, relevant and timely professional development, meaningful assessment of and inquiry into practice, and improved student performance through research-based teaching and learning.

Towards those ends, XXX University and SPS agree on the following:

A. HIGH QUALITY CANDIDATE PLACEMENTS IN DIVERSE SETTINGS

SPS agrees to provide field experiences and internship placements to XXX State University preservice candidates in PDS sites commensurate with its ability to maintain and support consistently high professional standards of practice. Partners also agree to establish a strong professional community in accordance with XXX STATE PDS Standards.

Both parties to this agreement recognize the value of placements that, based on XXX STATE guidelines, prepare professional educators to teach a diverse student population (ethnicity, socioeconomic status, English language learners, giftedness and inclusion of students with special needs in regular classrooms). Both parties to this agreement will endeavor to assure that all placements are made in settings that are diverse and sensitive to the needs of all learners.

Mentors will be tenured, experienced teachers with proper certification in the teaching field; prospective mentors must be recommended by their school system principal/supervisor. New mentors are expected to participate in a mentor-training program conducted by XXX University.

The number and type of supervised placements in SPS will be mutually agreed upon by the XXX University PDS Coordinator for Partnerships and Programs and the SPS Manager of PDS Programs and IHE Partnerships. Specific intern-mentor placements in PDS sites are determined collaboratively by the XXX University PDS Coordinator and the principal and site liaison at each school in accordance with school system procedures.

B. **GOVERNANCE**
All PDS implementation and activities, whether at the XXX University level or the local PDS site level, will be in accord with governance guidelines in the current XXX STATE PDS Standards/Guidelines.

Partnership activities at PDS sites will be governed by a Steering Committee/Advisory Body with representatives from both XXX University and LSS.

C. **CONFIDENTIALITY**
The Partner acknowledges its responsibility to ensure compliance with the confidentiality provisions of the Family Educational Records Privacy Act (FERPA) (34 CFR §99); The Health Insurance Portability and Accountability Act of 1996 (HIPAA) 45 CFR Part 160 and Part 164, Subparts A and E, and Code of XXX Regulations §13A.08, with respect to school records provided by the Board, if applicable.

Unless inconsistent with the XXX Public Information Act, any confidential information provided by SPS to XXX University including all copies thereof must be used by XXX University only as provided for by this Agreement and only for the purposes herein described. Such information shall not be disseminated or disclosed to any third party, not a party to this Agreement, without the expressed written consent of SPS, and can only be done so in accordance with applicable privacy laws. XXX University agrees to return to SPS all such information within fifteen (15) days of the expiration of termination of this Agreement; or with the express consent of SPS, XXX University may destroy such information within fifteen (15) days of termination or expiration of this Agreement, certifying to SPS in writing that the information has been destroyed.

XXX University preservice teacher candidates will maintain the confidentiality of information contained in students' educational records in accordance with FERPA and are by this agreement, designated as school officials for such purposes. COMAR permits the handling of student records by interns and student teachers: XXX State Code, Education § 6-107.

D. COMMUNICATIONS

Both XXX University and SPS affirm the right to promote the benefits of this Memorandum of Understanding ("MOU") as it serves the interest of each. This would include but not be limited to promotions, events, websites, alumni, and district communications such as bulletins and corporate newsletters. Each organization will make available the corporate logo for promotional use in relevant materials relating to this collaboration. Both organizations will designate a corporate contact through whom all communications will be coordinated.

All promotional or other materials, printed, electronic or otherwise, bearing the name or logo ("marks") of an organization who is a party to this MOU, shall be submitted to that organization for written approval prior to public distribution of such materials. Such approval may be withheld by the organization which owns the mark at the owner's sole discretion. Each organization, as a party to this MOU, reserves the right to withdraw its approval for any use of its marks if it believes that its marks are being used improperly.

E. INQUIRY AND RESEARCH

In alignment with PDS Standards, both parties to this agreement support preservice teacher candidate, mentor teacher, and XXX University faculty and professional staff engagement in inquiry and research projects, and performance-based assessments, to include edTPA, aimed at improving professional performance and enhancing student achievement. In accord with the Annotated Code of the State of XXX (Section 6-107) regulations regarding the authority of student teachers/interns, interns have the same authority as and follow the same procedures that are in place for certificated employees. Both parties support XXX University preservice candidates, in meeting XXX University requirements for courses, performance assessment, and accreditation tasks, in the design and implementation of program-required inquiry and research projects, and in their use of student work as evidence of preservice teacher candidate performance. Collaborative Institutional Training Initiative (CITI) Human Subjects Training is mandatory for all preservice teacher candidates who will be participating in a field experience or internship in a XXX public school.

F. PDS RESOURCE SUPPORT

Both parties agree to provide reasonable financial, human, and other resources to support the PDS partnership in accord with XXX STATE

PDS Standards. To provide continuing professional development per the MSED PDS standards, PDS partners will:

- Collaboratively create, conduct and participate in needs-based professional development to improve instruction and positively impact students.
- Plan and participate in activities where all school staff is encouraged to support and interact with interns.
- Inform school and campus-based instructional activities by PDS experiences.
- Work together to meet one another's professional development needs.

Professional development is fundamental to the growth and success of the PDS and is centered in supporting student learning and in the professional revitalization of experienced teachers. Both parties agree to collaborate in the identification of professional development needs at PDS sites and in the design as well as implementation of relevant professional development activities to meet those needs within the resource and policy constraints of each party.

G. **REPORTING AND EVALUATION**

Specific procedures for reporting and evaluating the supervised performance of XXX University preservice teacher candidates shall be determined by XXX University in cooperation with SPS. This shall not preclude SPS from administering its own procedures for evaluating and reporting these experiences. XXX University and SPS agree to an annual review of mentors, PDS Site Coordinators, and XXX University supervisors, in accord with standards for program accreditation. Both parties agree to collaborate in the preparation and submission of appropriate reports to XXX STATE and other governmental, accreditation, or professional bodies to meet reporting and accreditation requirements.

H. **PROFESSIONAL AND ETHICAL COMPETENCIES/ STANDARDS**

Both parties to this MOU have a right and obligation to insist on standards of professional and ethical decorum on the part of all school system personnel and XXX University preservice teacher candidates and participating faculty that are consonant with prevailing standards in the school/university community. XXX University preservice teacher candidates are bound by the XXX University professional dispositions assessment.

I. FINGERPRINTING AND BACKGROUND CHECKS

XXX University preservice candidates, who during their field experience or internship with SPS have direct contact with minors, shall be subject to fingerprinting and background checks pursuant to Section 5-551 of the Family Law Article of the XXX Code. XXX University shall assure SPS that it is in full compliance with Section 11-722 of the Criminal Procedures Article of the XXX Code which provides that a person who enters into a contract with a county board of education or a nonpublic school may not knowingly employ an individual to work at a school who is a registered sex offender.

J. NONDISCRIMINATION

Neither party shall discriminate in the choice of schools, supervising personnel, or students on the basis of race, religion, age, marital status, disability, gender, sexual orientation, or national origin.

K. TERMS OF AGREEMENT

1. XXX University preservice teacher candidates will:
   (a) Participate in school system mandated trainings.
   (b) Abide by school system policies required for background checks and Child Protective Services clearances.
2. XXX University preservice teacher candidates may not be used to cover classes or as substitute teachers, even in emergency situations unless the candidate is hired under a "paid paraprofessional" or "paid internship/paid long-term substitute" partnership agreement between XXX University and SPS.
3. This agreement shall continue for three (3) years from the date of signing. The MOU may be amended upon the mutual written agreement signed by both parties. This MOU may be terminated prior to its expiration date upon the occurrence of any of the following events:
   (a) By mutual agreement of the parties;
   (b) By either party upon the other party's breach of any of the conditions of this Agreement, and the breaching party's failure to remedy such default to the satisfaction of the other party within seven (7) days from the time that notice of the default is given;

(c) By either party no less than 60 days after providing the other party with written notice of the intent to terminate.
4. If the MOU is terminated, XXX University candidates enrolled in a course or field experience/internship at the time of termination shall be permitted to complete the course or field experience under the conditions set forth in this MOU.

SAMPLE B

Memorandum of Understanding
between XXX University and
Sample Professional Development Schools (PDS)

THIS MEMORANDUM OF UNDERSTANDING ("MOU") is made this 17th day of September by and between Sample Public Schools and XXX University on behalf of its College of Education (the "University") (each a "Party" and collectively the "Parties").

WHEREAS, XXX University and Sample Schools will have PDS Partnerships where practicum students and yearlong interns will complete their school- based internships

WHEREAS, XXX University and Sample Schools will collaborate on identifying mentor teachers and providing workshops for mentor teachers

WHEREAS, Sample Schools and XXX University wish to collaborate to implement the XXX State Department of Education Redesign in Teacher Education and PDS Standards and the National Association for Professional Development Schools Nine Essentials: What it Means to Be a Professional Development School.

SECTION 1—INDEMNIFICATION

1. The Board is in accordance with XXX Annotated Code, Education Article, Section 4-105, self-insured for comprehensive liability on all matters up to the statutory sum of $100,000 per occurrence. The Board shall indemnify and hold harmless, up to the amount of its statutory limits, the University, its officers, trustees, employees and agents from and against any and all claims, damages, judgments, actions and causes of action, including but not limited to the costs, expenses and legal fees arising by reason of the negligent acts or omissions of the Board, its officers or employees. The University agrees to provide the Board and Sample Board of Education written notice of all such claims, damages, judgments, actions costs, expenses and legal fees within thirty (30) days after the University has notice thereof.

   The University agrees to indemnify and hold harmless, up to the amount of $100,000 per occurrence, the Board and Sample Public

Schools and each of their respective officers, employees and agents, from and against any and all claims, damages, judgments, actions and causes of action, including but not limited to the costs, expenses and legal fees arising from the negligent acts or omissions of the officers, employees or agents of the University. The Board and Sample Public Schools agree to give the University written notice of all such claims, damages, judgments, actions, costs, expenses and legal fees within thirty (30) days after the Board and Sample Public Schools has notice thereof, as appropriate.

SECTION 2—TERM OF MOU

The initial term of this MOU shall be for a period of (4) years, from ___/___/___ through ___/___/___. This MOU may be renewed by written agreement of the Parties.

SECTION 3—TERMINATION

This MOU may be terminated prior to its expiration date upon the occurrence of any of the following events:

(d) By mutual agreement of the Parties.

(e) By either Party for any reason by giving the other thirty (30) calendar days written notice. Notice of termination shall be sent by registered mail.

(f) If the University fails to provide the services as required by this MOU, in any manner whatsoever, or, otherwise fails to comply with the terms of this MOU, or violates any regulation or law that applies to performance herein, Sample Public Schools may terminate this MOU by giving five (5) calendar days written notice.

(g) Sample Public Schools shall have the right to terminate this MOU at any time, without incurring any liability to the University. Termination of the MOU under this section shall constitute termination for non-appropriation and/or availability of funds.

(h) The University shall have the right to terminate this MOU at any time, without incurring any liability to Sample Public Schools.

SECTION 4—NONDISCRIMINATION

The University and Sample Public Schools agree to make no distinction among the participants or employees who are covered by the MOU on the basis of age, sex, sexual orientation, race, color, religious belief, national origin, marital status, status as a qualified individual with a disability or handicap or as a disabled veteran.

SECTION 5—AMENDMENTS

This MOU may not be amended except upon mutual written agreement signed by both Parties.

SECTION 6—REPRESENTATIONS AND WARRANTIES

Each Party represents and warrants that: (a) it is duly authorized to operate under the laws of its respective jurisdiction; (b) it is in good standing under the applicable laws of such jurisdiction; (c) it is expressly and duly authorized by its respective institution to execute this MOU; and (d) there are no legal restrictions or bars to each Party entering into this MOU.

SECTION 7—HEADINGS

The headings used in this MOU are for purposes of ease of reference only, and in no event or respect shall the substance of any provision or the intent of the Parties be interpreted or controlled by any such headings.

SECTION 8—LIMITATION OF LIABILITY

Neither Party shall be responsible for, nor entitled to, any indirect, consequential (including lost profits) or punitive damages, regardless of whether the theory giving rise to such damages is tort or contract or otherwise. In no event will the University be responsible to Sample Public Schools for any amounts in excess of the amount paid by to the University hereunder.

CRIMINAL BACKGROUND CHECKS

It is the responsibility of the University to make certain that its employees, agents, volunteers, and contractors and any instructors who have contact with students be fingerprinted and have a background check in compliance with Title 5, Subtitle 5, Part VI, of the Family Law Article of the XXX Code.

A. University Students Having Direct Contact with Students: Any and all current and future University Students of the University who have direct contact with Students must have a criminal background check and fingerprinting conducted by the Human Resources Department of SPS before beginning work in a Sample Public School. Previous background checks will not be accepted. The fee for the background check shall be paid by check or money order at the time the fingerprinting is performed. No employee can begin work in a Sample Public School until results have been received. Violation of this provision may result in Termination for Cause.

B. University Students that do not have Direct Contact with Students: University Student of the University who will be placed in a SPS school but will not have direct contact with students must have on record a Criminal Justice Information Service (CJIS) and NCIC background checks. Copies of the background checks must be forwarded to the Contracting Officer before services can commence. Every two years the University shall submit copies of background checks to the Contracting Officer. Should any employee be flagged during the term of this contract, the University shall contact the Contracting Officer within 24 hours of notification. Violation of this provision may result in Termination for Cause.

C. Employment of Sex Offenders: The University shall at all times be compliant with the Criminal Procedure Article of Annotated Code of XXX Section 11-722 that states that a person who enters a contract with a County Board of Education or a nonpublic school may not knowingly employ an individual to work at a school if the individual is a registered sex offender. If a registered sex offender is employed by the University, they are prohibited from assigning that employee to perform management, delivery, installation, repair, construction or any other type of services on any SPS property. Violation of this provision may result in Termination for Cause.

The University acknowledges its responsibility to ensure compliance with the confidentiality provisions of the Family Educational Records Privacy Act (34 CFR §99); The Health Insurance Portability and Accountability Act of 1996 (HIPAA) 45 CFR Part 160 and Part 164, Subparts A and E, and Code of XXX Regulations §13A.08, with respect to school records provided by the Board, if applicable.

Any confidential information provided by SPS to the University, including all copies thereof must be used by the University only as provided for by this Agreement and only for the purposes herein described. Such information shall not be disseminated or disclosed to any third party, not a party to this Agreement, without the expressed written consent of SPS, and can only be done so in accordance with applicable privacy laws. University agrees to return to SPS all such information within fifteen (15) days of the expiration of termination of this Agreement; or with the express consent of SPS. University may destroy such information within fifteen (15) days of termination or expiration of this Agreement, certifying to SPS in writing that the information has been destroyed.

SECTION 9—FORCE MAJEURE

Neither Party shall be responsible for any failure or delay in its performance under this MOU due to causes beyond its reasonable control, including but not limited to, labor disputes, strikes, lockouts, shortages of or inability to obtain labor, energy, raw materials or supplies, war, riot, acts of terrorism, civil unrest, an act of God (including but not limited to fire, flood, earthquakes or other natural disasters) or governmental action (including but not limited to any law, regulation, Decree or denial of visas or residence permits). In the event that either Party wish to invoke force majeure, that Party shall within ten (10) calendar days after the occurrence of the event of force majeure has become known to that Party, send written notice of such event to the other Party. In the event that a force majeure event prevents either Party's performance for a period of thirty (30) days, either Party shall be entitled to terminate the MOU upon written notice to the other Party. The provisions of this paragraph shall not apply to the payment of fees or to any other payments due from either Party.

SECTION 10—ASSIGNMENT

Neither Party shall assign this MOU, in whole or in part, without the other Party's prior written consent. Any attempt to assign this MOU, without such consent, shall be null and void.

SECTION 11—WAIVERS

There shall be no waiver of any term, provision or condition of this MOU unless the waiver is set forth in a written document signed on by the waiving Party. No such waiver shall be deemed to be or construed as a continuing waiver of any such term, provision or condition unless the written waiver states to the contrary. The waiver by either Party of its rights or remedies under this MOU in a particular instance shall only apply to matters arising from or in connection with this MOU.

SECTION 12—SEVERABILITY

If any part, term or provision of this MOU shall be held void, illegal, unenforceable or in conflict with any law of a government having jurisdiction over this MOU, the validity of the remaining portions or provisions shall not be affected. However, if such invalidity changes the basic intent of the Parties, as set forth in this MOU, the rights, duties or obligations of the

Parties shall be subject to a good faith negotiation.

SECTION 13— NO AGENCY

The Parties are strictly independent contractors and are not, in any way, employees, partners, joint venturers or agents of the other. Neither shall, in any way, bind the other in any way unless such Party has received the written consent of the other.

SECTION 14—CONFIDENTIALITY OF STUDENT EDUCATIONAL RECORDS

The Parties agree to treat personally identifiable information contained in a Participant's educational records as confidential and will not release such information to third parties without the written consent of the Participant whose educational records are sought.

SECTION 15—ENTIRE AGREEMENT; ORDER OF PRECEDENCE

This MOU contains the entire agreement between the Parties and, except as otherwise expressly provided, supersedes any prior oral or written agreements, commitments, understandings or communications with respect to its subject matter.

SECTION 16—NOTICES

All notices required or permitted under this MOU shall be in writing and delivered by confirmed email, confirmed facsimile transmission or by certified mail, and in each instance shall be deemed given upon receipt. All communications shall be sent to:

For BSU: For Sample:

SECTION 17—ENTIRE AGREEMENT; ORDER OF PRECEDENCE

This MOU contains the entire agreement between the Parties and, except as otherwise expressly provided, supercedes any prior oral or written agreements, commitments, understandings, or communications with respect to its subject matter.

IN WITNESS WHEREOF THE PARTIES HAVE SIGNED AND SEALED THIS MEMORANDUM OF UNDERSTANDING AS OF THE DATE FIRST WRITTEN ABOVE

Sample Public Schools   XXX University

_____   _____

SAMPLE C

Memorandum of Understanding
between Example Independent School District
and XXX University School of Education

This agreement is between Example Independent School District, ("ISD"), and XXX University ("XXX "), through the XXX University School of Education. ISD and XXX may each be referred to as Party or together as Parties.

SECTION 1: PURPOSE OF INTERAGENCY AGREEMENT:

The purpose of this agreement is to establish the best quality cooperative effort of providing instructional services to the Professional Development Schools, herein referred to as PDSs, andto the Partner Schools.

It is the intent of this agreement to:

1. Define the services to be provided by each Party.
2. Ensure that each Party assumes the responsibility to communicate with the other andshare leadership responsibilities and by doing so ensure that available resources are utilized in the most effective manner.
3. Ensure that these cooperative arrangements between ISD and XXX are developed, implemented, and reviewed prior to the end of this agreement.

SECTION 2: AGENCY RESPONSIBILITIES

1. Responsibilities of XXX:

    (i) Provide senior teacher education candidates from the School of Education to workas interns and/or junior teacher education candidates from the School of Education to work as teaching associates at all designated PDS/Partner sites.
    (j) Provide freshman and sophomore education candidates from the School ofEducation to work as novice teachers at PDS and/or ISD sites.

(k) Provide School of Education faculty to serve as university liaisons and/or residentfaculty at active PDSs and School of Education faculty to serve as resident faculty at ISD.

(l) If requested by ISD, maintain for itself and provide to Students or require that Students obtain and maintain appropriate general and professional liability insurance coverage in the amounts of at least $1,000,000 per occurrence and $3,000,000 in the aggregate, with insurance carriers or self-insurance programs approved by ISD in accordance with ISD bylaws, rules and regulations. A copy of the certificate of insurance shall be provided to ISD.

2. Responsibilities of the ISD:

   (a) Provide employees to work as PDS Coordinators at all fully-staffed PDS sites.
   (b) Provide mentor teachers to act as supervisors of the teaching interns.
   (c) Provide clinical instructors to act as supervisors of the teaching associates.
   (d) Prohibit the disclosure of personally identifiable information, as defined by the Family Education Rights and Privacy Act (FERPA), of XXX students without the prior consent of the students, and to limit ISD's use of such information only for the purpose for which it obtained such information from XXX or the student.
   (e) Maintain appropriate general liability insurance coverage in the amounts of atleast $1,000,000 per occurrence and $3,000,000 in the aggregate.

3. Exhibit A, attached hereto, defines and more fully describes the roles and responsibilities of the clinical instructors, mentor teachers, site-based coordinators, university liaisons and resident faculty. The terms "partnership" and "partner" are notused herein in the legal sense; but rather, the terms mean affiliation and affiliate, respectively.

4. Exhibit B, attached hereto, describes in greater detail the purpose, mission, and functions of the Professional Development School partnership between ISD and XXX .

5. ISD and XXX School of Education will jointly monitor the progress of each PDS Site-Coordinator, intern, and teaching associate.

XXX may gather general data pertaining to student performance in connection with the PDS project and may perform research related to that data, but the data will exclude individual students' names, personal information, and any other information that could identify the students.

6. Exhibit C, attached hereto, describes the cost of the PDS project that will be shared between XXX and ISD, who as previously defined are equal partners in this agreement. XXX's share is to be paid upon receipt of two separate invoices submitted by ISD no later than October in the fall semester and March in the spring semester of each school year. As part of each invoice, ISD will list the salary of each site-based coordinator assigned to this agreement, but to protect anonymity will not list the names of each. It is the expectation that each site-based coordinator will receive the minimum salary indicated in Exhibit C (i.e., half of the Unit Cost per Year). XXX will pay a maximum of half of the Unit Cost per year for each site-based coordinator or half of each site-based coordinator's salary, whichever is less.

7. If ISD is unable to provide the full complement of mentor teachers and/or clinical instructors as detailed in Exhibit C to provide the appropriate learning experience for theinterns and teaching associates, XXX may reduce the total fee paid to ISD by the unit cost for each mentor teacher and/or clinical instructor ISD cannot provide.

SECTION 3. AGENCY INFORMATION

1. Example Independent School District
   Contact Person:
   <Name>, <Position in District>
   <Mailing Address, City, ST, Zip>

   Person Responsible for Implementing Agreement:
   <Name>, <Position in District>
   <Mailing Address, City, ST, Zip>

2. XXX University School of Education
   Contact Person:
   <Name>, <Position at XXX >

<Mailing Address, City, ST, Zip>

Person Responsible for Implementing Agreement:
<Name>, <Position at XXX >
<Mailing Address, City, ST, Zip>

SECTION 4: EFFECTIVE DATE AND TERM

This agreement will be effective on June 1, 2021 through May 31, 2022. This agreement will automatically renew on June 1, 2022 and be effective until May 31, 2023, unless either party gives written notice of its intent not to renew, which notice must be given on or before May 1, 2022. This agreement will again automatically renew on June 1, 2023 and be effective until May 31, 2024, unless either party gives written notice of its intent not to renew, which notice must be given on or before May 1, 2023. This agreement will again automatically renew on June 1, 2024 and be effective until May 31, 2025, unless either party gives written notice of its intent not to renew, which notice must be given on or before May 1, 2024.

The ISD and XXX agree to enter into the collaborative PDS initiative as outlined above.

_____   _____
Signature   Signature
Dean, School of Education   Superintendent, ISD

_____   _____
Date   Date

Exhibit C

Example Independent School District and XXX University Professional Development School Projected Cost Share Analysis 202_ – 202_

Description	Unit	FTE Equivalent	Unit Cost per Year	Total Cost
PDS coordinators	3	1.5	$50,000.00	$75,000.00
PDS Teams				
• Mentor teachers for interns	41	N/A	$1,000.00	$41,000.00
• Professional development	41		$500.00	$20,500.00
• Materials and supplies	41		$100.00	$4,100.00
• Clinical instructors for teaching associates	33		$500.00	$16,500.00
• Materials and supplies	33		$20.00	$660.00
• Total PDS estimated costs				$157,760.00
Cost Sharing				
• XXX university				$78,880.00
• Example independent school district				$78,880.00

*Example ISD will join XXX University in contributing to the cost of training mentor teachers who do not attend the mentor training sessions offered by XXX University during the summer of 201_ (*summer before upcoming academic year*).

Note: This example is based on a cost share model that includes three PDSs, 41 interns (senior level full-year candidates, and 33 teaching associates (junior level candidates).

SAMPLE D

Memorandum of Understanding
Between XXX University and
XXX Public Schools

This Memorandum of Understanding ("MOU") affirms the longstanding collaboration between the XXX Public Schools ("County") concerning a network of professional development schools ("PDS"). These efforts will encompass the implementation of the XXX State Standards for Professional Development Schools. The parties hereby affirm their commitment to a dual goal of preparing the next generation of world-class teachers while helping local schools fulfill their missions and enhance P–12 student learning. This MOU shall govern the use of the County's facilities by UNIVERSITY XXX faculty and teacher candidates enrolled in Teacher Education Programs. "Teacher Candidate" is an umbrella term used to describe UNIVERSITY XXX students (including interns) during any and all phases of an educator preparation program that leads to initial licensure.

WHEREAS: The County/UNIVERSITY XXX partnership finds common ground between the County's core beliefs and the University's School of Education ("School") Mission and Goals.

School Mission
The mission of the School of Education is to provide opportunities for its students to become excellent professionals in the field of education. To implement this mission, the School of Education fosters outstanding teaching, scholarship/creative activity, and service and cultivates a learning-centered community which strives to meet national standards for excellence by offering high quality, innovative professional programs. The School of Education is committed to community involvement, professional collaboration, regional partnerships, and national and international outreach in an increasingly diverse and interdependent society.

School of Education School Goals

- To provide to the School of Education's diverse, capable students with the opportunities and experiences necessary to become ethical, resourceful professionals in education by offering high quality, innovative professional programs characterized by active learning that meet or exceed national standards for excellence.

- To provide qualified, diverse faculty who are student centered, reflective, intellectually vibrant, and enthusiastic models for teaching, professional excellence, and commitment to community service;
- To pursue national eminence and secure the resources necessary to achieve the mission of the School of Education.

NOW, THEREFORE, in consideration of the mutual covenants and agreements set forth herein, the Parties seek to affirm a legacy of shared values and agree as follows:

ARTICLE I: UNIVERSITY RESPONSIBILITIES

A. As resources allow, UNIVERSITY XXX will provide from among its faculty a PDS Liaison for the established County PDS sites. The PDS Liaisons will be the primary UNIVERSITY XXX collaborators with the assigned representatives of the individual schools. Each UNIVERSITY XXX Liaison will maintain a reasonable presence in the PDS site(s), assist in coordinating the placement of Teacher Candidates following the guidelines of UNIVERSITY XXX and County, and assist the PDS sites in meeting the XXX State PDS standards. PDS Liaisons will, when appropriate, assist with identifying and securing professional development opportunities for the PDS sites.

B. The University Regional Professional Development Schools ("RPDS") Coordinator will be the primary collaborator and communicator between UNIVERSITY XXX and County working closely with all PDS stakeholders.

C. UNIVERSITY XXX is an agency of the State of XXX, subject to and shall comply with the XXX State Public Information Act, codified at Section 4-101 et seq., of the General Provisions (GP) Articles of the Annotated Code of XXX State, as amended from time to time.

D. UNIVERSITY XXX agrees to indemnify, defend and hold harmless the County, its directors, officers, agents and employees from any claims, demands, injuries, losses, or damages resulting from any negligent conduct by UNIVERSITY XXX's employees or agents while acting within the scope of their employment during the term of and in any way connected with this MOU, only to the extent of (1) any coverage that might be provided under the XXX State Tort Claims Act and/or other private insurance coverage, or (2) a supplemental appropriation of funds to UNIVERSITY XXX specifically for the purpose of providing the assurance claimed here, as required by Section 7-237 of the State Finance and Procurement Article, XXX State Code. It is further understood and agreed that UNIVERSITY XXX, by the terms of this MOU, is not waiving or relinquishing in any manner any defenses that may be available to UNIVERSITY XXX, whether relating to governmental or sovereign immunity or otherwise, nor is UNIVERSITY XXX relinquishing any defenses that may become available to it at any time during this MOU, but it is further understood that UNIVERSITY XXX is free to assert all defenses that may be available to it as a governmental or State agency or such defenses that become available to them by operation of law.

ARTICLE II: COUNTY RESPONSIBILITIES

A. County PDS agrees to maintain a sufficient level of staff employees to carry out regular duties and will not make any reductions in its staff as a result of the presence of Teacher Candidates and/or faculty. County PDS retains full and sole responsibility for its students and the educational environment.

B. The Site Coordinator(s) for each PDS site or their representative will attend the quarterly RPDS Council meetings at UNIVERSITY XXX to provide valuable input to PDS initiatives as well as to remain informed of RPDS decisions and practices. Faculty and administration at each PDS site will be encouraged to attend the Annual RPDS Celebration.

C. The County agrees to indemnify, defend and hold harmless the State of XXX, XXX University, its Board of Regents, and any officers, employees, agents or volunteers of each of the aforementioned entities from and against any losses, claims, liability, causes of action, and damages resulting from any act of negligent conduct by County, County PDS or its officers, employees, agents or volunteers while acting within the scope of their employment arising out of or in any way connected with this MOU, but only to the extent of private insurance coverage or an appropriation of funds by the County for such purpose. It is further understood and agreed that County and County PDS, by the terms of this MOU, are not waiving or relinquishing in any manner any defenses that may be available to them, whether relating to governmental or sovereign immunity or otherwise, nor are they relinquishing any defenses that may become available at any time during this MOU, but it is further understood that County and County PDS are free to assert all defenses that may be available to them as a governmental or State agency or such defenses that become available to them by operation of law.

ARTICLE III: JOINT RESPONSIBILITIES

A. The selection and designation of a particular building as a PDS site or partner school will be determined jointly by designated representatives of the UNIVERSITY XXX and the Board of Education of the County. These designations will be reviewed annually and updated with addenda as necessary. Similarly, the decision to remove a school as a PDS site, or shift to a partner school, will be a joint decision. PDS sites and partner schools exist in unique configurations based on tradition, available resources and geographical considerations.

B. In the instance of joint PDS sites/partner schools between UNIVERSITY XXX and University of YYY, equal consideration will be given to both institutions of higher education in the placement of Teacher Candidates. In all other PDS sites/partner schools, UNIVERSITY XXX placement of Teacher Candidates will take precedence.

C. UNIVERSITY XXX, in consultation with County, will place Teacher Candidates in PDS sites for their foundations and methods courses' clinical practice experiences, as well as their 100-day extended internships. On occasion, teachers in other County schools may be used as PDS mentors when circumstances require. In such cases, the guiding principle will be to identify the best possible mentor for the Teacher Candidate.

D. The parties agree that the County PDS shall have the right, after consultation with UNIVERSITY XXX, to require the removal of a Teacher Candidate from the clinical practice experience at the County PDS/partner school if the Teacher Candidate for, other than legally nondiscriminatory reasons, such as the Teacher Candidate is disruptive, disreputable or otherwise a risk to the operation of the County PDS/partner schools and its students.

E. The principal of each County PDS site/partner school and the UNIVERSITY XXX Liaison will identify a PDS Site Coordinator(s) for each building to assist in arranging placements and other matters of PDS collaboration.

F. Each PDS site will be supported by representative Coordinating Councils. These Councils will serve as steering committees/advisory boards meeting no less than once each semester. The Coordinating Councils will include UNIVERSITY XXX's PDS Liaison or designee, the site administrator(s) or designees, the PDS Site Coordinator(s), and key PDS stakeholders as appropriate. These Coordinating Councils and PDS business can be incorporated into the site's existing School Improvement Team structure.

G. In keeping with the dual goals of this MOU, internships will include a collaborative atmosphere between mentor and Teacher Candidate. The focus of internships will be for the mentor and Teacher Candidate to work together to improve P–12 student learning. Both mentor and Teacher Candidate will remain engaged in the instructional process to provide an enriched learning experience for P–12 students, while simultaneously providing the Teacher Candidate with consistent modeling of teacher best practices. UNIVERSITY XXX will provide mentor training in coteaching and best practices as needed and desired by County.

H. In preparation for instructional planning, the County PDS will allow Teacher Candidates to access relevant student files such as Individualized Education Programs and 504 plans. Teacher Candidates will use them to meet the needs of students and will honor expectations of confidentiality.

I. In order to complete performance assessment requirements for initial and advanced teacher certification, UNIVERSITY XXX Teacher Candidates and graduate students in advanced degree programs will be permitted to video record instruction of students on a limited basis. Teacher Candidates and graduate students will consult the County's list of students who are not to be included in such activities and will adhere to these requests. Instructional recordings will be housed on a secure University server and will not be shared with individuals beyond those who review the performance assessments for licensure. Video recordings will be deleted from the University server once a passing score has been obtained by the Teacher Candidate.

J. Opportunities for school faculty in PDS/partner sites to teach as adjuncts at UNIVERSITY XXX are endorsed as professional development activities. Similarly, team-teaching evening, weekend or summer session courses with full-time faculty is highly valued as a means of increasing stakeholder investment in the PDS program.

K. The County will attempt to find suitable classroom space for UNIVERSITY XXX education courses to be offered at PDS/partner sites when possible. In addition to the internship seminars, such courses may include preprogram and methods courses for undergraduates and graduate offerings for in-service teachers. The School of Education will attempt to provide accommodations for PDS committee meetings to be hosted on the

UNIVERSITY XXX campus. Neither Party makes any guarantee of availability of any faculty to the other.

L. UNIVERSITY XXX and County agree to pursue joint opportunities for grant funding in support of PDS and other projects in keeping with the County's professional development agenda.

M. All UNIVERSITY XXX Teacher Candidates will complete a fingerprint-based background check by the State of XXX and the Federal Bureau of Investigation. Results will be sent directly to the County.

N. The Parties shall at all times under this MOU comply with all federal, state and local laws and UNIVERSITY XXX policies. Both Parties expressly agree to conduct themselves in a manner free of unlawful discrimination against any person or entity on the basis of race, ethnicity, national origin, age, gender, religion, political affiliation, qualified disability, sex, sexual orientation, sexual identity, gender identity or veteran status. County PDS agrees to provide reasonable accommodations affecting structural improvements at its location to UNIVERSITY XXX's faculty and students. UNIVERSITY XXX shall, at its expense, provide any other reasonable accommodations in compliance with applicable disability law. The Parties agree to maintain the privacy and security of personally identifiable education records and health information and to prevent disclosure in compliance with federal laws. The Parties agree to report any suspected child abuse and/or neglect in compliance with XXX State law and UNIVERSITY XXX policy.

O. Both Parties agree to maintain accreditation and to notify the other Party of any significant change in its accreditation or licensure status within thirty (30) days of such change. Both Parties shall permit the other Party and its accreditation agencies to visit, tour, and inspect its facilities and records relating to this MOU on reasonable notice during regular business hours, subject to requirements of student confidentiality, legal compliance requirements, and minimize disruption or interference with operations.

P. This MOU shall remain in full force and effect for three (3) years from the date of execution by both Parties and shall automatically renew for two (2) additional one (1) year terms unless otherwise terminated consistent with the terms herein above. This MOU may only be modified in writing upon the mutual consent of both Parties with the same formality as the original MOU. Either Party may terminate this MOU, in whole or in part, at any time upon thirty (30) days prior written notice to the other

Party; however, in no event shall such termination affect the students who may be participating in a field placement from completing the placement under the terms of this MOU.

Q. The relationship between the Parties to this MOU is that of independent contractors and is not to be in any manner construed to create an employment relationship between UNIVERSITY XXX, County PDS and/ or the student. The relationship of the Parties to this MOU shall not be construed to constitute a legal partnership, joint venture or any other relationship, other than that of independent contractors. No Party hereto shall have the right to bind the other to any agreement with a third party or to incur any obligation or liability on behalf of another Party. The Parties identify themselves as affiliates for purposes of this MOU.

R. Neither Party may assign any rights or interests nor delegate its duties under this MOU, in whole or in part, without the express prior written permission of the other Party and any attempted unauthorized assignment or delegation shall be wholly void and totally ineffective for all purposes. In the event of authorized delegation, the delegating Party shall remain fully liable for performance of the delegated duties hereunder.

S. This Agreement and its construction shall be governed by the laws of the State of XXX State, without regard to its conflicts of laws principles, and any interpretation, claim or dispute arising out of this Agreement shall be filed in a XXX State court of competent jurisdiction.

T. This Agreement, and its attachments, if any, constitutes the entire understanding between the Parties with respect to its subject matter and supersedes any and all prior or contemporaneous understandings and agreements, whether oral or written, and cannot be modified except by written agreement signed by both Parties. This Agreement may be signed in one or more counterparts, each of which shall be deemed an original and all of which, together, shall constitute one document. Original signatures delivered by means of facsimile or other electronic communication shall be considered to be original signatures. In the event of any conflict between the terms and conditions of this Agreement and any other document referencing or regarding the subject matter herein, the terms and conditions of this Agreement shall prevail. No waiver, alteration, or modification of the provisions in this Agreement shall be binding unless in writing and signed by both Parties. The invalidity or unenforceability of any provision of this Agreement shall not affect the validity or enforceability of any other provision. This Agreement shall be binding upon, and shall inure to the benefit of, the Parties and their respective legal representatives, successors, and permitted assigns. No right or remedy conferred in this Agreement upon or reserved to the Parties is intended to be exclusive of any other right or remedy. Each and every right and remedy shall be cumulative and in addition to any other right or remedy provided in this Agreement. The failure by either Party to insist upon the strict observance or performance of any of the provisions of this Agreement or to exercise any right or remedy shall not impair any such right or remedy or be construed as a waiver or relinquishment with respect to subsequent defaults. This Agreement is not intended to confer any right or benefit upon, or permit enforcement of any provision by, anyone other than the Parties to this Agreement. Neither this Agreement nor any right, remedy, obligation or liability arising hereunder or by reason hereof shall be assignable by either Party without the prior written consent of the other Party.

The following authorized representatives of the Parties hereby approve and agree to the terms of this MOU effective as of the date the last party signs:

XXX University:
___/___/___
_____

Provost
XXX Public Schools:
_____

Superintendent of Schools

RESOURCE II

Roles and Responsibilities

SAMPLE A

Personnel Descriptions
(Excerpted from *Teacher Education Handbook,* August 2021, pp. 57–61
https://www.baylor.edu/soe/doc.php/361996.pdf

PDS/Partner School Principal Responsibilities

1. Create a welcoming environment for teacher candidates and PDS/Partner school personnel.
2. Understand and advocate for the Professional Development School philosophy and advocate for PDS/Partner school goals to be aligned with campus goals.
3. Manage the PDS/Partner school funds gathering input from CDMC.
4. Include PDS/Partner school personnel in the CDMC.
5. Support the PDS/Partner school professional development efforts.
6. Invite PDS/Partner school personnel to participate in staff interviews.
7. Collaborate with the University Liaison to interview and recommend for hiring a Site Coordinator.

8. Conduct, in cooperation with the University Liaison, an annual appraisal of the Site Coordinator related to PDS/Partner school responsibilities.
9. Meet regularly, and as needed, with PDS/Partner school personnel.
10. Help identify quality placements (Mentors and Clinical Instructors) for candidates.
11. Encourage creative and flexible scheduling to accommodate the needs of all participants.
12. Participate in an annual PDS/Partner school evaluation and include PDS/Partner school issues in the Campus Improvement Plan (CIP).
13. Identify space for PDS/Partner school activities.

Clinical Instructor Responsibilities

The role of the Clinical Instructor should include, but not be limited to the following:

1. Serve as a role model and coach to provide opportunities for the Teaching Associate(s) in planning, preparing, teaching, and assessing students.
2. Support the Teaching Associate(s) in making the transition from candidate to teacher by clearly sharing authority from the beginning of the semester and in modeling appropriate classroom management strategies.
3. Accept primary responsibility for classroom supervision and evaluation of the Teaching Associate.
4. Initiate co-teaching models with the Teaching Associate(s) as required.
5. Schedule and participate in weekly planning/feedback conferences with Teaching Associate(s).
6. Provide written feedback.
7. Participate in summative evaluations of Teaching Associate(s).
8. Contact the University Liaison should concerns arise.
9. Provide input to XXX faculty about the Teaching Associates' final grades.

Resident Faculty Responsibilities

The role of the Resident Faculty should include, but not be limited to, the following:

1. Assume collaborative responsibility for Teaching Associate supervision.
2. Work with University Liaison to provide orientation for Instructors and Teaching Associates.
3. Provide instruction in course content areas.
4. Observe classroom instruction and provide written feedback.
5. Conduct bi-monthly conferences with Teaching Associates.
6. Participate in summative evaluations as needed.
7. Consult regularly with PDS and Partner teams.

University Liaison Responsibility (Elementary and Middle School)

The role of the University Liaison should include, but not be limited to, the following:

1. Maintain high level of communication between the University and PDS.
2. In collaboration with Site Coordinator, provide recommendations about candidate placements to Office of Professional Practice (OPP).
3. Provide orientation, with Site Coordinator, for Clinical Instructors and Teaching Associates.
4. Assume collaborative responsibility, with Site Coordinator, Resident Faculty, and Clinical Instructor, for supervision of Teaching Associates.
5. Conference with Teaching Associates and Clinical Instructors.
6. Observe Teaching Associates informally on a regular basis and formally, as needed by the PDS team.
7. Schedule and participate in midterm and summative evaluations with Clinical Instructor, Site Coordinator, Resident Faculty, and Teaching Associates.
8. Communicate continuously with the Clinical Instructor about the Teaching Associates' schedules and responsibilities.

9. Determine Teaching Associate's final grade with input from Clinical Instructor, Site Coordinator, and Resident Faculty.
10. Cochair, with Site Coordinator, the monthly campus PDS Steering Committee meeting.
11. Monitor resources required at the PDS.
12. Inform the Campus Decision Making Council of PDS activities monthly.
13. Schedule, with Site Coordinator, all field-based experiences at the PDS, including experiences for Novice groups.
14. Coordinate the assessment of the effectiveness of the PDS experience on the assigned campus.
15. Attend PEF meetings and campus faculty meetings as needed.
16. Attend PDS Coordinating Council meetings.
17. Monitor adherence to the PDS Standards during partnership experiences.

University Liaison Responsibilities (Secondary)

The role of the University Liaison should include, but not be limited to, the following:

1. Maintain high level of communication between the University and PDS.
2. In collaboration with Site Coordinator, provide recommendations about candidate placements to Office of Professional Practice.
3. Provide orientation, with Site Coordinator, for Clinical Instructors and Teaching Associates.
4. 4. Assume collaborative responsibility, with Site Coordinator, Resident Faculty, and Clinical Instructor, for supervision of Teaching Associates.
5. Conference with Teaching Associates and Clinical Instructors.
6. Observe Teaching Associates informally on a regular basis and formally, as needed by the PDS team.
7. Schedule and participate in midterm and summative evaluations with Clinical Instructor, Site Coordinator, Resident Faculty, and Teaching Associates.
8. Communicate continuously with the Clinical Instructor about the Teaching Associates' schedules and responsibilities.
9. Monitor resources required at the PDS.

10. Schedule, with Site Coordinator, all field-based experiences at the PDS, including experiences for Novice groups.
11. Coordinate the assessment of the effectiveness of the PDS experience on the assigned campus.
12. Attend PEF meetings and campus faculty meetings as needed.
13. Attend PDS Coordinating Council meetings.
14. Monitor adherence to the PDS Standards during partnership experiences.

Site Coordinator Responsibilities (Elementary)

Candidate development is a shared responsibility of all PDS faculty and staff.

1. Maintain high level of communication between the Professional Development School (campus) and university personnel.
2. Collaborate with the University Liaison to provide recommendations about candidate placements to the Office of Professional Practice (OPP).
3. Work with the University Liaison to provide orientation for Clinical Instructors and Teaching Associates.
4. Assume collaborative responsibility with the University Liaison, Resident Faculty, Clinical Instructors, and Mentors, for supervision of Teaching Associates and Interns.
5. Conference with Teaching Associates, Clinical Instructors, Interns, and Mentors.
6. Observe Teaching Associates and Interns informally on a regular basis and formally as needed by the PDS team. Document observations on the approved forms.
7. Work with the University Liaison to schedule and participate in summative evaluations with Clinical Instructors, Resident Faculty, Mentors, and candidates when requested.
8. Communicate regularly with the Clinical Instructors about the Teaching Associates' schedules and responsibilities.
9. Co-chair the monthly PDS Steering Committee meeting (if the Steering Committee responsibilities have not been assigned to the CDMC).
10. Inform the Campus Decision Making Council of PDS activities at regularly scheduled CDMC meetings.

11. Schedule, with University Liaison and campus Principal, all field-based experiences at the PDS, including experiences for Novice groups.
12. Participate in the assessment of effectiveness of the PDS experience on the assigned campus.
13. Attend campus faculty meetings and Professional Education Faculty (PEF) meetings at XXX University as needed.
14. Attend PDS Coordinating Council meetings.
15. Monitor adherence to the PDS Standards during partnership experiences.

Site Coordinator Responsibilities (Middle and Secondary)

Candidate development is a shared responsibility of all PDS faculty and staff.

1. Maintain high level of communication between the Professional Development School (campus) and university personnel.
2. Collaborate with the University Liaison to provide recommendations about candidate placements to the Office of Professional Practice (OPP).
3. Work with the University Liaison to provide orientation for Clinical Instructors and Teaching Associates.
4. Assume collaborative responsibility with the University Liaison, Resident Faculty, Clinical Instructors, and Mentors, for supervision of Teaching Associates and Interns.
5. Conference with Teaching Associates, Clinical Instructors, Interns, and Mentors.
6. Observe Teaching Associates and Interns informally on a regular basis and formally as needed by the PDS team. Document observations on the approved forms.
7. Work with the University Liaison to schedule and participate in midterm and summative evaluations with Clinical Instructors, Resident Faculty, Mentors, and candidates when requested.
8. Communicate regularly with the Clinical Instructors about the Teaching Associates' schedules and responsibilities.
9. Co-chair the monthly PDS Steering Committee meeting (if the Steering Committee responsibilities have not been assigned to the CDMC).

10. Inform the Campus Decision Making Council of PDS activities at regularly scheduled CDMC meetings.
11. Schedule, with University Liaison and campus Principal, all field-based experiences at the PDS, including experiences for Novice groups.
12. Participate in the assessment of effectiveness of the PDS experience on the assigned campus.
13. Attend campus faculty meetings and Professional Education Faculty (PEF) meetings at XXX University as needed.
14. Attend PDS Coordinating Council meetings.
15. Monitor adherence to the PDS Standards during partnership experiences.

SAMPLE B

Principal PDS Stakeholders

The personnel of both XXX University and the P–12 School are the principal stakeholders in the PDS partnership. The members of both faculties will collaborate to support the learning of P–12 students and the preparation of pre-service teacher candidates. They will also support the professional development of their respective faculties through mentoring and participating in seminars and other collegial activities. These principal stakeholders are involved in the daily management and maintenance of the PDS partnership.

Supporting PDS Stakeholders

XXX UNIVERSITY deans and administrators, the school district, the educator's association (union) and parent groups are also important stakeholders in the PDS. Representatives from these groups should be present on the steering committee to collaborate within the learning community. These stakeholder groups are considered supporting partners and will not be involved in the daily management of the PDS partnership. These supporting stakeholders assume shared responsibility for providing resources (financial and facilities), parity, and dialogue to maintain the PDS.

University PDS Director

This person will serve as XXX UNIVERSITY's representative within the PDS partnership and will work closely with the university PDS coordinator to provide leadership for the PDS. They will visit classrooms regularly and be available to provide support for the staff of the PDS. This person will oversee the continual evaluation and assessment of the goals of the PDS and will co-chair the steering committee with the university PDS coordinator and the Site PDS Liaison

University PDS Coordinator

This person will serve as XXX UNIVERSITY's representative to a specific P–12 school that is partnered with the university. They will have frequent, consistent and equitable interaction with all stakeholders, ensuring ongoing and clear communication is taking place. The PDS Coordinator will visit the school weekly to meet with the P–12 principal and the Site PDS Liaison to discuss matters pertaining to the program. Additionally, they will visit each cooperating teacher and teacher candidate bi-weekly to provide any additional support that may be needed.

Site PDS Liaison

This person will serve as the P–12 school's representative within the PDS partnership. The site liaison will work closely with the university PDS coordinator to provide leadership for the PDS. They will have frequent, consistent and equitable interaction with all stakeholders, ensuring ongoing and clear communication to all participants. The site coordinator will be expected to attend monthly meetings at the university as well as meetings at the PDS site. This person will co-chair the steering committee with the university PDS coordinator.

Cooperating Teacher

This is a classroom teacher in the P–12 school that will serve as a mentor for a teacher candidate. This person shall be a permanent employee with at least three years of experience and have participated in the university's cooperating teacher orientation (ten hours). P–12 teachers still in participating in an induction program or those who do not hold a CA Clear Credential, cannot serve as cooperating teachers.

Teacher Candidate

These are XXX UNIVERSITY students participating in the PDS-Residency program.

Student Observers

These are students taking educational foundations courses at the university which require 10-40 hours of classrooms observation. Student observers are not required to aid the teachers or work with students, but may do so if all parties agree.

Undergraduate Intern[1]

These are undergraduate students majoring in liberal studies, interdisciplinary educational studies or a subject matter degree for teachers with the intent to continue into the Teacher Preparation Program. These students take a field work internship for 30–120 hours depending on how much credit they wish to earn.

The PDS will define specific duties and experiences in advance so that students may select an internship of interest. A culminating project will be required of each undergraduate intern.

This is a XXX UNIVERSITY representative responsible for providing individualized guidance, support, and evaluation of the teacher candidate. This must be done in collaboration with the cooperating teacher.
   Supervisors will be expected to visit the candidate on a regular basis (minimum of six observations per semester) or university guidelines in effect.

PDS Principal

This person serves as the administrator of the PDS site and provides ongoing support, resources and leadership to maintain the PDS partnership.

Steering Committee

This is a collaborative professional learning community open to representatives from all stakeholder groups. The role of this committee is to meet regularly to develop, govern, and evaluate all aspects of the PDS. The steering committee is co-chaired by the university coordinator and site PDS liaison. An invitation to all stakeholders will be made at the beginning of each year to form the steering committee that will serve for that specific school year.

NOTE

1. Interns will apply for the specific intern positions that will be made available each semester.

RESOURCE III

Recommended Readings for Professional Development

Bambrick-Santoyo, P., Settles, A., & Worrell, J. (2013). *Great habits, great readers: A practical guide for k–4 reading in the light of common core*. Jossey-Bass.

Beaty, J. J., Pratt, L. (2010). *Early literacy in preschool and kindergarten* (3rd ed.) Allyn & Bacon.

Beauchat, K., Blamey, K. L., & Walpole, S. (2010). *Building blocks of preschool success*. Guilford Press.

Beers, K., Probst, R. E. (2013). *Notice and note: Strategies for close reading*. Heinemann.

Bellanca, J. A., Fogarty, R. J., & Pete, B. M. (2012). *How to teach thinking skills within the common core: 7 key student proficiencies of the new national standards*. The Solution Tree Press.

Bender, W. N. (2009). *Differentiating math instruction: Strategies that work for k-8 classrooms* (2nd ed.). SAGE.

Bender, W. N. (2013). *Differentiating math instruction, K–8: common core mathematics in the 21st century classroom*. SAGE.

Blood, P., & Thorsborn, M. (2013). *Implementing restorative practice in schools: A practical guide to transforming school communities*. Jessica Kingsley.

Boushey, G., & Moser, J. (2009). *The café book: Engaging all students in daily assessments in literacy*. Stenhouse.

Bresser, R., & Fargason, S. (2013). *Becoming scientists: Inquiry-based teaching in diverse classrooms, grades 2-5*. Stenhouse.

Bresser, R. & Fargason, S. (2013). *Becoming scientists: Inquiry-based teaching in diverse classrooms, grades 3-5*. Stenhouse.

Burgess, D. (2012). *Teach like a PIRATE: Increase student engagement, boost your creativity, and transform your life as an educator.* Dave Burgess Consulting.

Calkins, L. (2010). *Launch an intermediate writing workshop: Getting started with units of study for teaching writing, Grades 3–5.* FirstHand.

Calkins, L., & Mermelstein, L. (2010). *Launch a primary writing workshop: Getting started with units of study for primary writing, grades k-2.* FirstHand.

Castagna, V. B. (2007). *Teaching the information generation.* Scholastic.

Connell, G., & McCarthy, C. (2013). *A moving child is a learning child: How the body teaches the brain to think.* Free Spirit.

Curwin, R., Mendler, A. N., & Mendler, B. D. (2008). *Discipline with dignity: New challenges new solutions* (3rd ed.). Association for Supervision and Curriculum Development.

Diller, D. (2016). *Growing independent learners: From literacy to stations, K–3.* Stenhouse.

Dove, M. G., & Honigsfeld, A. (2013). *Common core for the not-so common learner: English language arts strategies.* Corwin, A SAGE Company.

Elden, R. (2013). *See me after class: Advice for teachers by teachers.* Sourcebooks.

Fisher, D. B., & Frey, N. (2014). *Text-dependent questions, grades k-5: Pathways to close and critical reading.* Corwin, A SAGE Company.

Fisher, D., Frey, N., Anderson, H. & Thayre, M. (2015). *Text-dependent questions grades K-5. Pathways to close and critical reading.* Corwin.

Fisher, D., Frey, N., & Lapp, D. (2012). *Text complexity: Raising rigor in reading.* International Reading Association.

Fisher, D., Frey, N., & Rothenberg, C. (2008). *Content area conversations: How to plan discussion-based lessons for diverse language learners.* Association for Supervision and Curriculum Development.

Garcia, A. & O'Donnell-Allen, C. (2015). *Pose, wobble, flow: A culturally proactive approach to literacy instruction (Language and Literacy Series).* Teachers College Press.

Gill, V. (2009). *The eleven commandments of good teaching* (3rd ed.). Corwin, A SAGE Company.

Glasgow, N., & Hicks, C. (2009). *What successful teachers do: 101 research-based classroom strategies for new and veteran teachers* (2nd ed.). Corwin, A SAGE company.

Greeley, K. (2000). *Why fly that way?: Linking community and academic achievement.* Teacher's College Press.

Gregory, G. H., & Kaufeldt, M. (2012). *Think big, start small: How to differentiate instruction in a brain-friendly classroom.* Solution Tree Press.

Gurian, M. (2011). *Boys and girls learn differently.* Jossey-Bass.

Holley, S. (2017). *Becoming the teacher you wish you'd had a conversation about teaching.* Truman State University Press.

Karten, T. J., (2010). *Inclusion strategies that work!: Research-based methods for the classroom.* Corwin, A SAGE Company.

Kazemi, E., & Hintz, A. H. (2014). *Intentional talk: How to structure and lead productive mathematical discussion.* Stenhouse.

Lemov, D. (2010). *Teach like a champion: 49 techniques that put students on the path to college.* Jossey-Bass.

Mah, R. (2009). *Getting beyond bullying & exclusion, Prek-5: Empowering children in inclusive classrooms.* Corwin–Skyhouse.

Marshall, J. C. (2016). *The highly effective teacher: 7 classroom-tested practices that foster student success.* ASCD.

McCoy, A., Barnett, J., & Combs, E. (2013). *High-yield routines for grades K–8.* National Council of Teachers of Mathematics.

Meltzer, L. (2010). *Promoting executive function in the classroom (what works for special-needs learners).* The Guilford Press.

Miller, D., (2009). *The book whisperer: Awakening the inner reader in every child.* Jossey-Bass.

Novick, B. J. (2016). *Parents and teachers working together: Addressing school's most vital stakeholders.* Rowman & Littlefield.

Pariser, S. (2018). *Real talk about classroom management: 50 best practices that work and show you believe in your students.* Corwin, A SAGE Company.

Parrish, S. (2014). *Number talks: Whole number computation, grades K-5.* Math Solutions.

Richardson, J. (2009). *The next step in guided reading: Focused assessments and targeted lessons for helping every student become a better reader.* Scholastic.

Richardson, J. (2016). *The next step forward in guided reading: An assess-decide-guide framework for supporting every reader.* Scholastic.

Ryan, J. E. (2017). *Wait, what?: And life's other essential questions.* HarperCollins.

Schwartz, S., & Boodell, D. (2009). *Dreams from the monster factory: A tale of prison, redemption and one woman's fight to restore justice to all.* Scribner.

Selznick, R. (2012). *School struggles: A guide to your shut-down learner's success.* First Sentient Publications.

Serravallo, J. (2013). *The literacy teacher's playbook, 3–6: Four steps for turning assessment data into goal-directed instruction.* Heinemann.

Serravallo, J. (2014). *The literacy teacher's playbook, K–2: Four steps for turning assessment data into goal-directed instruction.* Heinemann.

Serravallo, J. (2015). *The reading strategies book: Your everything guide to developing skilled readers* (1st ed). Heinemann.

Shindler, J. (2010). *Transformative classroom management: Positive strategies to engage all students and promote a psychology of success.* Jossey-Bass.

Shumway, J. F. (2011). *Number sense routines: Building numerical literacy everyday in grades k–3.* Stenhouse.

Shumway, J. F. (2018). *Number sense routines: Building mathematical understanding every day in grades 3–5.* Stenhouse.

Smith, M. S., & Stein, M. K. (2018). *5 practices for orchestrating productive mathematics discussions* (2nd ed.). NCTM.

Sousa, D. A. (2011). *How the brain learns* (4th ed.). Corwin, A SAGE Company.

Spence, C. M. (2008). *The joys of teaching boys.* Stenhouse.

Sprenger, M. (2013). *Teaching the critical vocabulary of the common core: 55 words that make or break student understanding.* ASCD.

Thompson, J. G. (2011). *Discipline survival kit for the secondary teacher* (2nd ed.). Jossey-Bass.

Vatterott, C., & Association for Supervision and Curriculum Development. (2009). *Rethinking homework: Best practices that support diverse needs*. Association for Supervision and Curriculum Development.

Wagstaff, J. (2017). *We can do this! Student mentor texts that teach and inspire*. SDE Professional Development Resources.

Weakland, M. (2014). *Super core! Turbocharging your basal reading program with more reading writing, and word work*. International Reading Association.

Wickett, M., & Hendrix-Martin, E. (2011). *Beyond the bubble. How to use multiple-choice tests to improve math instruction*. Stenhouse.

Witzel, B. S., Riccomini, P. J., & Herlong, M. L. (2016). *Building number sense through the common core*.

Yisrael, S. B. (2014). *The Cleopatra teacher rules effective strategies for engaging students and increasing achievement*. Rowman & Littlefield.

Zager, T. (2017). *Becoming the math teacher you wish you'd had: Ideas and strategies from vibrant classrooms*. Stenhouse.

RESOURCE IV

Organizational Charts

SAMPLE A

Pathways to Partnership

The XX University Elementary PDS Program uses a pathway to partnership model. Schools within the Elementary PDS Network share a commitment to improved PK–12 education and teacher preparation but may vary in their degree of participation. In this model, all schools are members of the PDS Network through either the Partner School, Clinical Practice School, or Collaborative Inquiry School 'pathway.' All schools have access to university faculty for professional development opportunities and advanced mentor teacher training, and all schools have the opportunity, given interest and space, to support site-based course instruction.

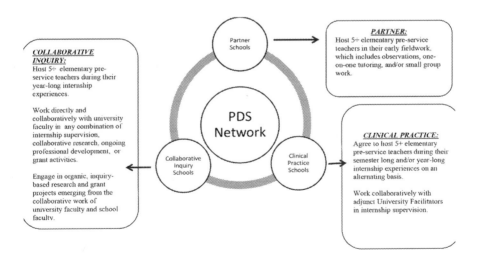

SAMPLE B

PDS Network Governance

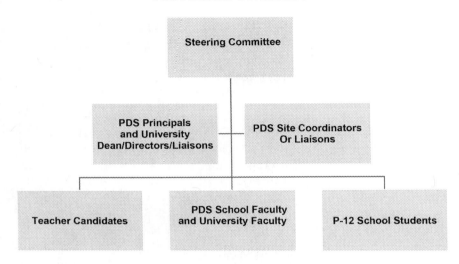

Steering Committee: Representatives from all stakeholder groups including university faculty and administrators, P-12 faculty and administrators, parents, union representatives, paraprofessionals, teacher leaders, and teacher candidates.

Resource IV 195

SAMPLE D

Regional Professional Development Schools Network

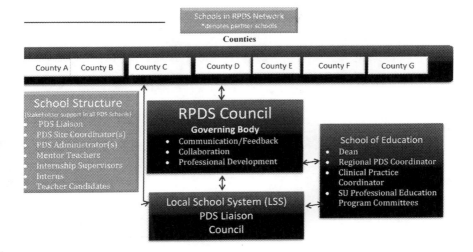

SAMPLE E
Baylor University

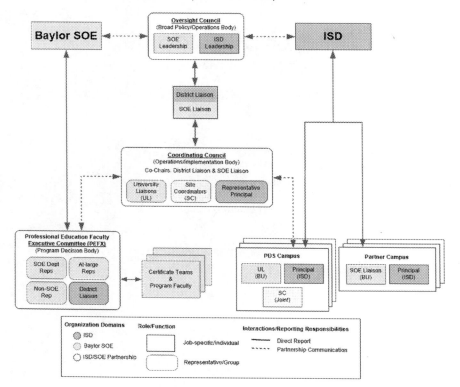

RESOURCE V

Problem–Solving Protocol

Issue Between Candidate—Cooperating Teacher

Step 1	An attempt should always be made to work out any issues or concerns with one another prior to elevating it to the next level.
Step 2	• **Cooperating Teacher** – Should contact the university supervisor, the Field Placement Director or the PDS Director to express her/his concerns regarding the candidate. • **Candidate** – Should contact their supervisor, the Field Placement Director or the PDS Director to express her/his concerns regarding the cooperating teacher.
Step 3	If the issue cannot be resolved at Step 2 then: • **PDS**: The Site PDS Coordinator and the University PDS Director will meet to discuss the conflict • **Partner School**: The Supervisor will meet with the Field Placement Director to discuss the conflict and develop a plan of action
Step 4	Appropriate meetings will take place with stakeholders to implement an action plan for resolution

Issue Between Candidate—University Supervisor

Step 1	An attempt should always be made to work out any issues or concerns with one another prior to elevating it to the next level.
Step 2	University Supervisor – • **PDS**: Should contact the UNIVERSITY PDS Director to express her/his concerns regarding the candidate. • **Partner School:** Should contact the UNIVERSITY Field Placement Director regarding candidate Candidate – • **PDS**: Should contact the UNIVERSITY PDS Director to express her/his concerns regarding the university supervisor. • **Partner School**: Should contact the Field Placement Director to express her/his concerns regarding the university supervisor.
Step 3	PDS Director or Field Placement Director will meet to discuss the issues and develop a plan of action.
Step 4	Appropriate meetings will take place with stakeholders to implement an action plan for resolution.

Issue Between University Supervisor—Cooperating Teacher

Step 1	An attempt should always be made to work out any issues or concerns with one another prior to elevating it to the next level.
Step 2	**Cooperating Teacher** – **PDS:** Should contact the Site PDS Coordinator to express her/his concerns regarding the university supervisor. **Partner School**: Should contact the Field Placement Director regarding the university supervisor. **University Supervisor** – **PDS**: Should contact the UNIVERSITY PDS Director to express her/his concerns regarding the cooperating teacher. **Partner School**: Should Contact the Field Placement Director to express her/his concerns regarding the cooperating teacher.
Step 3	PDS Director or Field Placement Director will meet to discuss the issues and develop a plan of action.
Step 4	Appropriate meetings will take place with stakeholders to implement an action plan for resolution

RESOURCE VI

Job Descriptions

SAMPLE A

The Role of the Cooperating Teacher

The primary role of a cooperating teacher is to purposefully take an aspiring teacher on a journey that will cause them to develop capacity and confidence to make their own informed decisions about teaching and learning (Portner, 2003). The cooperating teacher is a powerful force in encouraging self-evaluation and reflection by the teacher candidate. Cooperating teachers are specifically encouraged to:

1. **Provide ongoing evaluation of the Teacher Candidate's performance.**

   (a) Clearly define the management and instructional requirements and expectations of the teacher candidate.
   (b) Provide prompt feedback on specific strengths and weaknesses of daily lessons and procedures.
   (c) Constructively critique every lesson plan at least one day prior to presentation and each unit plan at least one week before implementation.
   (d) Offer and/or demonstrate specific alternatives or additional suggestions for the teacher candidate to implement.

(e) Avoid verbalizing negative comments to the teacher candidate in front of others (students, teachers, parents, etc).

2. **Communicate the value of continuous self-evaluation.**

    (a) Set an example by analyzing one's own instruction in relation to the elements of effective teaching.
    (b) Show willingness to accept comments or suggestions about one's performance from building administrator and/or district supervisor.
    (c) Acquaint the teacher candidate with district teacher evaluation procedures.

3. **Clinical Practice**

    (a) Through the coteaching model, develop and implement lessons and assessments collaboratively.
    (b) Permit teacher candidates to plan and implement lessons for observation by university supervisor.
    (c) Permit teacher candidate to plan and take-over as lead teacher for a 1-week period

SAMPLE B

JOB TITLE: PDS Director
DEPARTMENT: Dept. of Learning and Teaching
SUPERVISOR: Chair of Department

Major Purpose

The Director will act as the official university administrator providing overall oversight of the PDS program. The Director will work with the liaisons to provide support to teacher candidates, field supervisors, school principals, and cooperating teachers. The Director will provide oversight for workshops, orientation meetings and professional development for stakeholder groups within the PDS partnership.

The Director will maintain critical relationships between the University and the officially designated P–12 PDS partner school(s) where UNIVERSITY students will participate as observers, assistants, interns and teacher candidates.

Additional Duties

- Coordinate the placement assignments at the PDS site in accordance with MOU for each site (with Placement Director and Liaison)
- Provide support and guidance to the university supervisors (with Placement Director)
- Provide support and develop collegial relationships with Cooperating Teachers and Supervisors
- Maintain collegial relationships with PDS site administrators and office support staff
- Visit all candidates and their cooperating regularly (coordinated with liaison) to provide support, guidance and answer questions that may arise regarding the program
- Maintain records for PDS Advisory Board Meetings
- Meet with PDS liaison(s) regularly to maintain collaborative partnership, visit classrooms and address issues as they arise.
- Coordinate professional development for the PDS partnerships
- Provide onsite support to cooperating teachers, coordinate site-based meetings, sharing of best practices, meet and greets etc. (with Liaison))

- Assist liaison in developing a collaborative atmosphere and serve as the bridge between university professors and site teachers. Assist in arranging teachers to guest speak, model lessons and open their classrooms for group observation.
- Assist in solving problems using problem solving protocols.

SAMPLE C

JOB TITLE: PDS Coordinator
DEPARTMENT: Dept. of Learning and Teaching
SUPERVISOR: PDS Director and/or Dept. Chair

Major Purpose

The coordinator will act as an official university contact to school(s) that is operating as PDS. The coordinator will work with teacher candidates, field supervisors, school principals, and cooperating teachers to provide support and guidance for the PDS program.

The coordinator will maintain critical relationships between the University and the PDS school(s) assigned through weekly visits, accessibility through electronic media and committee meetings.

Additional Duties

- Assist with the arrangement of the placement assignments at the PDS site in accordance with MOU for each site (with PDS and Placement Coordinator)
- Provide support and guidance to the university supervisors regarding PDS policy (with PDS and Placement Coordinator)
- Serve as coordinator to PDS site(s)
- Provide support and develop collegial relationships with Cooperating Teachers and Supervisors
- Maintain collegial relationships with PDS site administrators and office support staff
- Visit all candidates and their cooperating teachers weekly to provide support, guidance and answer questions that may arise regarding the program
- Attend PDS Advisory Board Meetings
- Attend PDS staff meetings to provide status updates and to encourage dialogue and collaboration to improve programs
- Meet with school site PDS liaison regularly to maintain collaborative partnership, visit classrooms and address issues as they arise.
- Participate in and provide professional development
- Provide on-site support to cooperating teachers, coordinate site-based meetings, sharing of best practices, meet and greets etc. (with PDS Coordinator)

- Assist in developing a collaborative atmosphere and serve as the bridge between university professors and site teachers. Assist in arranging teachers to guest speak, model lessons and open their classrooms for group observation.
- Assist in solving problems using problem solving protocols.

SAMPLE D

POSITION TITLE: University Supervisor
DEPARTMENT: School of Education
Supervisor: Placement Coordinator and/or Director of University Partnerships

BASIC FUNCTION:

The University Supervisor provides coaching, mentoring and evaluative feedback to teacher candidates during their student teaching clinical fieldwork.

Duties

- Visit school site in accordance with frequency listed in Supervisor Handbook
- Complete online observation forms
- Conduct midterm/final evaluations of the student teacher collaboratively with the Cooperating Teacher
- Attend training sessions and monthly supervisor meetings
- Notify program directors of issues that affect teacher candidates performance
- Provide candidates feedback in a quick and timely fashion
- Maintain strong relationship with cooperating teacher to provide collaborative coaching
- Assist Placement Coordinator in obtaining paperwork from school site (including cooperating teacher stipend forms, student teacher attendance books etc.)
- Attend and assist with cooperating teacher training and orientations (site based or on main campus)
- Participate in any counseling sessions or remediation meetings that affect your student teacher
- Provide feedback on school site quality and cooperating teachers for future placement decisions
- Provide support and assistance to cooperating teachers
- Assist with the review of criteria for clinical placements
- Maintain positive relationships with administrators of partner, leadership and professional development schools
- Meet all requirements outlined in the Supervisor Handbook

RESOURCE VII

Application Solicitation

Dear School Principal,

This letter invites you and your faculty to apply to the XXX Professional Development Schools Network. As you may know, the University's Elementary Education Program has worked in partnership with local schools for over 30 years.

Faculty in Elementary Education at XXX University recognize the critical role elementary school contexts play in pre-service teacher education, and we appreciate the time, commitment, and work of PK–12 educators who embrace their role in advancing the profession. Applications to participate in our teacher preparation network are being solicited from all schools in the region and are due by **XXXX**.

Building on a long-standing history of partnership with local elementary schools, we look to increase opportunities for rich clinical practice and enhanced collaboration as an outgrowth of our new undergraduate program in Elementary Education. Based on a thorough review of feedback from various stakeholders in our current Professional Development Schools (PDS), we have made some minor modifications to our existing partnership structure. While the central vision of improving PK–6 education and preservice and in-service teacher professional development remains at the core of our work, we would like to share the opportunities that come with partnering with the Elementary Professional Development School (PDS) Network.

A number of documents are included in this packet to explain the Elementary PDS Network and facilitate the application process. These include

1. a list of key terms and definitions
2. a description of the revised Elementary PDS Network
3. a chart outlining benefits of participation
4. a description of financial considerations for districts
5. an application

We hope these serve as a helpful guide to understanding our PDS structure and the process for applying to the Elementary PDS Network. After reviewing the materials, we encourage you and your faculty to consider completing the application process. All applications are due by **XXXX**. Applications will be reviewed, and schools will be notified of the status of their application by **XXXX**. Applications can be submitted via email to XXXX or by mail to the address above, attn.: XXXX.

The Elementary PDS Network is a significantly more robust approach to teacher education than traditional models. It creates a framework for simultaneously supporting collaborative inquiry, as well as the learning of pre-service teachers, K–6 teachers, teacher educators, and K–6 students. As we look to the future, we are particularly enthusiastic about the possibilities undergraduate teacher preparation affords all stakeholders! Ultimately, we believe the Elementary PDS Network will prepare effective elementary teachers, positively impact local schools and communities, and contribute to the professional knowledge base in teacher education. We are keenly aware of the fact that none of this is possible without our elementary school partners. Please feel free to contact me if you have any questions about the Elementary PDS Network or the application process.

Sincerely,

RESOURCE VIII

Grant Narrative

**University Elementary PDS Internship Program—
XXXX County School Division**
___/___/___

Statement of Work

For over 18 years, the Elementary Education program in the College of Education and Human Development at XXX University has partnered with elementary schools in XXXX County Public Schools using a PDS (Professional Development School) framework.

The partnership engages 24 elementary schools in three pathways to partnership—collaborative inquiry, clinical practices, and partner schools—each of which supports field hours and internship students in the elementary teacher preparation program. This mutually beneficial partnership simultaneously supports undergraduate and graduate teacher candidates' growth, in-service classroom teachers' and university-based faculty's professional development, PK–6 student learning, and ongoing inquiry.

The partnership between XXX's Elementary Education program and XXXX's PDS sites supports teacher candidates (student interns) and pre-internship/field hours students from CEHD in the following ways 1) a full school year internship (referred to as 'yearlong' teacher candidates), 2) a one semester internship (referred to as "semester long" teacher candidates) and/or 3) as a field hours teacher candidate in either fall or spring. Semester long and yearlong teacher candidates work under the direction of trained mentor teachers who are known as mentor teachers/advanced mentor teachers.

Yearlong teacher candidates receive a monthly stipend in return for acting as substitute teachers for a limited number of days (minimum 35 days and up to 45 days) during their placement. Substitute teaching will include limited time coverage (less than half day), half day and full day subbing, and providing additional support in classrooms outside of the internship placement. All substitute teaching will be document by teacher candidates.

Semester long teacher candidates do not receive a stipend; however, they still work with trained advanced mentor teachers. Field hours teacher candidates are placed in a site for 15–45 hours and do not receive a stipend and can work with classroom teachers with or without advanced mentor teacher training.

At each elementary professional development school, a trained teacher leader is designated as a Site Facilitator (typically an assistant principal, teacher, or other personnel) and serves as a point person for communications, placement assignments, and other logistical and pedagogical tasks. At schools hosting year long and semester long teacher candidates, a university facilitator from XXX University serves as point person for each elementary professional development school. At schools with field hours, a point person based at the university serves as the liaison between the university and the schools.

To this end, a Professional Development Schools Network exists wherein the university students will provide teaching services to professional development schools in XXXX County Public Schools in exchange for training by and payment to the university.

Budget Justification

Personnel:

XXXX is Principal Investigator and will oversee the program as Academic Program Coordinator of Elementary Education (no monetary amount assigned).

There are 14 teacher candidates enrolled in our year-long cohort. They complete a year-long internship at their professional development school and receive student wages in the amount of $450 per month for 10 months in return for acting as substitute teachers for a limited number of (up to 45) days during their placement for a total of $63,000.

Other Direct Costs:

Six site facilitators who serve as a point person at their schools for communications, field assignments, and other logistical and pedagogical tasks for year long interns receive $95 per semester for a total of $1,140 for the year.

Six site facilitators who serve as a point person at their schools for communications, field assignments, and other logistical and pedagogical tasks for semester long teacher candidates receive $95 in the fall (field hours) and spring semester (internship) for a total of $1,140.

Additionally, a site facilitator receives $50 per semester per each of 14 "year long" MEd teacher candidates assigned to her/his school for a total of $1,400; $50 per semester for each of the 24 practicum/internship BSEd teacher candidates for a total of $2,400, and $50 for each of the MEd (4 fall and 23 spring) teacher candidates from the "semester long" cohort that are assigned to her/his school for a total of $1,550.

Additionally, 12 site facilitators serve as a point person at their school for communications, assignments, and other logistical and pedagogical tasks for field hours students and receive $95 per semester for a total of $2280.

Total other direct costs are $9,910.

Summary:

- Total direct costs requested from XXX are $72,910
- Total facilities and administrative costs requested from XXXX are $0:
- Total project costs requested from XXXX are $72,910.

ABOUT THE CONTRIBUTORS

THE EDITORS

Michael N. Cosenza, EdD, is a professor in the Graduate School of Education at California Lutheran University. He serves as the Chair of the Department of Learning and Teaching and is the director of the TEAMS (Teacher Experiences Advancing Mathematics and Science) program, which is an NSF funded residency program for preparing teachers in the STEM subjects. He is also the director of the PDS-Residency Program collaborating with a network of five P–12 schools. Outside of his university roles, Dr. Cosenza also serves as the executive director of the National Association for Professional Development Schools, vice-president of the California Council on Teacher Education and treasurer of the California Association of School-University Partnerships. Dr. Cosenza's career includes teaching in both the P–12 and university settings. His expertise and research interests include professional development schools, P–12 school-university partnerships, teacher residency programs, and teacher leadership.

JoAnne Ferrara, PhD, is professor emerita at Manhattanville College where she served as the associate dean of undergraduate programs and professor. Prior to joining Manhattanville, Dr. Ferrara held positions as a general and special education teacher, a literacy coach, and school administrator for the New York City Department of Education.

Dr. Ferrara serves as the Chief Program Officer for the Eastern Region Technical Assistance (ETAC), for Community Schools at Rockland 21C. ETAC is one of three regional community school technical assistance centers funded by New York State to support the development and sustainability of community schools.

Dr. Ferrara is an experienced educator specializing in community schools and university partnerships. For the last 2 decades Dr. Ferrara has worked to build stakeholders' capacity in community schools. She is the series coeditor for Professional Development School (PDS) Research Book Series, and the author of numerous articles, blogs and has contributed chapters to several books on professional development schools, community schools and community/school partnerships. She presents national and internationally on these topics. Her work has appeared in *Educational Leadership*, *The Journal of Research in Character Education*, *School-University Partnerships*, *The Journal of Leadership in Teaching and Learning*, and *Teacher Education and Practice*

Diane Gómez, PhD is a retired associate professor at Manhattanville College where she taught courses in second language acquisition and special education. She served as chairperson of the School of Education's department of Educational Foundations and Special Subjects, Professional Development School (PDS) liaison, and interim director of Field Placement and Certification. Prior to her appointment at Manhattanville College, she taught high school Spanish, special education in a high school residential setting, and graduate education courses in methods of teaching world languages, English to speakers of other languages, and bilingual education.

She has authored and coauthored several books, book chapters, and articles related to work in educational leadership and PDSs. Dr. Gómez has presented workshops and papers nationally and internationally. She served at chairperson of American Education Research Association (AERA) PDS Research SIG.

THE AUTHORS

Cathy Brant, PhD, is an assistant professor in the Department of Interdisciplinary and Inclusive Education at Rowan University. Her work focuses on LGBTQIA+ issues in education and teacher education.

Michelle L. Damiani, PhD, is an assistant professor of Inclusive Education at Rowan University. She is also a professor-in-residence at a local school. Formerly, she was a public school elementary special education teacher and a new teacher mentor. Her work focuses on developing sustainable inclusive education practices and understanding the experiences of teachers with disabilities.

Pixita del Prado Hill, PhD, has served as the SUNY Buffalo State PDS codirector from 2012–2022 and is a professor in the Elementary Education, Literacy, and Educational Leadership Department. Her scholarly, teaching, and service interests include international school-university partnerships, coteaching, and content area literacy.

Robert Eisberg, MA, is a lecturer in the Department of Language, Literacy, and Sociocultural Education at Rowan University. A former elementary school teacher and literacy leader, he also is coordinator of the Rowan University Reading Clinic.

Sara Elburn, MEd, serves as the Professional Development Schools Coordinator for Salisbury University's Regional PDS Network, overseeing P–12 partnerships with 39 schools in seven Maryland counties. Sara uses her previous experiences as an intern, mentor teacher, University faculty member and PDS liaison to inform her work.

Keli Garas-York, PhD, has served as the SUNY Buffalo State PDS codirector from 2018–present and is a professor in the Elementary Education, Literacy, and Educational Leadership Department. Her scholarly, interests include school-university partnerships, effective online instruction, and literacy strategy instruction.

Eva Garin, EdD, is a professor at Bowie State University where she coordinates the PDS Network and serves as the Director for the Center for Excellence in Teaching and Learning. Dr. Garin is very active in the National Association for Professional Development Schools (NAPDS) and serves as the coeditor of their peer reviewed journal, *PDS Partners: Bridging Research to Practice*. Dr. Garin is also the President Elect of NAPDS.

Selenid Gonzalez-Frey, PhD, is a member of the PDS Consortium at SUNY Buffalo State and an assistant professor in the Elementary Education, Literacy, and Educational Leadership Department. Her research interest focuses on literacy instruction for early childhood and elementary aged students that is developmentally appropriate and supported in the science of reading as well as school-university partnerships.

Krystal Goree, PhD, served as director of Professional Practice and PDS Liaison in the School of Education at Baylor University for 21 years. She served on the National Association for Professional Development Schools leadership team and was a member of the task force that updated the NAPDS Nine Essentials.

Stacey Leftwich, PhD, is the executive director for the Office of Educator Support and Partnerships at Rowan University. Her office provides sup-

216   ABOUT the CONTRIBUTORS

port to programs and initiatives related to education preparation as well as P–12 partnerships.

Madelon McCall, EdD, is a clinical associate professor of Curriculum and Instruction at Baylor University where she coordinates the secondary education program. Her research interests include student perceptions of teacher effectiveness, coteaching, and instructional design.

Suzanne Nesmith, PhD, associate professor of Curriculum and Instruction at Baylor University, serves as Associate Dean of Undergraduate Education. Her research interests include transformative change in preservice and in-service teachers' pedagogic practices and how settings can be created to enable change that allows students to learn STEM in conceptually based ways.

Audra Parker, PhD, is a professor and academic program coordinator in elementary education at George Mason University. Her research interests include elementary teacher preparation and school/university partnerships. In addition to teaching courses in elementary methods and management, she supervises interns at a PDS site and serves as School of Education Director.

Drew Polly, PhD, is a professor in the Elementary Education program at the University of North Carolina at Charlotte. His work focuses on how to support teachers and teacher candidates in their use of learner-centered pedagogies in their classrooms. His research interests include action research, the creation of literacy initiatives to advance student achievement and mentoring.

S. Michael Putman, PhD, is a professor and the chairperson for the Department of Reading and Elementary Education in the Cato College of Education at the University of North Carolina at Charlotte. His research focuses on the influence of clinical practice on teacher candidates' outcomes.

Doug Rogers, EdD, associate professor of Curriculum and Instruction, served as associate dean for Student and Information Services for 12 years during initial implementation of PDS work at Baylor University. Dr. Rogers served on the board of directors and as president of the National Association of Professional Development Schools.

Rachelle Meyer Rogers, EdD, is a clinical professor of Curriculum and Instruction at Baylor University where she coordinates the middle grades program. Her research interests include coteaching, action research, and lesson study. She has held many leadership positions including the 2022–2023 President of the Association of Teacher Educators.

Diallo Sessoms, PhD, is an associate professor of educational technology in the Department of Early & Elementary Education at Salisbury University and teaches technology integration courses. He serves as the liaison for Glen Avenue Elementary. He conducts research on makerspaces in education and created a makerspace for his department.

Ron Siers, PhD, is a professor and national championship baseball coach at Salisbury University. He is a university liaison and supervisor at Mardela Middle and High School. He is the codirector for Salisbury University's Academy for Leadership in Education coupled with coordinating the Athletic Coaching Minor program. Dr Siers uses his previous experiences as an intern and mentor teacher to guide and inform his PDS work.

Printed in the United States
by Baker & Taylor Publisher Services